Finding Your Irish Ancestors

A Beginner's Guide

David S. Ouimette

Ancestry

Library of Congress Cataloging-in-Publication Data

Ouimette, David S.
    Finding your Irish ancestors : a beginner's guide / by David S. Ouimette.
        p. cm.
    Includes bibliographical references and index.
    ISBN 1-59331-293-8 (softcover : alk. paper) 1. Ireland—Genealogy—
Handbooks, manuals, etc. 2. Irish Americans—Genealogy—Handbooks,
manuals, etc. I. Title.

    CS483.O95 2005
    929'.1'0720415—dc22

                                                        2005021165

Copyright © 2005
MyFamily.com, Inc.

Published by
Ancestry®, a division of MyFamily.com, Inc.
360 West 4800 North
Provo, Utah 84604
www.ancestry.com

First Printing 2005
10 9 8 7 6 5 4 3 2 1

Printed in the United States of America.

In memory of my grandfathers,
William O'Connor (1888–1944)
of Mulgrave Bridge, Ballyard, County Kerry,
and
George Gilbert Love (1893–1978)
of Abbeylara, County Longford

Kylemore Abbey, Ireland.

Table of Contents

List of Illustrations

Acknowledgments

This book would not have been possible without the help of many people. I particularly wish to thank my mother, Marilyn Ouimette, and her brother Thomas O'Connor for preserving and celebrating our Irish heritage; my wife, Deanna, and our children (Michael, Celeste, Derek, Chantelle, Nathan, Richard, and Peter) for their patience and support throughout this two-year project; my wife for reviewing so many draft manuscripts; Lou Szucs and Jennifer Utley for having confidence in me and encouraging me to write this book; David Rencher, AG, FUGA, and Elizabeth Kelley Kerstens, CGRS, CGL, for peer reviewing and offering many valuable suggestions; Anastasia Sutherland Tyler for her tremendous talents and thoughtful advice while editing this book and for the great layout; Rob Davis for working his magic on the cover design and illustrations; Jennifer Browning and Matthew Wright for helping me publish my first family history articles; the staff and consultants of many Irish archives and libraries, especially Gregory O'Connor (Archivist at the National Archives of Ireland), Colette O'Flaherty (Assistant Keeper at the National Library of Ireland), Aideen Ireland (Senior Archivist at the National Library of Ireland), Dr. Susan Hood (Assistant Archivist at the Representative Church Body Library); the staff of the Family History Library; Christine Branch for her helpful suggestions; and André Brummer for approving this project.

I also wish to thank a number of individuals and institutions for permission to use illustrations, including Rosemary ffolliott, the Diocese of Galway, the National Archives of Ireland, the Representative Church Body Library, the Valuation Office, Genealogical Publishing Company, Oxford University Press, the General Register Office, The National Archives (of England), and the Family History Department.

Fishing boats in Dublin, Ireland.

Introduction

If you are lucky enough to be Irish, you are lucky enough.
—Irish proverb

Finding your Irish ancestors is a rewarding experience. As you discover more about your roots in Ireland and the Irish legacy you have inherited, you will see yourself and your family differently, with a greater appreciation for those who went before you. This book will help you find your Irish ancestors, learn about their families, and strengthen your connection with the past.

If you are like most people of Irish descent, you have an ancestor who left Ireland many years ago. What was your ancestor like? Where did your ancestor live in Ireland? Does the house still stand, occupied by now-distant cousins? Why did he or she leave such a beautiful country, saying goodbye to family, friends, and home for a new life across the ocean? Can you get in contact with relatives now living in Ireland? These are some of the questions you might be asking as you search for your Irish ancestors. This book will help you find the answers to these and many other questions.

Now is the best time to trace your Irish ancestry. Many Irish family history records have become readily accessible in recent years, including an ever-growing collection on the Internet. Millions of people worldwide are searching for their roots—some of these people may be your Irish cousins.

What motivates us to learn about our ancestors? For some of us, the search for ancestors is a journey of self-discovery. As we learn about the lives of our forebears, we gain a clearer picture of our own life and discover what makes us who we are. Each of us wants to answer the age-old question, "Where did I come from?" Genealogy links us with the past, and with that connectedness comes a strong grounding and self-awareness.

Some people love a mystery and get caught up in the thrill of the chase, the enjoyment of hunting down those elusive ancestors. They enjoy the detective work called family history.

Others find pleasure in building a legacy of family history for their posterity, preserving family photos, writing biographical sketches of their ancestors, and constructing the family tree.

Some people trace their Irish ancestry in order to become Irish citizens. If either of your parents were born in Ireland, you automatically qualify for Irish citizenship. If any of your grandparents were born in Ireland, you can also become an Irish citizen. In fact, any children born to you after you obtain your Irish citizenship can apply for Irish citizenship themselves. Once you are an Irish citizen, you are also a citizen of the European Community. All you need to do to become an Irish citizen is fill out the required forms, submitting proof that you descend from a grandparent of Irish birth.

Some people trace their Irish roots because they are enamored by all things Irish and want to feel a greater bond with their Irish heritage.

It is a wonderful thing to have Irish ancestry.

How to Find Your Irish Ancestors

This book will lead you through five recommended steps to find your Irish ancestors. These steps, along with the chapters in this book that cover each topic, are:

1. Begin your search at home, following the basic principles of family history (chapter 1)
2. Learn about Irish history and your Irish family names (chapter 2–3)
3. Find your immigrant ancestor's place of origin in Ireland (chapters 4–5)
4. Search the major Irish record sources to find your ancestors in Ireland:
   a. Birth, marriage, and death certificates (chapter 6)
   b. Church records (chapter 7)
   c. Censuses (chapter 8)
   d. Land records (chapter 9)
5. Search other Irish sources to learn even more:
   a. Gravestone inscriptions (chapter 10)
   b. Newspapers (chapter 11)
   c. Directories (chapter 12)
   d. Wills (chapter 13)
   e. School registers (chapter 14)
   f. Occupation records (chapter 15)

There are many places you can go to learn about your Irish ancestors, including the Internet, the Family History Library, Irish Heritage Centres, and various archives and libraries (chapters 16–19). You might even decide to take a trip to Ireland to find your Irish ancestors (chapter 20).

Let's get started!

References and Selected Reading
Faulkner, Frank. *Irish Citizenship Handbook.* 2d ed. Springfield, Mass.: Hungry Hill, 1994.

Beautiful Irish Countryside.

Basic Principles

I saw behind me those who had gone, and before me, those who are to come.
I looked back and saw my father, and his father, and all our fathers,
and in front, to see my son, and his son, and the sons upon sons beyond.
And their eyes were my eyes.
As I felt, so they had felt, and were to feel, as then, so now, as to-morrow and forever....
I was of them, they were of me, and in me, and I in all of them.
                    —Richard Llewellyn, How Green Was My Valley

Here are a few basic principles and practices of good genealogy that will help you trace your Irish roots. Refer back to these guidelines often and you will have more success finding your Irish ancestors:

- Begin at home
- Interview your relatives
- Go from the known to the unknown
- Collaborate, collaborate, collaborate
- Check published family histories
- Keep it simple
- Find your ancestor's precise place of origin
- Document and organize your work
- Create a research plan
- Use multiple sources
- Research siblings too
- Learn the history and geography
- Set reasonable expectations
- Enjoy the journey

Begin at Home

Family history begins in the home. The details you discover from home sources will form the foundation of your Irish family history.

Does your family have any heirlooms from Ireland? Be sure to search the attic, the closet, old trunks, and family lock boxes, looking for memorabilia and family documents.

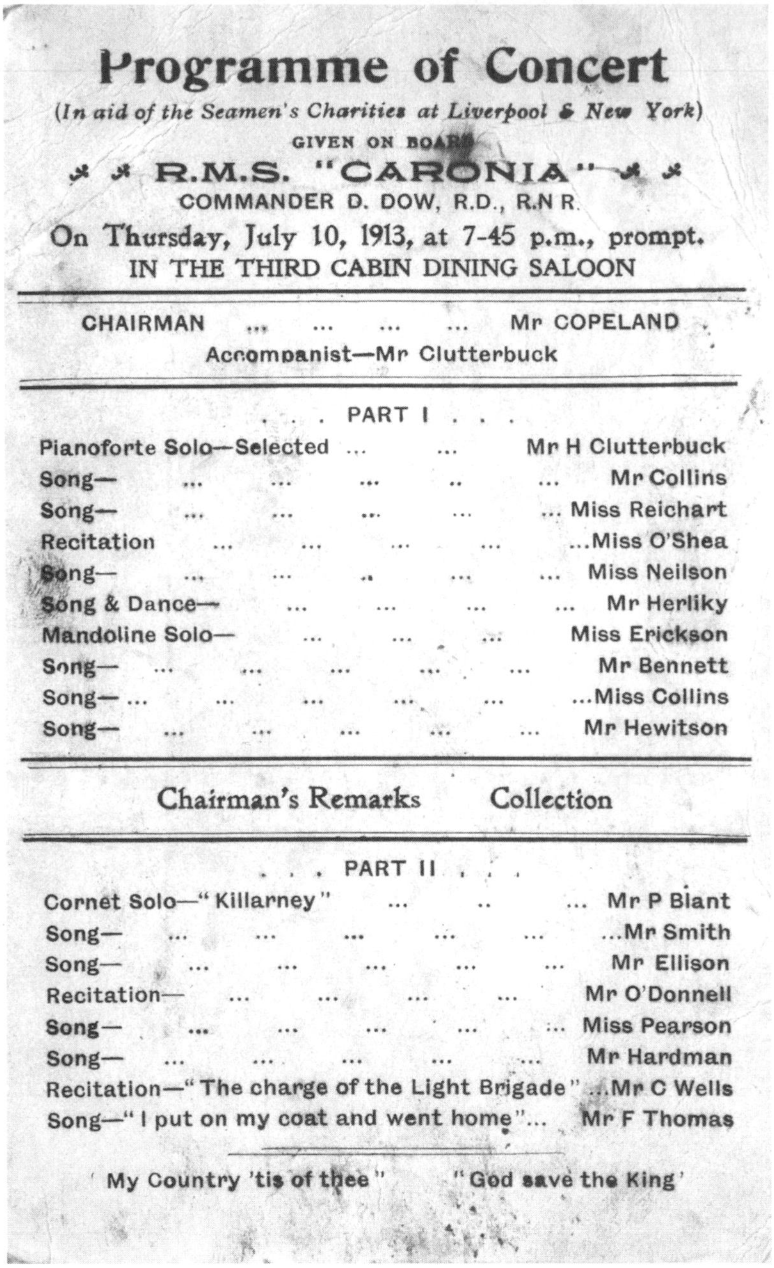

Programme of Concert

(In aid of the Seamen's Charities at Liverpool & New York)

GIVEN ON BOARD

✦ ✦ R.M.S. "CARONIA" ✦ ✦

COMMANDER D. DOW, R.D., R.N.R.

On Thursday, July 10, 1913, at 7-45 p.m., prompt.

IN THE THIRD CABIN DINING SALOON

CHAIRMAN ... ... Mr COPELAND

Accompanist—Mr Clutterbuck

. . . PART I . . .

Pianoforte Solo—Selected	Mr H Clutterbuck
Song—	Mr Collins
Song—	... Miss Reichart
Recitation	...Miss O'Shea
Song—	... Miss Neilson
Song & Dance—	... Mr Herliky
Mandoline Solo—	Miss Erickson
Song—	Mr Bennett
Song—	...Miss Collins
Song—	Mr Hewitson

Chairman's Remarks   Collection

. . . PART II . . .

Cornet Solo—" Killarney"	... Mr P Biant
Song—	...Mr Smith
Song—	Mr Ellison
Recitation—	Mr O'Donnell
Song—	... Miss Pearson
Song—	Mr Hardman
Recitation—" The charge of the Light Brigade "	...Mr C Wells
Song—" I put on my coat and went home " ...	Mr F Thomas

" My Country 'tis of thee "   " God save the King "

Figure 1-1. Home source—steamship postcard.

Check with your older relatives as well. You may locate old newspaper clippings, baptism announcements, diaries, naturalization papers, medals, death certificates, family Bibles, old photographs, steamship postcards (figure 1-1), birth certificates, communion tokens, wedding invitations, family heirlooms, prayer cards, scrapbooks, old letters, insurance papers, military service papers, inscribed jewelry, and much more. Each of these items may be the essential link to connect you to your ancestors in Ireland. Be creative, looking for anything that might shed light on your family history.

Old letters may tell you much about the personalities in your family. You can gain valuable insights about an ancestor by reading a letter written decades ago. The envelope might provide clues as well, like a return address in Ireland or a dated postmark.

Family photographs breathe life into genealogy. Photographs tell stories just like words in print. Does anyone in your family have photographs of your Irish ancestors? Has anyone in the family written any names, dates, or places on the back of these photographs? Who can tell you about the people in the pictures? You might see some of your own features in the faces of your ancestors.

Make an inventory of what you find, summarizing the facts, the stories, the details you infer about your Irish ancestry from home sources.

Interview Your Relatives

When I was a teenager and first discovered the excitement of family history, I quizzed my grandparents about their family, childhood, and ancestry. My notes from these visits reveal unique insights and details about my grandparents and their families that I could not have gained in any other way.

Interview your oldest living relatives individually. Find out what they know about your Irish ancestry. Let them roam freely through their memories. The experiences and family folklore they describe may clarify many details about your Irish origins, including family names, place names in Ireland, immigration dates, and much more. Tape record these interviews so you miss nothing—you can transcribe everything later.

Commit the family stories to writing. Write down all names, dates, and places that surface during these interviews. Your family stories, with all facts and fiction intact, are so perishable yet so valuable. Even if you suspect that a story is probably exaggerated or fabricated, it's best to write down the legend anyway. Family folklore usually contains a kernel of truth.

Go From the Known to the Unknown

Good genealogy consists of many small steps, not giant leaps. Start with the present, start with yourself, and gradually go back in time. Learn all you can about one generation before trying to jump back to the previous generation. Frankly, this is one of the rules I have the hardest time keeping, because I enjoy the thrill of finding lots of ancestors quickly.

Expand your search gradually from the core facts you already know. Start your research on solid ground. It is better to have patience, methodically learning all you can about an ancestor's family before continuing back in time. If you walk in the light of known facts, you will be less likely to stumble.

> → Basic Principle ←
>
> Learn all you can about one generation before trying to jump back to the previous generation.

Collaborate, Collaborate, Collaborate

Most of your ancestors have many living descendants—some you know and some you don't. Get in touch with close relatives to see what they know about your Irish ancestry. Seek out distant cousins and their research on your ancestors by letter, telephone, or the Internet. There is no need for you to do it all yourself. Besides, family history is all about family, and it can be fun working with others and getting to know cousins living in Ireland.

One of the best ways to collaborate in family history is to upload your family tree to the Internet. A number of websites have areas where you can submit your family tree for free. This is a great way to broadcast your efforts to the world, allowing distant relatives around the globe to find your family tree and contact you. The largest family tree collections on the Internet have hundreds of millions of names linked together in individual family trees (see Chapter 16, "Internet Sites").

Another great way to collaborate is to post your research questions on genealogy message boards. Use the community of the Internet and family history societies to share your research goals, challenges, and successes with others.

Check Published Family Histories

One of the most pleasant experiences in family history is finding a well-researched genealogy on one of your ancestral lines. Before you spend too much time doing original research on a family, take the time to search for published family histories. Many libraries have extensive collections of family history books dealing with particular surnames.

The Family History Library, based in Salt Lake City, Utah, has the largest collection of Irish genealogy in the world, including thousands of published family histories. You can search The Family History Library Catalog online at FamilySearch <www.familysearch.org>. Type in an ancestor's surname in the Surname Search, and the website will respond with a list of the family histories for the selected surname. Chapter 17, "The Family History Library," describes the Family History Library Catalog in detail.

A word of caution: remember that all family histories, whether published in books, on the Internet, or elsewhere, simply reflect the opinions of other genealogists. Not all family histories are correct. How do you know whether someone else's family history contains trustworthy information? If you find a family history that does not cite genealogical sources, you can't be sure where the information came from or whether it is valid. In this case, it's appropriate to treat the family history with suspicion. However, if the family history is well documented, you can check the sources yourself and draw your own conclusions about the credibility of the information.

Keep It Simple

Focus on one goal at a time, selecting just one ancestor or family you want to learn more about. Review what you know and identify the one question you most want answered. Maybe you want to learn where your ancestor was born in Ireland or when your ancestor emigrated from Ireland. Write down your question, your research goal. Your family history activities will focus on answering that one question.

Find Your Ancestor's Precise Place of Origin

Basic
✦ Principle ✦

The key to successful Irish family history is identifying the parish or townland where your ancestors lived in Ireland.

The key to successful Irish family history is finding where your ancestors lived in Ireland. Just knowing that your immigrant ancestor came from Ireland is rarely good enough. Knowing the county is certainly better, but what you really need to do is identify the parish or townland of origin. The more precisely you identify your ancestor's address in Ireland, the better. Once you know precisely where your ancestors lived in Ireland, you can use a wide variety of Irish genealogical sources to learn more about them.

As you search records about your immigrant ancestor in his or her adopted homeland, you will be looking for details about the individual's birthplace, last known residence in Ireland, residence of nearest kin in Ireland, parents' names, or anything else that can help you learn more about your ancestor's life in Ireland.

Chapter 4, "Place Names and Land Divisions," describes counties, parishes, townlands, and other Irish land divisions. Chapter 5, "The Irish Overseas," explains how to use the best record sources to find your immigrant ancestor's precise place of origin in Ireland.

Document and Organize Your Work

As you gather details about the lives of your ancestors, you will probably accumulate lots of information from many sources. Rather than keep all of this in your head, you will find it is much easier to write everything down.

Most people doing genealogy use a combination of descendancy charts, pedigree (ancestry) charts, and family group sheets to document and organize their work.

A pedigree chart isn't used just for dogs and horses—people use pedigree charts to display their ancestors on a single sheet of paper. The word pedigree comes from the French phrase "*pie de grue*," which literally means "foot of crane." The pedigree chart does look something like the webbed foot of a crane: it begins with you and then branches out to your parents, grandparents, great-grandparents, and so on.

A family group record shows the information you have recorded for a husband, wife, and children (figure 1-2). This is one of the best tools to use, because it helps you keep track of what you know about everyone in the family, not just your direct ancestors. Many people keep a family group record for each couple in their ancestry.

Many people use genealogy software to record their family history. Some of the more popular computer programs for genealogy and family history are Family Tree Maker™, Personal Ancestral File™, Legacy™, and The Master Genealogist™. These programs make it easy to add and describe individuals and families; cite sources; keep notes; insert digital photos, videos, and audio files; create family history websites; print charts and family history books; and share your genealogy with others.

Create a Research Plan

A research plan starts with a clearly stated goal. A research plan also lists the sources you plan to consult to find the information you seek. With this you can document when and where you obtained each source and what you did or did not find. You can begin a research plan for an individual, a couple, or a family, depending on what you want to learn about your ancestors. Drawing a time line of your ancestor's life may help you decide the best questions to ask about your ancestor.

Write down what you know, what you want to learn, and what you discover along the way. At some point in the future you may want to refer back to what you found. As you keep accurate notes and cite your sources, you make it easier for you or someone else to see what work has already been done. If you get in the habit of making photocopies of all documents you find, you will be able to examine them in detail later and always have a complete record of what you found.

Family Group Record

Husband	John Love		
	Born	Abt Jun 1855	Place West Riding of County Cork, Ireland
	Married	12 Aug 1884	Place Lissavally, Galway, Ireland
	Husband's father	John Love	
	Husband's mother	Unknown	

Wife	Harriet Emily McCarthy		
	Born		Place County Armagh, Ireland
	Wife's father	William McCarthy	
	Wife's mother	Marion	

Children List each child in order of birth.

1	F	Sarah Kate Love		
		Born	6 Mar 1886	Place Lissavally, Galway, Ireland

2	M	William John Love		
		Born	17 Jun 1887	Place Moylough, Galway, Ireland

3	F	Marion Isabella Love		
		Born	26 Jun 1889	Place Abbeylara, Longford, Ireland

4	M	Alfred Henry Love		
		Born	2 Jan 1891	Place Abbeylara, Longford, Ireland

5	M	Richard Bertram Love		
		Born	13 Jan 1892	Place Abbeylara, Longford, Ireland

6	M	George Gilbert Love		
		Born	6 Nov 1893	Place Abbeylara, Longford, Ireland
		Died	24 Jul 1978	Place San Jose, Santa Clara, California
		Buried		Place Fremont, Alameda, California
		Spouse	Merle Carlyss Bissonette	
		Married	1 Oct 1948	Place Springfield, Hampden, Massachusetts
		Spouse	Alice Woodfine	
		Married	1921	Place

7	F	Harriet Helena Love		
		Born	23 Mar 1895	Place Newtownforbes, Longford, Ireland
		Died	Deceased	Place

8	F	Olive Jane Love		
		Born	8 Oct 1896	Place Kilgolagh, Cavan, Ireland
		Died	Deceased	Place

9	M	Ernest Love		
		Born	25 Jan 1903	Place Carrickart, Donegal, Ireland

10	M	Wilfred Henry Love		
		Born	1 Nov 1905	Place Belfast, Antrim, Ireland
		Spouse	Ruth	
		Married		Place

Figure 1-2. Family group record (printed from Personal Ancestral File).

As you glean information from genealogical sources you will be looking for evidence about your ancestors' identities and family relationships. You will compare the information found in a variety of sources and form your own conclusions about whether your ancestors are the people named in these sources. At some point you may find contradictory information as you compare information from various records: you will want to resolve the discrepancies to your satisfaction. Document the reasons for your conclusions, and write down the questions you still have. These questions are your new research goals.

Use Multiple Sources

Use a variety of sources, not just one, to paint a true picture of each of your ancestors. Names, dates, and places may be recorded incorrectly in some genealogical sources. For example, a baptism certificate is more likely to state the correct birth date than a death certificate for the same person. If you have more sources confirming the birth date, you can be more confident that your information is accurate.

The more records you find about a family, the more balanced and comprehensive a view you will have of them. As you extract facts from multiple sources, you form better conclusions about your ancestors.

Research Siblings Too

The search for an ancestor is really the search for a family. Learn about the entire family before continuing to the next generation. Sometimes the best discoveries come as you learn about the lives of brothers and sisters. Study the siblings as closely as you study your own ancestor. You will find clues about your ancestor you otherwise might have completely missed.

Learn the History and Geography

Your ancestors were a part of history—learn about that history and you will learn more about your ancestors. Many families lived in the same area for generations. You will understand more about your ancestors as you study the history and geography of the area. As you study the local history you will become more aware of the religious practices, folklore, customs, and cultural setting where your ancestors lived. You may begin to understand some of the reasons why your ancestors left Ireland. An overview of the history of Ireland is presented in Chapter 2, "Timeline of Irish History."

Set Reasonable Expectations

Most of our Irish ancestors were poor tenant farmers. Few records document their lives, and most of these records date back only to the early nineteenth century. Set your expectations accordingly and allow yourself to be pleasantly surprised if you succeed in tracing an Irish ancestral line back two hundred years.

Consider the professionally researched Irish ancestry of former U.S. President John Fitzgerald Kennedy (figure 1-3). Although expert genealogists assembled this family tree by consulting all the best genealogical sources, unanswered questions appear as recently as the 1830s:

Table 1-1 illustrates the availability of Irish records. Most surviving records begin in the early 1800s or later. This chart shows the most valuable record sources to consult as you search for your Irish ancestors. Many of the time periods are approximate; for example, individual church parish registers may begin before or after the general start dates shown.

Table 1-1: Irish Family History Sources

Source	1700–24	1725–49	1750–74	1775–99	1800–24	1825–49	1850–74	1875–99	1900–24	1925–49	1950–74	1975–99
Civil Registration							■	■	■	■	■	■
Census Returns									■			
Catholic Parish Records				■	■	■	■	■	■	■	■	■
Church of Ireland Records			■	■	■	■	■	■				
Presbyterian Records					■	■	■	■				
Land Valuations					■	■	■	■	■	■	■	■
Tithe Applotments						■						
Registry of Deeds	■	■	■	■	■	■	■	■	■	■	■	■
Newspapers		■	■	■	■	■	■	■	■	■	■	■
Directories				■	■	■	■	■	■			
Wills and Administrations	■	■	■	■	■	■	■	■	■	■	■	■
Gravestone Inscriptions			■	■	■	■	■	■	■	■	■	■
National School Registers					■	■	■	■	■	■	■	■

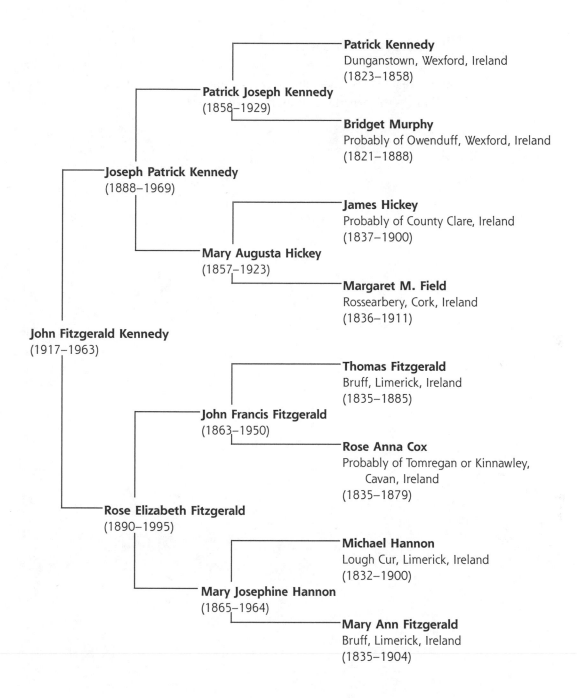

Figure 1-3: Pedigree chart of U.S. President John Fitzgerald Kennedy.

Enjoy the Journey

Family history is a marvelous journey of self-discovery. It is exciting to climb your family tree and learn more about yourself and your family in the process. There is no finish line—the experience brings its own rewards.

2

Time Line of Irish History

IRISHMEN AND IRISHWOMEN: In the name of God and of the dead generations from which she receives her old tradition of nationhood, Ireland, through us, summons her children to her flag and strikes for her freedom.
    —Opening sentence of the Proclamation of the Republic, Easter Monday, 1916.

Ireland has had a tumultuous and colorful history. Your Irish ancestors participated in that history. As you learn about that history, you learn more about your Irish ancestors. Your knowledge of English rule in Ireland, the Penal Laws, the Great Famine, the birth of the Irish Free State, the Irish Civil War, and other historical events may provide valuable insights as you search for your ancestors.

Here's a time line of the history of Ireland, including some of the major historical and genealogical events of interest to family historians:

c. 6000 B.C. Earliest traces of people settling in Ireland.

c. 2500 B.C. Neolithic people build passage grave at Newgrange.

c. 250 B.C. Celtic tribes first invade the island.

A.D. 432 Saint Patrick converts many Irish to the Christian faith.

795 Vikings begin raiding Ireland.

922 Vikings create a settlement in Limerick.

1002 Brian Boru first to ascend to High Kingship of Ireland.

1014 Brian Boru defeats the Vikings at Clontarf but dies in battle.

1152 Synod of Kells divides Ireland into four ecclesiastical provinces, the archdioceses of Armagh, Cashel, Dublin, and Tuam. The boundaries of the original twenty-two dioceses are essentially the same as those now used by the Catholic Church and the Church of Ireland, with minor alterations.

1170–71 Normans invade Ireland: Richard de Clare "Strongbow," Earl of Pembroke, seizes Dublin and becomes King of Leinster. Most Irish bishops and kings submit to his rule.

1366	Statutes of Kilkenny forbid Anglo-Normans from marrying Irish or speaking the Irish language.
1536	The Anglican Church becomes the official state church of Ireland.
1541	Henry VIII forces the Irish Parliament to declare him King of Ireland.
1550	Proclamation against Catholic religious ceremonies.
1579–80	Earl of Desmond rebels against English encroachment in Munster.
1605	Beginning of English and Scottish plantation of Ulster.
1607	Flight of the Earls: O'Neill, Earl of Tyrone; O'Donnell, Earl of Tyrconnell; and others flee Ireland.
1619	Earliest surviving Church of Ireland parish register: St. John the Evangelist, Dublin.
1641	Irish/Catholic rebellion, seeking return of lands confiscated in Ulster.
1649	Cromwell brutally crushes Irish rebellion; massacres at Drogheda and Wexford; more land granted to English Protestants.
1671	Earliest surviving Irish Catholic parish register: Wexford.
1674	Earliest surviving Irish Presbyterian church register: Antrim (First) Congregation.
1690	William of Orange defeats his father-in-law, James II, and Irish troops at Battle of the Boyne.
1690s	Penal Laws forbid Catholics from holding public office, receiving an education, voting, bearing arms, and buying land.
1695	Only 14 percent of Catholics in Ireland own land.
1704	Another Penal Law "to prevent further growth of popery" weakens rights of Catholic landholders.
1708	Registry of Deeds created.
1740s	Penal Laws are strictly enforced.
1772–95	Catholic Relief Acts restore many rights suspended by Penal Laws.
1801	Act of Union merges two governments, creating the United Kingdom of Great Britain and Ireland.
1821	First complete census of Ireland, listing everyone by name and age in each household (mostly destroyed in the 1922 bombing of Four Courts in Dublin).
1823	Tithe Composition Act requires that tithes be paid in cash to the Anglican Church.
1823–38	Tithe Applotment Survey, first detailed survey and valuation of (agricultural) land throughout Ireland.
1829	Catholic Emancipation Act grants equal rights to Roman Catholics in Ireland.
1831	Second census of Ireland (mostly destroyed).
1838	Poor Law Relief Act creates Poor Law Unions to collect taxes and provide relief of the poor.
1841	Third census of Ireland (mostly destroyed): population 8,175,124, the largest total of any Irish census.

1843   O'Connell assembles nearly one million people at the Hill of Tara to protest the Act of Union.

1845   Civil registration of non-Catholic marriages begins.

1845–49 Potato blight over consecutive years causes Great Famine: millions die, and millions more emigrate.

1847–64 Griffith's Primary Valuation of Tenements, earliest surviving list of all households in Ireland.

1851   Fourth census of Ireland (mostly destroyed): population 6,552,385, down 20 percent in ten years due to ravishes of famine and ensuing emigration.

1857   Probate Act transfers probate authority from the Church of Ireland to newly established government probate districts.

1858   The Irish Republican Brotherhood (Fenians) founded.

1861   Fifth census of Ireland (destroyed): population 5,798,967, down 11.5 percent in ten years.

1864   Civil registration of all births, marriages, and deaths required by law.

1870   Church of Ireland disestablished—ceases to be recognized as the established state church.

1871   Sixth census of Ireland (destroyed): population 5,412,377.

1879   Foundation of Irish National Land League; beginning of Land Wars.

1881   Seventh census of Ireland (destroyed): population 5,174,836.

1891   Eighth census of Ireland (destroyed): population 4,704,750.

1901   Ninth census of Ireland: population 4,458,775; earliest surviving census of entire population.

1907   John Millington Synge writes *The Aran Islands*, describing the people and folklore of Inishmór.

1908   Old Age Pension Act initiates a pension program; applications often included abstracts of 1841 and 1851 censuses to prove age.

1911   Tenth census of Ireland: population 4,381,951; second complete surviving census in Ireland.

1916   The Easter Rising—Proclamation of the Republic.

1919   Beginning of the war of Irish independence from British rule.

1922   Birth of the Irish Free State.

1922   Beginning of the Irish Civil War; Four Courts in Dublin is bombed, the Public Record Office is destroyed in the ensuing fire, and priceless church records, censuses, and wills are lost forever.

1923   End of the Irish Civil War.

1937   The Irish Free State is renamed Ireland (*Eire* in Irish) in a new constitution.

1949   Ireland Act, proclamation of the Republic of Ireland.

1955   The Republic of Ireland is admitted to the United Nations.

1969   "The Troubles" begin in Northern Ireland.

> ⬇
> ### Historical Fact
> The huge exodus caused by the Great Famine of 1845–49 dwarfed all previous waves of Irish emigration.

1972	January 30: thirteen Catholics killed by British soldiers during civil rights march in Londonderry (Bloody Sunday).
1973	The Republic of Ireland and the United Kingdom join the European Economic Community.
1985	Anglo-Irish Agreement gives the Republic an advisory role in Northern Ireland.
1993	English and Irish prime ministers agree to Irish self-determination in Downing Street Declaration .
1998	Good Friday Agreement lays out a plan for resolving the troubles in Northern Ireland.
2002	Republic of Ireland adopts Euro (€) as official currency.

As you learn about your Irish ancestors you will want to keep in mind the historical events that occurred during their lifetime. A knowledge of Irish history will help you see your ancestors in the context of the culture and times they lived. An awareness of the history of Ireland will make it easier for you to interpret what you learn about your ancestors: their family life, their occupations, their faith, and the challenges they may have experienced.

References and Selected Reading

Duffy, Seán, ed. *The Macmillan Atlas of Irish History*. New York: Macmillan USA, 1997.

Foster, R. F. *The Oxford History of Ireland*. New York: Oxford University Press, 2001.

Hackney Blackwell, Amy, and Ryan Hackney. *The Everything Irish History and Heritage Book*. Avon, Mass: Adams Media, 2004.

Killeen, Richard. *A Timeline of Irish History*. Dublin: Gill and Macmillan, 2003.

McCourt, Malachy. *Malachy McCourt's History of Ireland*. Philadelphia: Running Press, 2004.

Surnames and
Given Names

In every conceivable manner, the family is the link to our past, the bridge to our future.
—Alex Haley

In Ireland, the practice of inheriting family names began more than one thousand years ago, earlier than in most European countries. The surnames (family names) of Ireland have rich and impressive histories. You can learn a lot about your Irish ancestors by becoming familiar with the history and origin of their names. You may even be able to use your emigrant ancestor's surname to narrow down where the family lived in Ireland. Surnames are one of our best links to the past.

Years ago, children usually lived in the same place as their parents and grandparents. When a family settled in a new area, they put down roots, established a livelihood, occupied a plot of ground, and became part of the community. Their children tended to stay in the neighborhood even after they were married. This means that many family names are densely clustered in specific places. This is especially true in Ireland, where some families have occupied the same land for over a thousand years.

Learn all you can about your Irish surname. Learn the origin and meaning of the name. Learn the history of the name, including where the name is common in Ireland. You can see how your ancestors' surnames are distributed across Ireland and use the information to narrow your search considerably.

Surname Origins

Most Irish surnames are ancient, typically of Gaelic or Anglo-Norman origin. English and Scottish surnames are also common in Ireland, especially in the northern counties.

Gaelic surnames derive from many sources, such as:

- Given names (e.g., O'Brien, son of Brian)
- Occupations (e.g., O'Riordan, from *riogh bhard*–royal bard)

15

- Plants (e.g., MacDarragh, from *dair*–oak)
- Animals (e.g., Whelan, from *faol*–wolf)
- Places (e.g., Desmond, from *deas*–south, *Mumhan*–Munster)
- Personal attributes (e.g., Kennedy, from *ceann*–head, *eidigh*–ugly)

Anglo-Norman surnames derive from similar sources. Some of these surnames in modern Ireland were anglicized, thus obscuring their past. For example, some Smiths were originally MacGowans. Many Anglo-Norman names preserve their original form mostly intact, such as Browne, Fitzgerald, Power, and Ferriter.

English names such as Wilson, Spenser, Hughes, and Anderson have been very common throughout Ireland for many centuries. Many Scottish surnames such as Stewart, Graham, and Ferguson were introduced into Ireland in great numbers during the Plantation of Ulster in the seventeenth century. Quakers, French Huguenots, Palatine Germans, and Jews have also woven their names into the tapestry of Irish surnames.

Many surnames in Ireland have multiple origins. For example, some Campbell families are of Gaelic origin while others have roots in Scotland. Jones families may have either English or Welsh ancestors, as many Jones families emigrated from England and Wales and settled in Ireland.

Perhaps the best book describing the origins of Irish surnames is Edward MacLysaght's *The Surnames of Ireland*. For Northern Ireland, Robert Bell's *The Book of Ulster Surnames* is recommended reading. Other books on Irish surnames and given names are listed in the bibliography.

Surname Localities

Many surnames are identifiable with specific locations in Ireland, often having their origins in early Gaelic clans or Anglo-Norman families. If you do not know where your ancestor lived in Ireland, but his or her surname was concentrated in a particular geographic area, you may be able to find the ancestor by focusing your search in that area. Certain uncommon surnames are localized to a single Irish county or parish.

Research Tip

Many surnames are identifiable with specific locations in Ireland.

For example, the surname Ferriter originated in the town of Ballyferriter, near the western tip of the Dingle Peninsula in County Kerry. This ancient, Anglo-Norman family has occupied Ballyferriter for over seven hundred years. In the 1850s there were twenty-one Ferriter households in Ireland, nineteen in County Kerry. The Kerry Ferriters all lived on the Dingle Peninsula, mostly in and around Ballyferriter. A search of the 2000–2001 phone book for this part of Ireland shows that fourteen of the fifteen Ferriter families in present-day Kerry still live on the Dingle Peninsula, a century and a half later. If you have a Ferriter ancestor who immigrated to America from Ireland, it is highly likely that the family originated in the Dingle Peninsula.

So how can you identify the distribution of your ancestor's surname in Ireland? If you are looking for living relatives, search a modern phone book. A number of phone books for Ireland are searchable online, including:

- Golden Pages <www.goldenpages.ie/extra/phonebook.html>
- 11850 <www.11850.ie>

If you are looking for the location of families in earlier times, try using Griffith's Valuation, a land record from the mid-1800s (see Chapter 9, "Land and Property Records"). You can search this name list to find the distribution of a surname across all of Ireland or within a county or parish.

Relatively common surnames may still be concentrated in just a few parishes of a particular county. Let's say you know only which county your ancestor lived in, and his surname was rather common in Ireland. By searching modern phone books and Griffith's Valuation within the county, you can see how common the surname seems to be within the county. If you are fortunate, you will see most people with that surname clustered in one or two areas of the county. Although this does not guarantee that you've pinpointed your ancestor's residence, at least you have a starting point for your research.

Eneclann, a professional genealogical research firm in Ireland, has published a CD-ROM that helps identify localities in Ireland where certain surnames were common. The CD, entitled *Grenham's Irish Surnames*, uses historical sources and maps to display surnames by locality. You can enter a surname and see a county map highlighting where the surname appears in Ireland. These maps of surname distributions are derived from Griffith's Valuation (1847–64) and Sir Richard Matheson's distribution of surnames taken from the 1890 civil registration of births.

If you know the surnames of a husband and wife and need to focus the geography of your search, find out where both surnames exist simultaneously. If both surnames occur within a single parish, for instance, you may be able to find the husband's family and the wife's family by searching records of that parish.

Surname Spellings

Your ancestor may be named differently in different records. Do not assume that your family name was always spelled exactly one way. It almost certainly has been spelled many ways over the years. The concept of a fixed surname spelling is largely a phenomenon of the twentieth century.

Most Irish surnames have a variety of creative spellings. You may expect to find many curious name spellings as you search the original records. Most spellings of a particular name will sound almost the same when spoken. Name spellings in original documents often reflect how locals perceived the sound of the name. For example, some letters have similar sounds and are therefore interchangeable. The letters "c," "k," and "g" are

Warning

Do not assume that your family name was always spelled exactly one way, because it almost certainly has been spelled many ways over the years. "O" and "Mac'"prefixes may also have been added and removed, depending on the name.

often substituted one for another, as in the name Patrick (also Padric or Padraig). You may also find a number of transcription errors as people prepare name indexes for historical records and mistake one letter for another. An "n" may be misread as "m," the letter pair "ch" may be misread as "d," and so on.

Name spellings changed over time for many reasons. Some names were anglicized when the Irish emigrant arrived in America. Some Irish emigrants intentionally dropped the "O" prefix to avoid any stigma associated with being Irish in their newly adopted homes. Even in Ireland the "O" and "Mac" prefixes went in and out of fashion and may or may not appear in any particular record. Regardless of the reason, we need to be aware that surname spellings have not always been as rigid as they are nowadays.

Here are four typical examples of name changes you might see in Irish records:

- Margaret O'Connor's name may be written "Maggie Connor" on her birth certificate.
- Bridget Lysaght's name may be written "Delia MacLysaght" on the census.
- Michael Sullivan's name may be written "Ml. Ó Suilleabháin" on his marriage certificate.
- William O'Rourke's name might be written "Gulielmus Rorke" in a Catholic parish register.

Given Names

One hundred years ago the Irish used far fewer given names than today. Traditional naming patterns restricted the selection of names dramatically. Tables 3-1 and 3-2 show the dozen most common given names used in Ireland in the 1800s. Well over half the population of Ireland went by these twelve given names.

Table 3-1: The Most Popular Male Names in Nineteenth-Century Ireland

English	Gaelic	Latin	Common Abbreviations	Nicknames, Other Spellings, and Interchangeable Names
John	Eoin, Seaghan, Sean, Seon	Johannes, Joannes, Ioannes, Joannis	Jno	Jack, Johnny, Owen, Sean, Shane, Shawn
James	Seamus, Simidh, Siomaidh	Jacobus	Jas	Jacob, Jamey, Jamie, Jim, Jimmy, Shamus, Shemus
Patrick	Padraig	Patricius	Pat, Patt, Patk, Patrk	Paddy, Padric, Pat, Patty, Paudrick
Thomas	Tomas	Thomas	Tho, Thos	Tom, Tomas, Tommy
William	Uilliam	Gulielmus	Wm, Willm	Bill, Billy, Liam, Will, Willy
Michael	Michael	Michaelis	Mich, Michl, Ml	Mick, Mickey, Mike

Family Naming Customs

Nowadays, expectant parents come up with names for their children using all sorts of novel approaches. Historically, baby names were often selected according to much more traditional rules. In previous centuries, Irish parents often named their sons according to this general pattern:

- The first son was named after the father's father
- The second son was named after the mother's father
- The third son was named after the father

Irish daughters were frequently named following a similar pattern:

- The first daughter was named after the mother's mother
- The second daughter was named after the father's mother
- The third daughter was named after the mother

Some Irish families strictly adhered to this naming convention. If your Irish ancestors named children in this traditional way, you might be able to more readily find them in records even when the surname is common. You may also be able to predict the names of the grandparents. However, these patterns should serve only as a guideline and should not be considered "proof" of family relationships. Many families simply named their children after close relatives or godparents, following no obvious pattern.

You may find a family that has two children with the same given names. If a child died in infancy it was common for the next born child of the same gender to receive the same name. Look for the death of the first child before the birth of the second child of the same name.

The ethnic and religious origins of Irish families also influenced the names given to children. Protestant families often named their sons and daughters after kings and queens. Catholic families usually named their children after prophets and saints. If you do not know a family's religion, the children's names may give you a clue. The

Table 3-2: The Most Popular Female Names in Nineteenth-Century Ireland

English	Gaelic	Latin	Common Abbreviations	Nicknames, Other Spellings, and Interchangeable Names
Mary	Maire	Maria	M	Margery, Marie, Maura, Maureen, May, Moira, Molly, Polly
Anne	Aine, Eithne	Anna		Ann, Annie, Hannah, Hanora, Johanna, Nan, Nancy, Nanny, Norah
Margaret	Maire, Mairead	Margareta	Marg, Margt, Mgt	Madge, Maggie, Marge, Meg, Molly, Peg, Peggy, Polly
Catherine	Caitilin, Catroine, Cait	Catharina	Cath	Caitlin, Cassie, Cate, Cathy, Kate, Kathleen, Kathy, Kay, Kitty, Triona
Bridget	Brid, Brighid	Brigida	Brid, Bgt	Bess, Bessie, Biddy, Bidelia, Breeda, Brideen, Brigit, Cordelia, Delia
Ellen	Eibhilin	Elena		Eileen, Eleanor, Ella, Elly, Helen, Nel, Nellie

rules weren't rigid, but you may notice these tendencies in the naming patterns of your Irish ancestors.

Another naming custom in some families was to bestow a family surname upon a child in the form of a middle name. This middle name was often the mother's maiden name. For example, my ancestor Ambrose Lysaght Browne was actually named after his mother, Margaret Lysaght. If you encounter a middle name that sounds suspiciously like a surname, you may actually have evidence of another family surname.

In Summary

Your ancestors' names are full of meaning. Since many surnames are rooted in particular localities in Ireland, you can often focus on the place where the surname is concentrated to find your ancestors. This is especially true if you already know an ancestor's county of origin. Modern phone books, land records, censuses, surname dictionaries, and other historical records may help you identify specific localities where your ancestors' surnames occur most frequently. Remember to keep an open mind about the spelling of any surname, as the name may have been spelled many different ways over the years. Given names deserve some caution as well, as nicknames and alternate names were commonly used in historical records. Given names may also hold important clues about the family, including the names of parents and grandparents.

References and Selected Reading

Bell, Robert. *The Book of Ulster Surnames*. Belfast: Blackstaff, 1988.

Grehan, Ida. *The Dictionary of Irish Family Names*. Boulder, Colo.: Roberts Rinehart, 1997.

MacLysaght, Edward. *The Surnames of Ireland*. 6th ed. Dublin: Irish Academic Press, 1985.

Matheson, Sir Robert E. *Varieties and Synonymes of Surnames and Christian Names in Ireland*. 1901. Reprint, Bowie, Md.: Heritage Books, 1995.

Ó Corráin, Donnchadh, and Fidelma Maguire. *Gaelic Personal Names*. Dublin: Academy Press, 1981.

Place Names and Land Divisions

Erin grá mo chrói,
You're the dear old land to me,
You're the fairest that my eyes did e'er behold.
You're the land Saint Patrick blessed,
You're the bright star of the west,
You're that dear little isle so far away.
        —*From the traditional Irish song* Erin Grá Mo Chrói (Ireland, Love of My Heart), *as*
        performed by Cherish the Ladies on the album The Girls Won't Leave the Boys Alone

The key to successful Irish family history is finding where your ancestors lived in Ireland. A basic understanding of Irish place names will help you feel more familiar with the places you encounter in your research. Knowledge of the various land divisions in Ireland will make it easier to search genealogical records to find your ancestors.

Place Name Origins

Many places in Ireland were originally named in Irish Gaelic. For example, the place name "Ballymore" comes from two Gaelic words, *baile* (town) and *mhór* (big), or "big town." Some places were originally named for prominent features of the local geography, such as a lake, ridge, hill, valley, rock, or plain. Other place names derive from local flora, such as groves, heathers, or pastures. Places are commonly named after man-made structures as well, such as forts, churches, roads, and castles. Some places are also named after prominent people. Table 4-1 gives some examples of Gaelic words commonly found in place names.

Many place names in Ireland have Anglo-Norman or English roots. These place names often derive from personal or family names but may also describe the local geography, vegetation, or man-made structures. Some examples are Blanchardstown, Castleisland, Newtownabbey, Cookstown, and Newcastle. Vikings settled most towns with names that end in "ford." Waterford and Wexford, for example, were originally Viking strongholds.

Table 4-1: Gaelic Words Commonly Used in Irish Place Names

Gaelic	English Meaning	Place Name Example	Gaelic Name and English Translation
Ard	Height, summit	Ardfert, Kerry	Ard Fhearta, height of the grave
Baile	Town, village, homestead	Ballyloughbeg, Antrim	Baile an Locha Beag, town of the small lake
Beag	Small	Ballybeg, Tipperary	Baile Beag, small town
Bóthar	Road, lane	Boherboy, Cork	Bóthar Buí, yellow road
Caiseal	Castle, circular fort	Cashel, Tipperary	Caiseal, stone fort
Carraig	Rock, crag	Carrickfergus, Antrim	Carraig Fhearghasa, rock of Fergus
Cathair	Stone fort	Cahermore, Cork	Cathair Mhór, big stone fort
Cill	Church, cell	Kildare, Kerry	Cill Dara, church of the oak tree
Cloch	Stone	Cloghane, Kerry	Clocháne, stony place
Cluain	Pasture	Clonygowan, Offaly	Cluain na nGamhan, pasture of the calves
Cnoc	Hill	Knockvicar, Roscommon	Cnoc an Bhiocáire, hill of the vicar
Doire	Oak, oak grove	Dunderry, Meath	Dún Doire, fort of the oak grove
Droim	Ridge	Drumshanbo, Leitrim	Droim Sean Bhó, ridge of the old cow
Dún	Fort	Donegal	Dún na nGall, fort of the foreigners
Gort	Tilled field, garden	Gortnananny, Galway	Gort an Eanaigh, field of the marsh
Gleann	Valley, glen	Glenroe, Limerick	Gleann Rua, red valley
Inis	Island	Inisheer, Galway	Inis Oirthir, eastern island
Lios	Ring fort, ancient place	Lisnakill, Waterford	Lios na Cille, fort of the church
Loch	Lake	Fin Lough, Clare	Loch Fionn, white lake
Mhór	Big	Kylemore, Galway	Coill Mhór, big wood
Ráth	Ring fort, earthen fort	Rathmullen, Sligo	Ráth an Mhuilinn, fort of the mill
Sean	Old	Shanbally, Cork	Sean Bhaile, old town
Sliabh	Mountain	Slieve Snaght, Donegal	Sliabh Sneachta, snow mountain
Teampall	Church, temple	Templebrendan, Mayo	Teampeall Brendáin, Brendan's church
Trá(igh)	Strand, beach, shore	Tralee, Kerry	Tráigh lí, shore of the (river) Lí

Spelling Place Names

Plays naems kin bee spelld een menny create if waies een geneolgy reckerds. In fact, most townlands did not have "official" spellings before the Ordnance Survey standardized Irish place names in the 1830s. As you encounter Irish place names in your family history, keep in mind that most were written as they sounded (phonetically). While researching the Catholic parish registers for Killury, I found these spellings of the townland Tiershanaghan: Tiershannahan, Tiershanahan, Tiershanhan, Tiershanna, Teershannahan, Tirshanahan, and Tiershanon. I never saw the "official" townland spelling in these records.

The same principle is true when dealing with Irish place names recorded abroad. For example, you may find an Irish locality spelled phonetically in an American document. Imagine this situation: A town clerk in New England is trying to fill out a marriage certificate in the 1850s. He asks the bride, recently arrived from Ireland, where she was born. She says, "Ballyloughbeg, County Antrim." He writes "Ballilockbag, Entrim County."

↓

Warning

Plays naems kin bee spelld een menny create if waies een geneolgy reckerds.

How, then, do you correctly identify the bride's birthplace in Ireland? First you try to imagine how a nineteenth-century New Englander would have heard an Irish girl pronounce the name. Then you would search an Irish townland index, repeating the sound of the place name while keeping an open mind about how it might be spelled.

Land Divisions

Once you discover where your ancestors lived in Ireland, you should take time to familiarize yourself with the area, learning the names of each of the land divisions they lived in. This is important because different genealogical records are organized under different land divisions. Each of the major land divisions is defined below, generally from largest to smallest.

Nation

Modern Ireland is divided into two nations: the Republic of Ireland and Northern Ireland. The Republic of Ireland spans four-fifths of the island, including the three provinces of Connaught, Leinster, and Munster, and three counties of the province of Ulster: Cavan, Donegal and Monaghan. Northern Ireland is part of the United Kingdom of Great Britain and Northern Ireland and consists of the other six counties of Ulster: Antrim, Armagh, Derry (Londonderry), Down, Fermanagh, and Tyrone.

Province

Ireland consists of four provinces: Connaught in the west, Leinster in the east, Munster in the south, and Ulster in the north (see figure 4-1). The four provinces roughly correspond to regions dominated by four major Irish clans before the Norman invasion: O'Conor in Connaught, MacMurrough in Leinster, O'Brien in Munster, and O'Niell in Ulster. Each province is divided into counties.

Diocese

A diocese is an administrative unit in either the Catholic Church or Church of Ireland, consisting of a number of church parishes and presided over by a bishop. In the twelfth century, four ecclesiastical provinces were established in Ireland: Armagh, Cashel, Dublin, and Tuam. These provinces were under the authority of four archbishops. Twenty-two bishops were responsible for the individual dioceses within the four provinces. From these beginnings, the Catholic Church and the Church of Ireland have developed distinctly different dioceses over the centuries.

County

The thirty-two counties of Ireland were created between the late twelfth and early seventeenth centuries. County boundaries typically follow lines drawn anciently between powerful Gaelic families. The county has become one of the most basic land divisions in Ireland and is similar in many ways to a state in the United States (see figure 4-1). Each county is comprised of a number of civil parishes. County Leitrim has the fewest civil parishes, with only seventeen. One-fourth of the counties in Ireland contain over one hundred civil parishes each.

Some counties have changed names over the years. Any of these names may appear in historical records:

- County Derry is also called County Londonderry—the names are interchangeable
- County Laois, sometimes written County Leix, was once known as Queen's County
- County Offaly was once known as King's County

Barony

The barony is a long-obsolete land division often corresponding to ancient tribal or clan boundaries. A barony may include a number of civil parishes and parts of parishes. Many baronies span parts of multiple counties. Some older records are organized by baronies, such as land and property valuations; for this reason, you may need to identify the barony corresponding to your ancestor's townland or civil parish (see figure 4-2).

Poor Law Union

The Poor Law Relief Act of 1838 called for the creation of administrative areas for the purpose of collecting taxes for the relief of the poor. These Poor Law Unions, originally 130 in number, were centered in large towns where workhouses were built to administer relief to the poor. The number of unions grew over the years to better accommodate the needs of the poor. The boundaries of Poor Law Unions often diverged from the boundaries of civil parishes. Poor Law Unions were each divided into electoral divisions.

Superintendent Registrar's Districts were created to administer the civil registration of births, marriages, and deaths in Ireland. They were established with the same names and boundaries as the Poor Law Unions. For genealogical purposes, Poor Law Unions and Superintendent Registrar's Districts can be considered one and the same.

Definition

A parish is a civil or religious jurisdiction. There are three distinct types of parishes in Ireland: civil parishes, Church of Ireland parishes, and Catholic parishes. Civil parishes in Ireland are similar to counties in the United States. Church of Ireland and Catholic parishes have different congregations and boundaries. Catholic parishes are typically larger geographically than Church of Ireland parishes.

Parish

There are three distinct types of parishes in Ireland: civil parishes, Church of Ireland parishes, and Catholic parishes. Civil parishes in Ireland are similar to counties in the United States. Church of Ireland and Catholic parishes have different congregations and boundaries. Catholic parishes are typically larger geographically than Church of Ireland parishes. Each was created for different purposes and kept different records of genealogical value.

THE COUNTIES OF IRELAND

Figure 4-1. County map of Ireland, from A New Genealogical Atlas of Ireland, *2d ed., by Brian Mitchell (Baltimore: Genealogical Publishing Company, 2002).*

426 CENSUS OF IRELAND FOR THE YEAR 1871.

No. of Sheet of the Ordnance Survey Maps.	Names of Townlands and Towns.	Area in Statute Acres. A. R. P.	County.	Barony.	Parish.	Poor Law Union.	Poor Law Electoral Division.	Census of 1871. Part I. Vol.	Page
80	Keelnagore	351 1 26	Kerry	Iveragh	Killinane	Cahersiveen	Bahaghs	II.	456
18, 19	Keelogalabaun	82 2 23	Longford	Moydow	Moydow	Longford	Moydow	I.	530
108, 109	Keeloge	236 2 32	Galway	Longford	Meelick	Portumna	Meelick	IV.	88
17	Keeloge	141 3 29	Kildare	Offaly East	Rathangan	Naas	Dunmurry	I.	237
43	Keeloge	168 0 17	King's	Ballybritt	Roscrea	Roscrea	Gorteen	I.	437
42	Keeloge	510 3 37	King's	Clonlisk	Shinrone	Roscrea	Mountheaton	I.	443
15	Keeloge	51 1 37	King's	Garrycastle	Wheery or Killagally	Parsonstown	Ferbane	I.	452
32	Keeloge	55 3 39	Leitrim	Leitrim	Mohill	Mohill	Bunnybeg	IV.	228
18, 19	Keeloge	150 0 13	Longford	Moydow	Moydow	Ballymahon	Doory	I.	530
32, 37	Keeloge	495 1 36	Queen's	Slievemargy	Killeshin	Carlow	Ballickmoyler	I.	801
37, 38, 40	Keeloge	142 3 17	Westmeath	Moycashel	Durrow	Tullamore	Durrow	I.	891
40	Keeloge	82 0 15	Wicklow	Arklow	Kilbride	Rathdrum	Kilbride	I.	1099
19	Keeloge Lower	146 3 1	Wicklow	Newcastle	Newcastle Upper	Rathdrum	Newcastle Upper	I.	1109
15	Keelogenasause	124 3 20	Longford	Ardagh	Mostrim	Granard	Edgeworthstown	I.	518
15	Keeloge North	400 0 31	Queen's	Upperwoods	Offerlane	Mountmellick	Nealstown	I.	809
92	Keeloges	440 2 24	Donegal	Banagh	Inver	Donegal	Inver	III.	362
44, 52	Keeloges	553 2 9	Donegal	Kilmacrenan	Conwal	Letterkenny	Church Hill	III.	385
70, 79	Keeloges	109 0 34	Donegal	Raphoe North	Clonleigh	Strabane	Clonleigh South	III.	396
21	Keeloges	217 1 8	Dublin	Newcastle	Newcastle	Celbridge	Newcastle	I.	94
29	Keeloges	98 2 31	Galway	Dunmore	Tuam	Tuam	Killeen	IV.	57
60, 61	Keeloges	83 3 3	Galway	Kilconnell	Ahascragh	Mount Bellew	Clonbrock	IV.	60
14, 15	Keeloges	134 2 14	Kildare	Naas North	Whitechurch	Naas	Bodenstown	I.	229
3, 4	Keeloges	517 3 30	Leitrim	Rosclogher	Rossinver	Ballyshannon	Aghanlish	IV.	236
25	Keeloges	254 1 32	Limerick	Coonagh	Oola	Tipperary	Oola	II.	567
49, 50	Keeloges	961 2 1	Limerick	Coshlea	Galbally	Mitchelstown	Galbally	II.	517
14, 19	Keeloges	170 0 36	Longford	Ardagh	Ardagh	Longford	Ardagh East	I.	517
67	Keeloges	122 2 19	Mayo	Burrishoole	Burrishoole	Newport	Newport East	IV.	288
77, 88, 89	Keeloges	292 1 32	Mayo	Burrishoole	Islandeady	Westport	Islandeady	IV.	290
52	Keeloges	45 3 26	Roscommon	Athlone	Drum	Athlone	Crannagh	IV.	432
6	Keeloges	164 0 5	Roscommon	Boyle	Kilbryan	Boyle	Rockingham	IV.	456
6	Keeloges	258 3 21	Sligo	Carbury	Rossinver	Sligo	Rossinver East	IV.	542
37	Keeloges	97 0 26	Wexford	Shelmaliere West	Kilbride-glynn	Wexford	Forth	I.	1011
30	Keeloges	67 3 34	Wicklow	Arklow	Kilcommon	Rathdrum	Rathdrum	I.	1099
29	Keeloges, Bauville, and Clonglash	727 3 22	Donegal	Inishowen West	Fahan Lower	Inishowen	Buncrana	III.	373
7	Keelogesbeg	185 3 27	Galway	Ballymoe	Ballynakill	Glennamaddy	Ballynakill	IV.	19
7, 19	Keeloges East	941 1 21	Galway	Ballymoe	Ballynakill	Glennamaddy	Toberroe	IV.	20
7, 14	Keeloges Lower	29 3 13	Mayo	Tirawley	Lackan	Killala	Lackan North	IV.	352
70, 79	Keeloges New	297 0 30	Mayo	Carra	Kildacommoge	Castlebar	Manulla	IV.	301
70, 79	Keeloges Old	337 1 22	Mayo	Carra					
15, 16, 21, 22	Keeloge South	221 2 4	Queen's	Upperwoods	Offerlane	Donaghmore	Moneymore	I.	809

Figure 4-2. General Alphabetical Index to the Townlands and Towns, Parishes and Baronies of Ireland, *1871*.

There are about twenty-five hundred civil parishes in Ireland (see figure 4-3). Many records are compiled or maintained by civil parish, especially land and property tax records. Civil parishes contain, on average, about two-dozen townlands.

In the early 1800s, when the Church of Ireland was still the Established Church, the civil parishes were essentially the same as the parishes of the Church of Ireland. They usually had the same names and boundaries. Over time, some parishes of the Church of Ireland have changed boundaries or names, but they are typically the same as civil parishes in most genealogical research. However, some Church of Ireland parishes cover multiple civil parishes.

Catholic parishes are usually larger than civil parishes for a number of ecclesiastical, historical, and political reasons. Catholic parishes may have the same names as associated civil parishes, but they are generally much more ancient.

City and Town

Cities and towns are urban jurisdictions and are not to be confused with townlands (see below). A city or town may contain all or part of a number of townlands. In

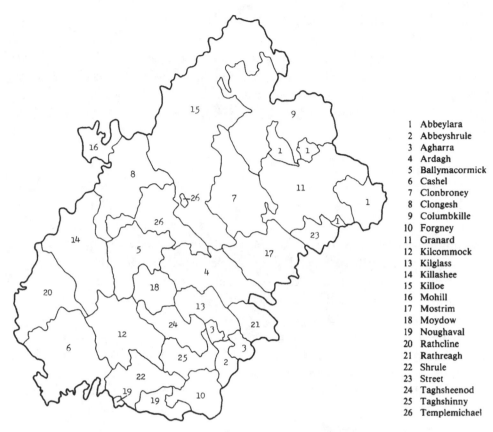

1	Abbeylara
2	Abbeyshrule
3	Agharra
4	Ardagh
5	Ballymacormick
6	Cashel
7	Clonbroney
8	Clongesh
9	Columbkille
10	Forgney
11	Granard
12	Kilcommock
13	Kilglass
14	Killashee
15	Killoe
16	Mohill
17	Mostrim
18	Moydow
19	Noughaval
20	Rathcline
21	Rathreagh
22	Shrule
23	Street
24	Taghsheenod
25	Taghshinny
26	Templemichael

Figure 4-3. Map of the civil parishes of County Longford, from A New Genealogical Atlas of Ireland.

genealogical documents, the basic address listed for city dwellers is the house number and street name, or just the street name, depending on the size of the city.

Electoral Division

The electoral division is a subdivision of the Poor Law Union, consisting of a number of townlands. Some land records, such as the canceled land books, are arranged by electoral division.

Townland

The townland is the most fundamental land division in Ireland. Townlands range in size from under one acre to over seven thousand acres. Most townlands are small neighborhoods ranging in size from two to four hundred acres. There are over 60,000 townlands in Ireland.

The townland is the basic unit of land in most genealogical records, so it is essential to identify the townland of your ancestors. In rural areas, the townland name serves as the postal address even in modern times.

⍌
Definition
The townland is the most fundamental land division in Ireland, the basic address for a rural family.

Tools For Finding Places in Ireland

The best tools for locating places in Ireland are townland indexes, maps of Ireland, and Lewis's *Topographical Dictionary of Ireland*. These reference aids can help you find which townland or parish in Ireland corresponds to a place name found in your genealogy. They can also help you learn the names of all land divisions you may need to know to search the different kinds of Irish records for your ancestors. Each of these is described below.

Townland Indexes

If you have discovered an Irish place name in your family history, but you don't know precisely where it is, the first source to consult is a townland index. The best Irish townland indexes were prepared from the 1851, 1871, and 1901 censuses. Once you find the townland in the index, you will learn the names of the various land divisions containing the townland. For example, if you look up Abbeygrove in the 1901 townland index you will see that this fifty-nine-acre townland is located in County Kilkenny, Gowran Barony, Blanchvilleskill Parish, Kilkenny County District, Dunbell District Electoral Division.

When you find the place you are looking for, write down all the information in the listing. The townland, civil parish, barony, Poor Law Union, and all other details will come in handy as you search for your ancestors in various types of Irish records. Some records are arranged by Poor Law Union, some by parish, and others by barony. With knowledge of each of these localities, you are prepared to search Irish records by locality to find your ancestors.

If you are not certain of the spelling, be very open-minded when searching these indexes. Your spelling may be phonetic but very different from the "standard" spelling.

The 1851 townland index is available online. You can search this index on a few websites, including Irish Origins <www.irishorigins.com>, the IreAtlas Townland database <www.leitrim-roscommon.com/ireatlas>, and the *Irish Times* <http://scripts. ireland.com/ancestor/placenames/index.cfm>.

Another handy book for identifying townlands is George Handran's *Townlands in Poor Law Unions*. This book makes it easy to find all neighboring townlands and parishes. This is especially useful when you have a rough idea how a townland is spelled but cannot find it in any of the townland indexes.

Maps of Ireland

If the townland indexes don't seem to list your ancestor's place, try looking at historical and modern maps of Ireland. The best modern maps of Ireland are the Discovery Series published by the Ordnance Survey. These topographic maps are very detailed, with a 1:50,000 scale, or about three-quarters of a mile per inch. The best historical maps are from the original Ordnance Survey in the early 1800s. These maps are extremely detailed, with a scale of one-sixth of a mile per inch. Search the area where your ancestor lived to see if any localities look similar to your ancestor's place name. Keep in mind that some place names are in Gaelic, while others are in English.

Maps are excellent tools to familiarize yourself with the place where your ancestors lived. With a map you can quickly see the names of the surrounding townlands and parishes. You can easily see which Poor Law Unions, baronies, and other land divisions are the right ones to search for your ancestors.

Using the Ordnance Survey maps, I was able to find the exact spot where my ancestor taught school in the mid-1800s. I looked up Ventry, County Kerry, and immediately noted the location of the schoolhouse. On a visit to Ireland, my wife and I drove around and could not find the school. We stopped at the post office and asked if anyone knew where the building was. We were told the schoolhouse had been leveled and replaced with a bungalow. We went and visited with the owner, whose house was exactly where the Ordnance Survey map showed a school in the 1840s. She confirmed that the schoolhouse was originally built on the precise spot where her house now stood. The remains of the old parish church were fifty paces away in the adjoining lot, exactly as indicated on the Ordnance Survey map (figure 4-4).

The best map book for larger jurisdictions is Brian Mitchell's classic work, *A New Genealogical Atlas of Ireland*. This book contains 156 maps, mostly of individual counties. Each county has four maps of civil parishes, baronies, Poor Law Unions, and Roman Catholic parishes. Each county in Northern Ireland has an additional map identifying the Presbyterian congregations. The first three maps in the book show the counties, dioceses, and probate districts of Ireland.

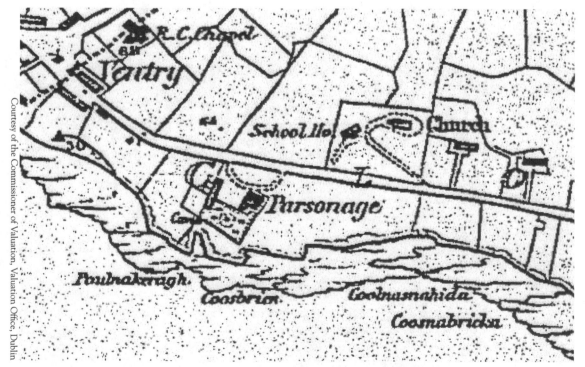

Courtesy of the Commissioner of Valuation, Valuation Office, Dublin

Figure 4-4. Ordnance Survey Map of Ventry, County Kerry.

Lewis's *Topographical Dictionary of Ireland*

Another valuable reference aid is Samuel Lewis's A *Topographical Dictionary of Ireland, Comprising the Several Counties, Cities, Boroughs, Corporate, Market and Post Towns, Parishes and Villages* (see figure 4-5). This two-volume geographical dictionary was originally published in 1847 and recently reprinted by Genealogical Publishing Company. All civil parishes, counties, and cities, as well as many market towns, have extensive descriptions and histories included in this work. Use Lewis's *Dictionary* to learn about where your ancestor lived. Lewis's *Dictionary* also identifies the Roman Catholic parish for each civil parish and is available on CD-ROMs published by Brøderbund and Quintin Publications.

In Summary

Equipped with a basic knowledge of Irish place names and land divisions, you are now more prepared to search Irish genealogical records to find your ancestors. That is, of course, if you know where your ancestors lived in Ireland. Most people beginning their Irish family history need to start in their own country, searching for their immigrant ancestors in records created overseas. Once you identify the specific parish or townland of origin in Ireland, you will then be able to search Irish records and learn more about your heritage.

References and Selected Reading

Flanagan, Diedre, and Laurence Flanagan. *Irish Place Names*. Goldenbridge, Dublin: Gill and Macmillan, 1994.

General Alphabetical Index to the Townlands and Towns, Parishes and Baronies of Ireland: Based on the Census of Ireland for the Year 1851. 1861. Reprint, Baltimore: Genealogical Publishing Company, 2000.

Handran, George B., CG. *Townlands in Poor Law Unions*. Salem, Mass.: Higginson Book, 1997.

Lewis, Samuel. *A Topographical Dictionary of Ireland: Comprising the Several Counties, Cities, Boroughs, Corporate, Market and Post Towns, Parishes and Villages*. 2 vols. 1837. Reprint, Baltimore: Genealogical Publishing Company, 1995.

List of Townlands in Each Poor Law Union of Ireland and Superintendent Registrar's District. 1891. Reprint, Salt Lake City: Redmond, 1997.

McMahon, Sean. *The Poolbeg Book of Irish Placenames*. Guernsey, Channel Islands: Guernsey Press, 1990.

Mitchell, Brian. *A New Genealogical Atlas of Ireland*. 2d ed. Baltimore: Genealogical Publishing Company, 2002.

Nolan, William, and Anngret Simms. *Irish Towns: A Guide to Sources*. Dublin: Geography Publications, 1998.

O'Dalaigh, Brian, Denis Cronin, and Paul Connell, eds. *Irish Townlands: Essays in Local History*. Dublin: Four Courts Press, 1998.

O'Laughlin, Michael C., ed. *Master Book of Irish Placenames: Master Atlas and Book of Irish Placenames*. Kansas City: Irish Genealogical Foundation, 1994.

rick, in boats of 10 or 12 tons burden, and where lime-stone and sea manure are landed for the supply of the neighbourhood. It has a daily penny post to Ennis and Kilrush, and a public dispensary: and fairs are held on June 14th, Sept. 16th, and Nov. 8th, chiefly for cattle. A little to the north of the village is the ruined tower or castle of Dangan, the upper part of which is supported only by the winding stone staircase.—See KILCHRIST.

BALLINACARGY, or BALNACARRIG, a market and post-town, in the parish of KILBIXY, barony of MOYGOISH, county of WESTMEATH, and province of LEINSTER, 7½ miles (W. by N.) from Mullingar, and 45¾ miles (W. by N.) from Dublin; containing 308 inhabitants. This town is situated on the road from Mullingar to Colehill, in the county of Longford, and near the right bank of the Royal Canal; it contains about 60 houses, neatly built and roofed with slate. Nearly adjoining it is an extensive deer-park belonging to Mrs. O'Connor. Malone, in whom the fee of the town is vested. The markets are held on Wednesday for corn and butter, and on Saturday for provisions; and fairs are held on the 9th of May and Oct. 20th. It is a constabulary police station; and petty sessions are held every Wednesday. The R. C. parochial chapel for the union or district of Kilbixy is situated in the town. A large school-house was built by Lord Sunderlin, open to children of all denominations; the master's salary is paid by Mrs. Malone. Here is a dispensary.—See KILBIXY.

BALLINACARRIG, otherwise STAPLESTOWN, a parish, partly in the barony of RATHVILLY, but chiefly in that of CARLOW, county of CARLOW, and province of LEINSTER, 1 mile (E. N. E.) from Carlow; containing 615 inhabitants. This parish, which is situated on the river Burren, and on the road from Carlow to Tullow, comprises 2576 statute acres, as applotted under the tithe act, and valued at £2200 per annum. Two-thirds of the land are arable, and nearly one-third pasture or wet grazing land; there is little waste or unprofitable bog; the state of agriculture is improving. There are some quarries of excellent granite for building; and mills at which about 10,000 barrels of flour are annually made. The principal gentlemen's seats are Kilmany, the residence of S. Elliott, Esq.; Staplestown Lodge, of H. Waters, Esq.; and Staplestown Mills, of — Mason, Esq. The living is an impropriate curacy, in the diocese of Leighlin, united by act of council in 1804 to the rectories of Tullowmagrinagh and Ballycrogue, constituting the union of Staplestown, in the gift of the Bishop; the rectory is appropriate to the Dean and Chapter of Leighlin. The tithes amount to £170, of which £100 is payable to the dean and chapter, and £70 to the impropriate curate: the entire tithes of the benefice payable to the incumbent amount to £411. 17. 6. The church, situated in Staplestown, is a small neat edifice, erected in 1821; it contains a tablet to the memory of Walter Bagenal, the last male representative of that ancient family. There is a glebe-house but no glebe. In the R. C. divisions the parish is in the union or district of Tullowmagrinagh, also called Tinriland. There are two schools, in which are about 40 children. Some remains of the old church yet exist. Sir Wm. Temple resided at Staplestown, from which many of his letters are dated; there are still some remains of the house in which he lived.

106

BALLINACLASH, a district parish, in the barony of BALLINACOR, county of WICKLOW, and province of LEINSTER, 2¾ miles (S. W. by S.) from Rathdrum; containing 3855 inhabitants. This district is situated on the river Avonbeg, over which there is a bridge, and on the road from Rathdrum to Glenmalur. It is of recent creation as a parish, and comprehends the constablewicks of Ballykine and Ballinacor, forming a perpetual curacy, in the diocese of Dublin and Glendalough, and in the patronage of the Rector of Rathdrum, who pays the curate's stipend. The church, on the townland of Ballinaton, is a neat building with a square tower, in the later English style of architecture, erected in 1834, at an expense of £900, granted by the Church Temporalities Commission. There is no glebe-house or glebe. There are two schools in the village, one a daily school and the other a Sunday school.—See BALLYKINE and BALLINACOR.

BALLINACLOUGH.—See BALLYNACLOUGH.

BALLINACOR, a constablewick or sub-denomination of the parish of RATHDRUM, barony of BALLINACOR, county of WICKLOW, and province of LEINSTER, 2½ miles (W.) from Rathdrum; containing 1221 inhabitants. This place is situated in the mountain district leading to Glenmalur, and comprises 27,225 statute acres, of which 20,473 are mountain, and 6752 are arable and pasture land, and of which also 16,619 acres are applotted under the tithe act. Ballinacor, the seat of W. Kemmis, Esq., is beautifully situated on the side of a hill commanding an extensive view of the vale towards the Cormorce copper mines. The military road intersects the constablewick, in which are the barracks of Drumgoff and Aughavanah. Fairs are held on Feb. 4th, May 1st, Aug. 4th, and Nov. 4th. As regards its tithes, which amount to £103. 17. 6¾., this is one of the denominations that constitute the union or benefice of Rathdrum; it also forms, with the constablewick of Ballykine, the perpetual cure of Ballinaclash, in the diocese of Dublin and Glendalough, and in the patronage of the Incumbent of Rathdrum. A school is supported by Mr. Kemmis, in the village of Grenane.

BALLINACOURTY, a parish, in the barony of DUNKELLIN, county of GALWAY, and province of CONNAUGHT, 3 miles (S. by W.) from Oranmore; containing 3250 inhabitants. This parish is situated on the eastern shore of the bay of Galway, and on the road from Oranmore to an inlet of the bay forming the approach to Claren-Bridge. The inlet of Tyrone or Ballinacourty is well sheltered, and has good anchorage for vessels drawing not more than ten feet of water, which, however, must not venture in when it comes within two hours of low water of spring tides, as there are then only nine feet in the channel. Westerly winds occasion a great swell at the entrance, in which case it should not be attempted before half flood, nor after half ebb. On the south side of the haven there is a small pier called St. Kitt's, built by the Fishery Board, but adapted only for boats, the strand being dry at low water; it was never properly finished, and is now in a ruinous condition. Small craft sail up this inlet three miles further, to a point near Claren-Bridge and Kilcolgan. In the parish is the Cottage, the residence of J. Ryan, Esq. The living consists of a rectory and a perpetual curacy, in the diocese of Tuam; the former is part of the union of St. Nicholas and corps of the wardenship

Figure 4-5. Lewis's A Topographical Dictionary of Ireland, 1847.

Tower in Cork, Ireland.

The Irish Overseas

Remember always that all of us, and you and I especially, are descended from immigrants and revolutionaries.

—*Franklin Delano Roosevelt*

Most of the seventy million people of Irish descent live outside Ireland, with the greatest numbers living in the United States, Canada, England, and Australia. There are about seven times as many Irish-Americans as there are people living in Ireland. Most people researching their Irish ancestry need to begin in their home country, seeking genealogical sources that point to a specific place of origin in Ireland.

If you are like most people beginning their Irish family history, you do not yet know the precise birth date, birthplace, or parentage of your emigrant ancestor. Perhaps your second great-grandfather Michael O'Brien was born in Ireland in the early 1800s and emigrated to the United States during the Great Famine of 1845–49. With such a common name and such imprecise information, you might find hundreds of Michael O'Brien in Ireland and not know which one was your immigrant ancestor. The best way to begin is to search for Michael and his family in American records.

A basic tenet of family history research is to "go from the known to the unknown." Learn all you can about your emigrant ancestor using records created *after* he left Ireland. You will be looking for specific details about your ancestor and his family that will identify him uniquely. Focus on discovering your emigrant ancestor's place of origin in Ireland. The more precise the location, the better. At a minimum, you will want to determine the city or county of origin. Identifying the parish or townland is much better.

Beyond the place of origin, set a goal to learn other clues about your ancestor, such as:

- Your ancestor's name before emigrating from Ireland
- The date of emigration

> **Basic Principle**
>
> → Go from the known to the unknown. Learn all you can about your emigrant ancestor using records created *after* he or she left Ireland.

- The port of departure
- The port of arrival
- Friends and relatives who also left Ireland
- Birth date and birthplace
- Marriage date and marriage place
- Parents' names
- Religion
- Names of brothers and sisters
- Occupation

Once you have identified your emigrant ancestor and his family precisely, you will be ready to search Irish genealogical sources and learn much more.

Each country has different records that might contain the details you seek about your Irish ancestor. We will focus on American records first and then consider a few of the best sources available in Canada, England, and Australia.

Irish Immigration to America

↓

Historical Fact

Most people of Irish descent live in the United States.

Most people of Irish descent live in the United States. In fact, 84 percent of the people who emigrated from Ireland between 1851 and 1921 sailed directly for the United States (see table 5-1). Four out of five Irish immigrants bound for America during this time period arrived in the port of New York.

Before the American Revolution, perhaps three hundred thousand to five hundred thousand people emigrated from Ireland to the American Colonies. During the 1600s, the majority of these Irish immigrants were Catholics from southern Ireland. During the 1700s, the majority were Presbyterians, Scots-Irish

Table 5-1: Irish Emigration Statistics, 1851-1921

Emigration Date	United States	British North America	Australia, New Zealand	Other Overseas	Total Overseas
1851–1860	989,834	118,118	101,541	6,726	1,216,219
1861–1870	690,845	40,079	82,917	4,741	818,582
1871–1880	449,549	25,783	61,946	5,425	542,703
1881–1890	626,604	44,505	55,476	7,890	734,475
1891–1900	427,301	10,648	11,448	11,885	461,282
1901–1910	418,995	38,238	11,885	16,343	485,461
1911–1921	191,724	36,251	17,629	9,691	255,295
Total: 1851–1921	3,794,852	313,622	342,842	62,701	4,514,017

Adapted from *Emigrants and Exiles: Ireland and the Irish Exodus to North America*, by Kerby A. Miller (New York: Oxford University Press, 1985), table 1, p. 569.

from Ulster. By the 1790s, about one out of six Europeans who had ever immigrated to the United States was from Ireland, mostly from the northern counties.

After the American Colonies gained their independence, Irish immigration continued to increase, with over a million Irish immigrants arriving in the United States between 1783 and 1844. But the huge exodus caused by the Great Famine of 1845–49 dwarfed all other waves of Irish immigration. The potato was the mainstay of the Irish diet, and in 1845 a large portion of the crop was destroyed by a devastating blight. In 1846 the same fungus caused an almost total failure of the potato harvest, and many people starved. Although the blight did not overcome the potato crop in 1847, few seeds were planted and twice the people died in that year than in the year before. The fungus struck again in 1848 and 1849. Throughout the famine years, millions of Irish died of starvation, and millions more emigrated overseas. Between 1845 and 1855, about 1.8 million people left Ireland for a new life in America. By 1921, a total of over six million people had left Ireland for America.

Records in the United States

Researching your Irish family history begins in the home. Search home sources that you or your relatives may have, looking for information about your immigrant ancestor and his family (see chapter 1). After interviewing your relatives and learning all you can from home sources, you will want to search more genealogical documents. The following U.S. sources may help you trace your Irish immigrant ancestor:

- Birth, marriage, and death certificates
- Cemetery records
- Census records
- Church registers
- City directories
- Family and local histories
- Military records
- Naturalization documents
- Newspapers
- Ships' passenger lists
- Social Security applications

Birth, Marriage, and Death Certificates

United States birth, marriage, and death certificates may help you pinpoint your ancestor's origins in Ireland. My grandfather was born in Ireland and died in the United States. His death certificate tells me his birth date, the names of his parents, and that he was born in Tralee, Ireland. If your immigrant ancestor married or died in the United States, marriage and death certificates may be a gold mine of information about your ancestor's Irish origins.

Death certificates report all kinds of genealogical information, but the details vary depending on when and where the certificates were filed and who supplied the information. A death certificate might give the exact birth date, give the age in years, or merely state that the birth date is "unknown." However, even a precise birth date on a death certificate should be regarded with some suspicion, given that the information may have been provided by a grieving relative many years after the birth actually occurred. Today it is much more common for people to remember birthdays than it was a century ago. If the birthplace is reported, it may be the townland, city, parish, county, or just "Ireland."

If your Irish immigrant married in the United States, the marriage certificate might identify where the bride and groom were born in Ireland—occasionally their ages are also recorded. Parents' names are often listed, providing another generation of Irish ancestry from U.S. records.

Birth, marriage, and death certificates of children may also indicate where the parents were born. Search these certificates for each of your immigrant ancestor's children to discover the family's origins in Ireland.

The United States has no national registry of births, marriages, and deaths. Records of these events are available only locally, usually from the county or state. In New England, the city and town clerks maintain the vital records of births, marriages, and death.

Some local government offices have actual certificates on file. Other offices have birth, marriage, and death registers, books with dozens of vital events recorded on each page. Other offices have file drawers containing alphabetical card-indexes of vital records. Some of these offices will let you search the records yourselves, but that service is becoming less common. You can write to the appropriate government office to order a copy of a birth, marriage, or death certificate. The U.S. Department of Health and Human Services publishes a list of current addresses and fees in a booklet entitled *Where to Write for Vital Records*.

Many states have online indexes of these vital records. Some websites specialize in ordering birth, marriage, and death certificates—one great site is VitalCheck <www.vitalchek.com>. You can search birth, marriage, and death indexes for many states on Ancestry.com. The Family History Library Catalog, found on FamilySearch <www.familysearch.org>, lists many microfilm collections of vital records indexes and certificates; these are listed by locality, some by state, many by county, and some by township (see Chapter 17, "The Family History Library").

Cemetery Records

It is a wonderful and moving experience to visit the cemetery where your ancestors were buried, find the family plot, and ponder your ancestors' lives as you study the inscriptions preserved on their tombstones.

The most useful cemetery records are gravestone inscriptions and the cemetery burial books, known as sexton records. Gravestone inscriptions and sexton records may reveal the birth date and even the birthplace of your immigrant ancestors. Catholic gravestones often reveal counties of origin in Ireland; Protestant gravestones occasionally indicate the parish or townland of origin.

Many genealogical societies and individual researchers have transcribed and published tombstone inscriptions. They often include cemetery maps to help identify where each plot is located. Perhaps someone has transcribed tombstone and memorial inscriptions from your ancestor's cemetery, saving you the difficulty of roaming the graveyard in search of the family plot. Some of these published transcriptions are rather abbreviated, so you may still want to visit the cemetery and read the family tombstones yourself to capture every detail about the family.

Census Records

United States Federal Census records are easy to use and reveal much about the origins of foreign-born residents. The details vary for each census year. Table 5-2 highlights some of the most valuable facts recorded on each individual listed in the later censuses.

Perhaps the most valuable information recorded for immigrant ancestors is the year of immigration, which is recorded on all twentieth-century censuses. The year of immigration, with the naturalization status, may help you find immigration and naturalization papers. You may also be able to find the passenger list for the ship that carried your immigrant ancestor to America.

Although most of the 1890 census was destroyed in 1921, many of the 1890 veterans schedules survived. This special census names Union veterans and widows of veterans.

Table 5-2: U.S. Census Information Helpful for Tracing Irish Immigrant Origins

Personal Detail	1850	1860	1870	1880	1900	1910	1920	1930
Full name	■	■	■	■	■	■	■	■
Gender	■	■	■	■	■	■	■	■
Race	■	■	■	■	■	■	■	■
Age	■	■	■	■	■	■	■	■
Birthplace (state or country)	■	■	■	■	■	■	■	■
Occupation	■	■	■	■	■	■	■	■
If father was of foreign birth			■					
If mother was of foreign birth			■					
Relation to head of household				■	■	■	■	■
Birthplace of father				■	■	■	■	■
Birthplace of mother				■	■	■	■	■
Year of immigration to U.S.					■	■	■	■
Naturalization status					■	■	■	■
Whether able to speak English					■	■	■	■
Years residing in United States					■			
Birth month and year					■			
Language						■	■	■
Year of naturalization							■	■
Union or Confederate veteran						■		
Veteran of which war								■

You can use this census to help you find pension papers for military families. The veterans' schedules survive for about half of Kentucky and are complete for all states alphabetically from Louisiana through Wyoming, as well as Washington, D.C.

Check each census for birthplace information. You may get lucky and find that the census enumerator recorded more detail than just the country of birth. (I searched the 1880 U.S. census index on Ancestry.com and found over three thousand Irish emigrants with their county or city of birth in Ireland actually listed on the census.)

Many state censuses also exist. State censuses were typically enumerated at five-year intervals between the decennial federal censuses. They usually contain information similar to that collected by the federal censuses.

Church Registers

The most valuable church records are baptism, marriage, death, and burial registers. Church records often predate civil registration of births, marriages, and deaths and are an excellent source of information on these vital events.

Many of our Irish immigrant ancestors attended churches of the same denomination as their ancestors. Many changed their religion after leaving Ireland. Interview older family members to learn as much as you can about the religious faith and practices of your ancestors. This will help you identify the churches they attended in the United States.

As you search the parish registers of your immigrant ancestor's church, you will want to concentrate on marriage and death certificates. These records may list the names and birthplaces of individuals and their parents. Catholic marriage records may also list the birth date and birthplace of the bride and groom.

A valuable resource for Catholic research is Virginia Humling's book, *U.S. Catholic Sources: A Diocesan Research Guide.*

City Directories

Cities and counties published directories long before the invention of the telephone. Just like modern phone books, directories provide street addresses of heads of household and business listings for merchants and companies. Many localities issued annual directories, so the information was usually kept quite current.

If you know where your immigrant ancestor immediately settled, you can use local directories to see which year your ancestor first appeared. This helps you approximate the date of immigration to the United States, which in turn can help you find immigration and naturalization papers.

Since names are usually listed alphabetically in city directories, you can quickly identify all families that share your immigrant ancestor's surname. If the name is uncommon, these families may be related and may have come from the same townland or parish in Ireland.

When you find your ancestor in a city directory, you can use the street address to help you identify the nearest churches and cemeteries. These records can help you trace your immigrant's origins in Ireland.

Local libraries are a great place to find city and county directories. You may be able to get book or microfiche copies of directories from other states through interlibrary loan.

Family and Local Histories

Many people are interested in your ancestors, and some may have already researched and published a portion of your family history. Before tracing your ancestry from scratch, consider taking the time to see what research others have done. A number of libraries have extensive family history collections, including the Family History Library in Salt Lake City, Utah; the New England Historic Genealogical Society in Boston, Massachusetts; the Allen County Public Library in Fort Wayne, Indiana; and the U.S. Library of Congress in Washington, D.C. (see Chapter 19, "Archives and Libraries").

Hundreds of thousands of family trees have also been published on the Internet. The largest collection, the Ancestry World Tree, is found on Ancestry.com. The Ancestry World Tree contains over 400 million names and grows by over a million names every week. Other large collections of family trees are found on Genealogy.com, FamilySearch <www.familysearch.org>, OneGreatFamily.com, and GenCircles.com.

Local histories, especially county and town histories, usually have a section devoted to family histories. The origins of immigrant ancestors are a source of pride for their descendants and are frequently mentioned in these family histories. Even the town histories in these books occasionally discuss the immigrant origins of founding members of the town.

Military Records

Irish Americans have fought in all American wars from the Revolutionary War to the present. United States military records are an outstanding source of genealogical information on soldiers and their families. Military service records, pension applications, and draft registration cards are a few of the most valuable records for family history research (see figure 5-1). Each of these records may provide the exact date and place of birth for an immigrant ancestor.

Veterans of the Revolutionary War and their widows recorded many personal details about their families when filing for pensions. These pension applications have been cataloged and microfilmed. For example, in 1779 James McConnell volunteered for service as a minuteman on the North Carolina line. In 1838 he applied for a pension (FHL 971670, pension file S11047). Among many personal details, his pension application states that

> *he was born on the fifteenth of August 1757 in County Down Ireland* that his parents removed to America when he was four or five years of age & settled on Big Saluda river South Carolina whence they removed to Mecklenburg County North Carolina some years before the revolutionary war. (emphasis added)

Civil War soldiers, their widows, and their heirs filed claims for military pensions. The many pages of paperwork include significant genealogical details of family members,

Honorable Discharge from The United States Army

TO ALL WHOM IT MAY CONCERN:

This is to Certify, That* _William O Connor_

† _1061211 Sgt. 1106 Aero Replacement S._

THE UNITED STATES ARMY, as a TESTIMONIAL OF HONEST AND FAITHFUL

SERVICE, is hereby HONORABLY DISCHARGED _from the military service of the_

UNITED STATES by reason of ‡ _Circular 106 W.D 1918_

Said _William O Connor_ was born

in _Tralee_, in the State of _Ireland_

When enlisted he was _27_ years of age and by occupation a _chauffer_

He had _blue_ eyes, _brown_ hair, _ruddy_ complexion, and

was _5_ feet _8½_ inches in height.

Given under my hand at _Camp Dix N.J._ this

_9_ day of _Sept._, one thousand nine hundred and _nineteen_

Guardley

Major U.S.A

Commanding.

Form No. 525, A. G. O.
Oct. 9-18.

3—3164

*Insert name, Christian name first; e. g., "John Doe."
†Insert Army serial number, grade, company and regiment or arm or corps or department; e. g., "1,620,302"; "Corporal, Company A, 1st Infantry"; "Sergeant, Quartermaster Corps"; "Sergeant, First Class, Medical Department."
‡If discharged prior to expiration of service, give number, date, and source of order or full description of authority therefor.

Figure 5-1. World War I honorable discharge certificate.

often providing birth and marriage information. If your immigrant ancestor was a Union veteran, he or his widow may have applied for a pension. You can obtain a copy of these pension applications and possibly find out where he was born in Ireland. The name of the county or townland is often specified. Remember that the spelling may be quite different from the usual spellings of the locality in Ireland since the person filling out the paperwork frequently wrote place names as they sounded.

In 1917 and 1918, about twenty-four million men—98 percent of the eligible male population—responded to the call to register for the draft. Men born between 1872 and 1900 were required to register, whether they were U.S. citizens or alien residents. Each provided much personal information on the draft registration cards, including the following details:

- Name in full
- Date of birth
- Birthplace (on 11 million of the 24 million cards)
- Citizenship status
- Father's birthplace (on 1 million cards)
- Address of nearest kin—even if the nearest kin lived abroad (on 14 million cards)
- Details of personal appearance
- Various additional details, depending on the date of registration

These cards are searchable by name on Ancestry.com, with digital images available for all cards. They are also available on microfilm at the Family History Library (see Chapter 17, "The Family History Library").

If your immigrant ancestor, his brother, or his son registered for the draft, examine each of their World War I draft registration cards to learn more about the family's Irish origins.

My grandfather William O'Connor was born in Ireland in 1888 and came to America in 1913. He participated in the first draft registration on 5 June 1917 in Springfield, Massachusetts. His draft registration card states his birth date and place in Ireland.

Naturalization Documents

Naturalization is the legal process of becoming a U.S. citizen. Naturalization papers capture the spirit of your ancestor's transition from life in Ireland to life in America. These documents bridge the gap between the two countries, providing genealogical details about life before and after immigration.

Before the American Colonies gained their independence, colonists were subjects of the British Crown as were the Irish in Ireland. Anyone leaving Ireland for the American Colonies was already a citizen upon arrival. Only after the United States became a separate nation did new immigrants from Ireland have a need to apply for citizenship.

Before 1941, an immigrant desiring U.S. citizenship had to file two sets of paperwork. A declaration of intention, or "first papers," was filed in any local, state, or federal

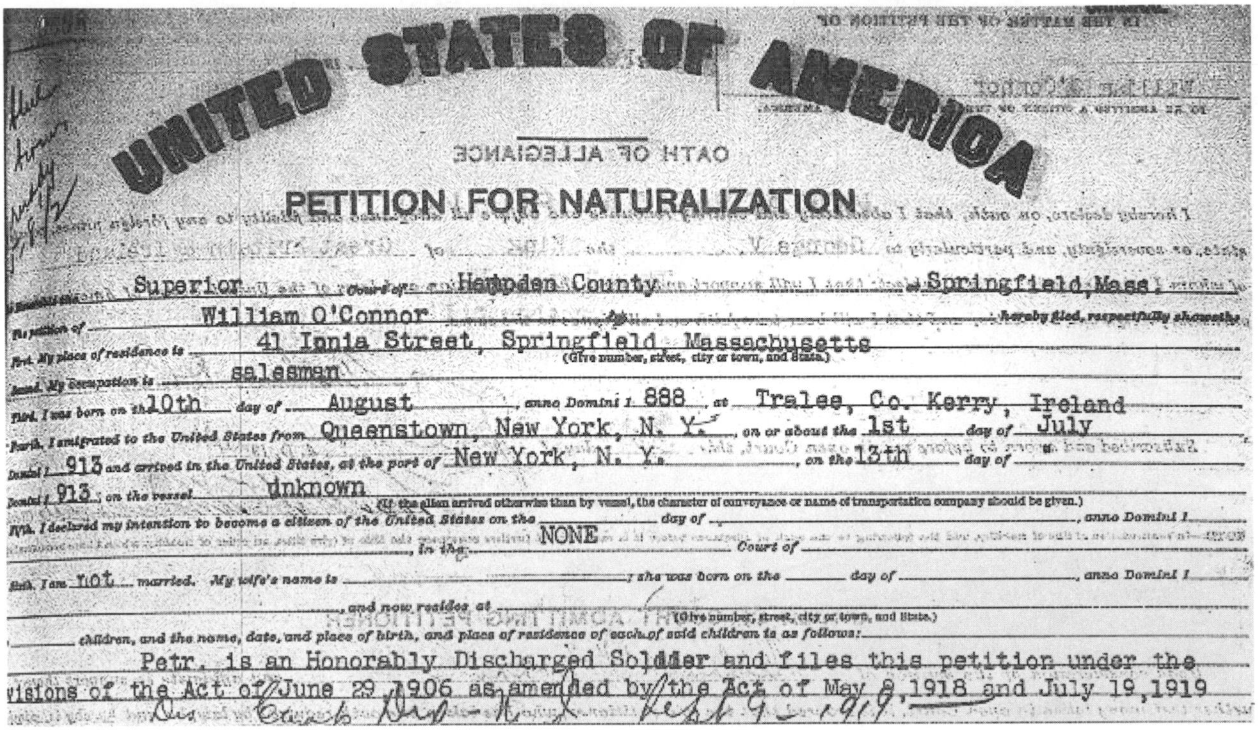

UNITED STATES OF AMERICA

PETITION FOR NATURALIZATION

Superior Court of Hampden County at Springfield, Mass.

The petition of William O'Connor hereby filed, respectfully showeth:

First. My place of residence is 41 Ionia Street, Springfield, Massachusetts (Give number, street, city or town, and State.)

Second. My occupation is salesman

Third. I was born on the 10th day of August anno Domini 1888 at Tralee, Co. Kerry, Ireland

Fourth. I emigrated to the United States from Queenstown, New York, N. Y. on or about the 1st day of July anno Domini 1913 and arrived in the United States, at the port of New York, N. Y. on the 13th day of anno Domini 1913, on the vessel unknown (If the alien arrived otherwise than by vessel, the character of conveyance or name of transportation company should be given.)

Fifth. I declared my intention to become a citizen of the United States on the NONE day of anno Domini in the Court of

Sixth. I am not married. My wife's name is she was born on the day of anno Domini I and now resides at (Give number, street, city or town, and State.)

children, and the name, date, and place of birth, and place of residence of each of said children is as follows:

Petr. is an Honorably Discharged Soldier and files this petition under the provisions of the Act of June 29 1906 as amended by the Act of May 9, 1918 and July 19, 1919

Figure 5-2. Petition for naturalization.

court. After a waiting period of between two and seven years, the immigrant would file a second set of papers, a petition for naturalization (figure 5-2). If the petition was approved, citizenship would be granted. After 1941, immigrants no longer had to file a declaration of intention, but they still needed to petition for naturalization.

The genealogical details contained in naturalization papers before 1906 depend upon when and where these documents were filed. In 1906, the naturalization forms were standardized and required substantial information from the applicant. The immigrant had to provide these personal details: full name, birth date, birthplace, occupation, personal description, citizenship, street address, last address before immigrating to America, date of arrival in the United States, name of the vessel, spouse's name, and children's names, birth dates, and birthplaces.

Newspapers

Newspapers are genealogy gold mines. You can learn so much about your ancestors and their communities by reading historical newspapers. Obituaries and marriage announcements are great family history sources, especially when they preserve biographical or immigration details about your ancestors. Other useful items found in newspapers are family business advertisements, crime reports, court cases, neighborhood gossip, and details about the lives of leading citizens.

Obituaries often contain miniature biographies of the deceased, beginning with the date and place of birth. Once you know the date of death, search the next few days of the local newspaper to find an obituary. You can find newspapers at local libraries, state libraries, and state archives.

Some cities have large Irish populations with newspapers specifically catering to the interests of their Irish subscribers. For example, from 1831 to 1920, the *Boston Pilot* published enquiries about lost friends and relatives—these enquiries were submitted from all over the nation. A wonderful book series entitled *The Search for Missing Friends: Irish Immigrant Advertisements Placed in the Boston Pilot* contains transcriptions of these ads for all ninety years. Here is an example from the "Missing Friends" column from 7 May 1870 (see vol. 6, p. 608):

OF JOHN SHEEHY, and family, a native of the parish of Ventry, near Dingle, county Kerry, who emigrated to the country in or about the year 1835, and in the year 1845 married a Miss Bridget Manning, in Cabbotville, Mass., and resided in Berrytown, Duchess county, N. Y., in the years 1850 and 1851, and when last heard of lived in the State of Illinois. Any information furnished of him, or family, will be received by his brother-in-law, James Manning, at Stone Mountain, De Rabb county, Georgia. – Illinois papers please copy.

Ships' Passenger Lists

Many nineteenth- and twentieth-century passenger lists have been microfilmed and indexed for U.S. ports of entry. For example, the Ellis Island website <www.ellisisland.org> contains an index of all documented immigrants who came to Ellis Island between 1892 and 1924. This remarkable database lists almost one million Irish-American immigrants. The records are linked to digitized images of passenger manifests. As soon as you find your ancestor, you can click to view the passenger list.

I searched for my grandfather William O'Connor on <www.ellisisland.org> and found him listed as William Connor, a British citizen of Irish ethnicity. His place of residence was Tralee, Ireland. He was twenty-four years old when he arrived in Ellis Island on 13 July 1913. All of this information was transcribed off the original ship's manifest. When I clicked to view the manifest, I discovered much more, including his birthplace, the name and address of the cousin he was going to live with, and his physical description.

Ancestry.com and Genealogy.com have name indexes listing millions of Irish immigrants to America. Perhaps the most valuable passenger lists on Ancestry.com are for the port of New York, from 1820 through 1891. The New York passenger lists from 1851 to 1891 are easiest to search. If you find your ancestor you can click to see his or her name on an image of the ship's manifest. Not only can you learn the exact date of immigration and the name of the vessel, but you will also learn the names, ages, and occupations of all who accompanied your ancestor to America. Even the children are named in these manifests.

⋎

Internet

Ancestry.com and Genealogy.com have name indexes listing millions of Irish immigrants to America.

Social Security Applications

Many twentieth-century immigrants applied for Social Security cards to obtain retirement benefits. The form required each applicant to supply the following personal details:

- Full name
- Mailing address
- Full name at birth, including the maiden name if a woman
- Date of birth
- Birthplace (city, county, and state)
- Father's full name, regardless of whether living or dead
- Mother's full maiden name, regardless of whether living or dead
- Sex and race
- Employer's name and address
- Date and signature

The Social Security Administration publishes monthly updates of their master index, the Social Security Death Index. You can search a current online index at a number of websites, including Ancestry.com and RootsWeb.com. Once you find your ancestor you will have a birth date and a death date. To get the birthplace and parents' names, you need to write to the Social Security Administration for a copy of the SS-5 form. Ancestry.com and RootsWeb.com can help you order a photocopy of the original by printing a form letter with all the details already filled in. Print out the letter and mail it to the Social Security Administration with the appropriate fee ($27 at the time of this writing). You will be sent a photocopy of the Social Security application filled out by your ancestor.

References and Selected Reading

Betit, Kyle. *Ireland: A Genealogical Guide for North Americans*. Salt Lake City: The Irish at Home and Abroad, 1995.

Eales, Anne Bruner, and Roberta M. Kvasnicka, eds. *Guide to Genealogical Research in the National Archives of the United States*. 3d ed. Washington, D. C.: National Archives Trust Fund Board, 2000.

Eichholz, Alice, ed. *Red Book: American State, County, and Town Sources*. 3d ed. Salt Lake City: Ancestry, 2004.

Harris, Ruth-Ann, Donald M. Jacobs, and B. Emer O'Keeffe, eds. *The Search for Missing Friends: Irish Immigrant Advertisements Placed in the* Boston Pilot. 8 vols. Boston: New England Historic Genealogical Society, 1989–99.

Humling, Virginia. *U.S. Catholic Sources: A Diocesan Research Guide*. Salt Lake City: Ancestry, 1995.

McKenna, Erin. *A Student's Guide to Irish American Genealogy*. Phoenix: Oryx, 1996.

Szucs, Loretto Dennis. *They Became Americans: Finding Naturalization Records and Ethnic Origins*. Salt Lake City: Ancestry, 1998.

Szucs, Loretto Dennis and Sandra Hargreaves Luebking. *The Source: A Guidebook of American Genealogy*. 2d ed. Salt Lake City: Ancestry, 1997.

Records in Canada

Hundreds of thousands of Irish emigrants sailed directly from Ireland to the eastern ports of Canada. While many later migrated to the United States, a large percentage made Canada their home. The following Canadian sources are some of the most helpful for tracing Irish-Canadian immigrants back to Ireland:

- Census records
- Church records
- Civil registration of births, marriages, and deaths
- Passenger lists

Census Records

The earliest major census in Canada was taken in 1666 in the fledgling province of New France, which later became Quebec. The names, ages, and occupations of all men, women, and children were recorded family-by-family and parish-by-parish. Over the next two centuries a number of regional censuses were taken in various parts of Canada.

The censuses covering the greatest area and containing the most valuable information on all family members were taken in 1851, 1861, 1871, 1881, 1891, 1901, and 1911. These censuses named all members of the household, with age, occupation, birthplace, religion, marital status, gender, race, and other details listed for each person. These later censuses are very similar in format and content to the U.S. Federal Censuses. Some indexes exist for portions of these later censuses. The 1901 census records the exact day, month, and year of birth for each person then living in Canada. Hundreds of districts of the 1901 Canadian census have been indexed—these records are searchable on Ancestry.com.

The Church of Jesus Christ of Latter-day Saints has indexed the 1881 Canadian census. This 4.3-million-name index may be searched online at FamilySearch <www.familysearch.org>.

Library and Archives Canada (formerly the National Library of Canada and the National Archives of Canada) has posted digital images of the 1901 and 1911 censuses on the Canadian Genealogy Centre website <www.genealogy.gc.ca>. Other recent releases include digital images of the 1906 census for the Northwest Provinces (i.e., Alberta, Manitoba, and Saskatchewan) and a heads-of-household index to the 1871 census for Ontario.

Church Records

The first church parish register in Canada began in 1621 with the marriage of Guillaume Couillard and Guilemette Hebert, in the newly established Catholic Church at Fort Quebec.

Some Catholic immigrants from Ireland settled in French Canada and attended French-Catholic churches. The marriage records of immigrants usually named their parents and place of origin. For example, Timothy O'Connor, an Irish immigrant and bachelor, settled in the parish of Saint-Charles-sur-Richelieu, Quebec. He married a young lady in 1784. The marriage register (presented below in the original French followed by an English translation) reveals much about his Irish origins:

> Le vingt six octobre mil sept cent quatre vingt quatre apres la publication deu ban de Mariage au prone de la misse paroisse ete entre *Mssr thimothe oconnor docteur en medecine de la faculte de Rheims de cette paroisse fils de Mssr Cornelius oconnor & de Mde honora Reidy de la paroisee de Castleishan diocese de Kerry* d'une part & Mademlle Barbe Dorion. (emphasis added)

> The twenty-sixth of October 1784 after the publication of two banns of marriage in this parish between Mr. *Timothy O'Connor, doctor of medicine of the faculty of Rheims, of this parish, son of Mr. Cornelius O'Connor and Madame Honora Reidy [Reilly?] of the parish of Castleishan [Castleisland], diocese of Kerry,* on the first part, and Miss Barbe Dorion.

This marriage record is a gold mine of information on Timothy O'Connor, revealing his parentage and precise place of origin in Ireland. Surviving Catholic parish registers for Castleisland begin in 1822, so other Irish sources would need to be consulted to extend Timothy O'Connor's ancestry further back in time.

Protestant denominations also kept records that can be used to trace Irish immigrants back to Ireland. Many Irish immigrants attended the Church of England (the Anglican Church) when they settled in Canada. Baptism, marriage, and burial records should be searched for all members of the immigrant's family. Many Irish immigrants attended Presbyterian churches in Canada. If your immigrant ancestor was Presbyterian, you would want to search the baptism, marriage, and burial registers, as well as the session minutes and communion rolls. The session minutes and communion rolls are particularly helpful in discovering the place of origin in Ireland.

Check the Family History Library Catalog, found online at FamilySearch <www.familysearch.org>, to see which church records have been microfilmed for the places in Canada where your ancestors lived. Chapter 17, "The Family History Library," discusses how to search the catalog.

One of the most helpful things to remember when searching church records is that our ancestors may have attended more than one church in their lifetime. While born and raised Catholic in Ireland, an immigrant might have chosen to attend the Anglican Church in Canada. If you don't find your ancestor in one church, consider searching the registers of other churches in the area.

Civil Registration of Births, Marriages, and Deaths

Civil registration of births, marriages, and deaths is the responsibility of each province in Canada. The information on these certificates may be very detailed and rich or very sketchy and sparse, depending on the locality and the date of the record. Civil registration began rather late in Canada, starting in the late 1800s for most provinces. Nonetheless, civil registration is a principle source of information on Irish immigrant origins in Canada.

The most important documents to obtain are the marriage and death certificates of the immigrant. These records may identify where the immigrant was born in Ireland. Also, if your immigrant ancestor came over with family members or friends, their marriage and death certificates may tell you their birthplaces in Ireland. These clues may help you eventually locate your immigrant ancestor in Irish records.

Many provinces have had their birth, marriage, and death certificates microfilmed. Consult the Family History Library Catalog for details, searching first under the province and then under the topic "Vital Records" to see which years of civil registration have been microfilmed.

Passenger Lists

Hundreds of thousands of Irish immigrants arrived in Quebec, New Brunswick, and Nova Scotia in the 1800s. Many were en route to the United States, taking the cheaper passage from Ireland to Canada. Many, of course, made Canada their home. Unfortunately, few passenger lists survive for vessels arriving in Canada before 1865.

If your Irish ancestors arrived in Canada after 1865, you have a better chance of finding them on passenger lists. Many Irish immigrants to Canada disembarked at the ports of Quebec and Halifax. The Family History Library has microfilms of surviving passenger lists for Quebec, 1865–1900, and Halifax, 1881–1899.

References and Selected Reading

Baxter, Angus. *In Search of Your Canadian Roots: Tracing Your Family Tree in Canada.* 3d ed. Baltimore: Genealogical Publishing Company, 2000.

Geyh, Patricia Keeney, et al. *French-Canadian Sources: A Guide for Genealogists.* Salt Lake City: Ancestry, 2002.

Records in England

Some of the most useful and readily available sources for tracing Irish immigrants in England back to Ireland are censuses, church records, civil registration, and gravestone inscriptions.

British censuses were enumerated every ten years beginning in 1841—censuses from 1841 through 1901 are available to the public (figure 5-3). Some of the more recent censuses have been posted on the Internet. The 1901 England census is searchable online at the National Archives website <www.nationalarchives.gov.uk>. The 1881 England census is online on the FamilySearch website <www.familysearch.org>. Ancestry.com has digital images and indexes for the 1851, 1861, 1871, 1881, 1891, and 1901 England censuses. Irish emigrants appearing on these censuses often gave specific birthplaces in Ireland.

The Church of England and the Church of Ireland are both part of the Anglican communion. Irish immigrants to England may appear in Church of England records such as marriage and burial registers. You may also find the names of other family members in the same church records.

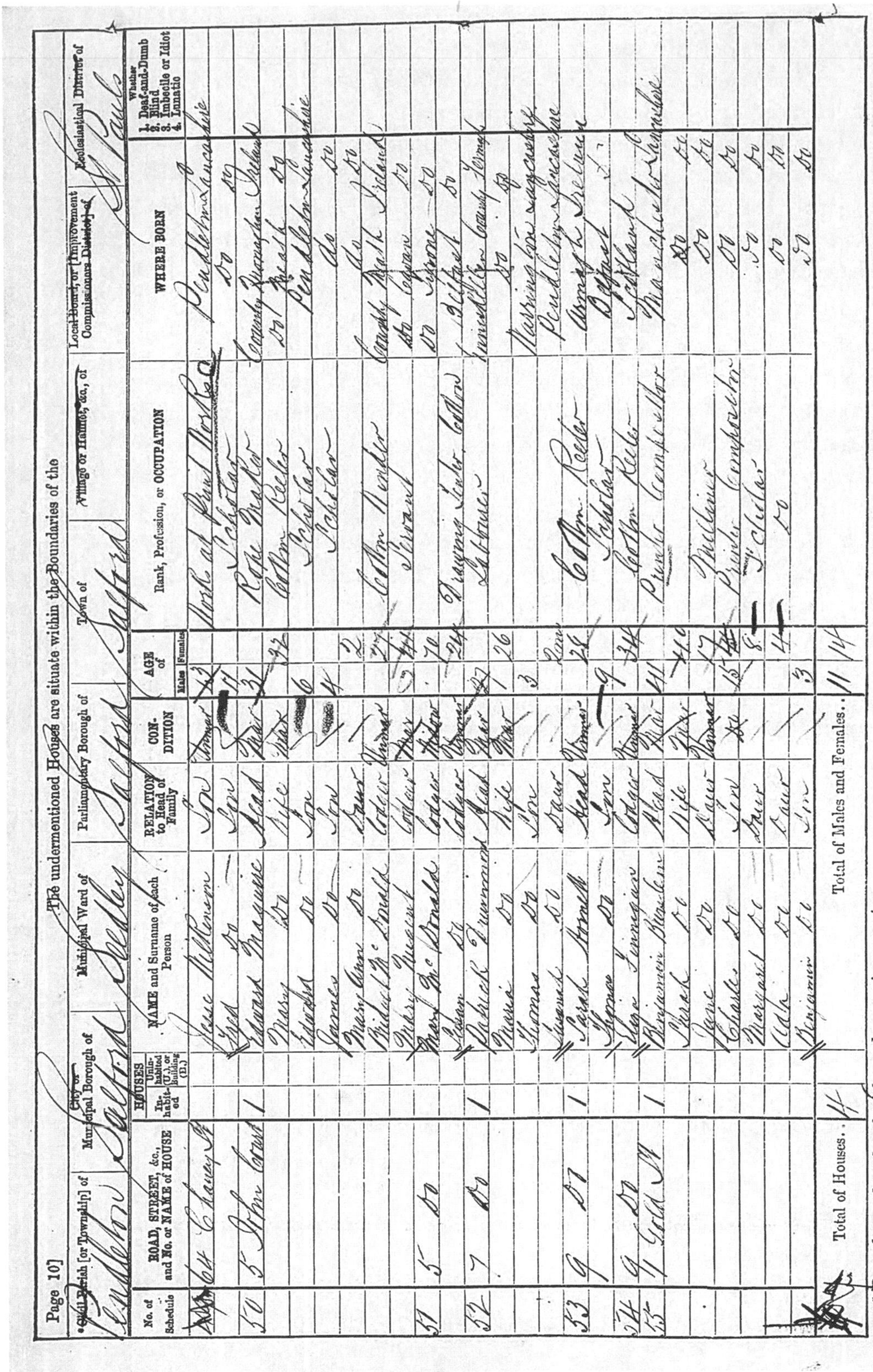

Page 10]

The undermentioned Houses are situate within the Boundaries of the

Civil Parish [or Township] of	City or Municipal Borough of	Municipal Ward of	Parliamentary Borough of	Town of	Village or Hamlet, &c., of	Local Board, or [Improvement Commissioners District] of	Ecclesiastical District of
Pendleton	Salford	Seedley	Salford	Salford			St Paul

No. of Schedule	ROAD, STREET, &c., and No. or NAME of HOUSE	HOUSES In-habited	HOUSES Uninhabited (U.), or Building (B.)	NAME and Surname of each Person	RELATION to Head of Family	CONDITION	AGE of Males	AGE of Females	Rank, Profession, or OCCUPATION	WHERE BORN	Whether 1. Deaf-and-Dumb 2. Blind 3. Imbecile or Idiot 4. Lunatic
	Total of Houses	4		Total of Males and Females			11	14			

*Draw the pen through such of the words as are inappropriate.

Courtesy of The National Archives of England

Figure 5-3. 1871 census of England.

In England, civil registration of births, marriages, and deaths began in 1837. These records are invaluable for tracing your immigrant ancestors back to Ireland. For example, a marriage record provides the names of the couple's fathers. Death records provide an age at time of death, helping you calculate a possible birth date. Remember to search for all family members in civil registration. An Internet project called FreeBMD is computerizing the civil registration indexes for England. Tens of millions of entries have already been added to the database, available on Ancestry.com and RootsWeb.com.

Gravestone inscriptions occasionally provide ages, birth dates, and birthplaces. If you can find your immigrant ancestor's family plot, you may learn where he was from in Ireland.

References and Selected Reading

Bevan, Amanda, ed. *Tracing Your Ancestors in the Public Record Office*. 5th ed. Kew, England: Public Record Office, 1999.

Irvine, Sherry. *Your English Ancestry: A Guide for North Americans*. Rev. ed. Salt Lake City: Ancestry, 1998.

Wuehler, Anne. *A Beginner's Guide to British Reference Works*. North Salt Lake, Utah: HeritageQuest, 2000.

Records in Australia

Some of the best sources for tracing Irish-Australian immigrants back to Ireland include the Australasian Genealogical Computer Index, civil registration, and convict transportation records.

Australasian Genealogical Computer Index

The Australasian Genealogical Computer Index is a microfiche collection of approximately two million records of cemetery transcriptions, newspaper articles, Irish Transportation Records, and other records. These genealogical sources have been gathered together from many different places. Combined, they are a valuable collection of early family history in Australia. The Australasian Genealogical Computer Index collection is available at the Family History Library and at a number of libraries in Australia.

Civil Registration of Births, Marriages, and Deaths

Birth, marriage, and death certificates are some of the best sources of detailed information on the origins of Irish Australians. You can search for Australian births, marriages, and deaths in a number of places.

The Genealogical Society of Utah has published a CD-ROM collection entitled "Australian Vital Records Index, 1788–1905," which indexes 4.8 million births, christenings, marriages, and deaths (figure 5-4). This four-CD collection may be

File   Edit   View   Search   OneClick   Window   Help

Australian Vital Records Index 1788-1905 (L-Q)
Click on the name to view the individual's event record

Name	Event	Year	State	Relative	
LYSAGHT, Alice Mary	B	1873	NSW	Fa:	James LYSAGHT
LYSAGHT, Alice T	B	1863	NSW	Fa:	Andrew LYSAGHT
LYSAGHT, Andrew	C	1860	NSW	Fa:	Andrew LYSAGHT
LYSAGHT, Andrew	B	1860	NSW	Fa:	Andrew LYSAGHT
LYSAGHT, Andrew	M	1860	NSW	Sp:	Johanna CARROLL
LYSAGHT, Andrew	D	1863	VIC	Fa:	James
LYSAGHT, Andrew	B	1863	VIC	Fa:	James LYSAGHT
LYSAGHT, Andrew	B	1873	NSW	Fa:	Andrew LYSAGHT
LYSAGHT, Angela Florence	B	1871	NSW	Fa:	Andrew LYSAGHT
LYSAGHT, Annie	M	1868	VIC	Sp:	Henry BEARD
LYSAGHT, Annie M	B	1868	NSW	Fa:	James LYSAGHT
LYSAGHT, Bridget	M	1844	VIC	Sp:	James PHILING
LYSAGHT, Bridget	M	1844	VIC	Sp:	James PHILING
LYSAGHT, Bridget	D	1881	NSW	Mo:	Bridget
LYSAGHT, Bridget	D	1883	NSW	Fa:	Michael O
LYSAGHT, Catherine	M	1853	NSW	Sp:	John RUSSELL
LYSAGHT, Catherine	C	1853	NSW	Fa:	Thomas LYSAGHT
LYSAGHT, Catherine	M	1853	VIC	Sp:	Patrick BOURKE
LYSAGHT, Catherine	C	1854	NSW	Fa:	Patrick LYSAGHT
LYSAGHT, Catherine	M	1870	NSW	Sp:	John REILLY
LYSAGHT, Catherine M M	D	1882	NSW	Fa:	Andrew
LYSAGHT, Catherine Mary Maud	B	1875	NSW	Fa:	Andrew LYSAGHT
LYSAGHT, Charles Vincent	B	1886	VIC	Fa:	John LYSAGHT
LYSAGHT, Chas Vincent	D	1887	VIC	Fa:	Jno
LYSAGHT, Cuthbert V	D	1883	NSW	Fa:	John
LYSAGHT, Daniel	B	1864	NSW	Fa:	Thomas LYSAGHT
LYSAGHT, Daniel	M	1887	NSW	Sp:	Sarah WILKINSON
LYSAGHT, Edith M	B	1870	NSW	Fa:	James LYSAGHT
LYSAGHT, Elen A	B	1865	NSW	Fa:	James LYSAGHT
LYSAGHT, Elen A	D	1867	NSW	Fa:	James
LYSAGHT, Elizabeth	C	1854	NSW	Fa:	John LYSAGHT
LYSAGHT, Elizabeth	B	1870	NSW	Fa:	Thomas LYSAGHT
LYSAGHT, Elizabeth M	B	1870	NSW	Fa:	Martin LYSAGHT
LYSAGHT, Elizabeth St J	B	1865	NSW	Mo:	Margaret LYSAGHT
LYSAGHT, Elizth	D	1886	VIC	Fa:	Mccann
LYSAGHT, Ellen	C	1830	NSW	Fa:	Patrick LYSAGHT
LYSAGHT, Ellen	B	1861	NSW	Fa:	Andrew LYSAGHT
LYSAGHT, Ellen	B	1864	VIC	Fa:	John LYSAGHT
LYSAGHT, Ellen	B	1867	NSW	Fa:	Thomas LYSAGHT
LYSAGHT, Ellen	M	1870	VIC	Sp:	Hugh CARROLL
LYSAGHT, Ellen	B	1881	NSW	Fa:	James LYSAGHT
LYSAGHT, Ellen U	C	1861	NSW	Fa:	Andrew LYSAGHT
LYSAGHT, Esther M	B	1872	NSW	Fa:	James LYSAGHT
LYSAGHT, Francis	D	1871	VIC	Fa:	Michael

Record: 1/128   Hit: 1/128   Query: [Field ListSurname:Lysaght]

Figure 5-4. Australian Vital Records Index.

purchased online at FamilySearch <www.familysearch.org>. These CDs contain indexes of births, christenings, marriages, and deaths for:

- New South Wales, 1788–1888
- Tasmania, 1803–99
- Victoria, 1837–88
- Western Australia, 1841–1905

Once you have found a record listed in the index, you have enough information to order the certificate from the corresponding records office in Australia.

New South Wales required the civil registration of births, marriages, and deaths beginning in 1856. In an effort to reconstruct a complete civil record of these vital events prior to 1856, the government requested that churches provide baptism, marriage, and burial records from 1788 to 1855. These early church records, combined with civil registration, constitute an impressive record of the population of New South Wales spanning over two centuries.

You can search the civil registration of New South Wales online at <www.bdm.nsw.gov.au>. This is the official website of the New South Wales Registry of Births, Deaths, and Marriages. While the complete registry contains over seventeen million records from 1788 to present, the online index permits family history searches of the index for only these time periods:

- Births: 1788–1905
- Deaths: 1788–1945
- Marriages: 1788–1945

Full birth, marriage, and death certificates may be purchased online (for $22.50 each, at the time of this writing).

Convict Transportation Records

After the American colonies gained their independence from Britain, the transportation of convicts from Britain and Ireland was diverted from America to Australia. When the first group of British convicts arrived in Australia in 1788, the penal colony of New South Wales was established, becoming the first European settlement on the continent.

Between 1791 and 1853, about 40,000 to 50,000 convicts were transported from Ireland to Australia. Each convict was sentenced to stay in Australia for at least seven years, with some given a life sentence of exile. Many of these convicts successfully petitioned the British government for free transport of their families to Australia.

The passage of convicts from Ireland to Australia was well documented. A number of Irish records on convicts transported to Australia have recently been microfilmed and indexed by name. You can search the database at <www.nationalarchives.ie/topics/transportation/search01.html>.

References and Selected Reading

Civil Registration Districts of Ireland. Salt Lake City: Genealogical Library, The Church of Jesus Christ of Latter-day Saints, 1983.

Hall, Nick Vine. *Tracing Your Family History in Australia: A Guide to Sources.* Albert Park, Victoria, Australia: Nick Vine Hall, 1994.

Ó Dúill, Eileen, and Steven ffeary-Smyrl. *Irish Civil Registration—Where Do I Start?* Killester, Dublin: Council of Irish Genealogical Organisations, 2000.

Registration of Births, Deaths and Marriages, Ireland. Dublin: Her Majesty's Stationery Office, 1891.

In Summary

The first tenet of Irish family history is to find the precise place of origin of your immigrant ancestor. You should search records in your own country to find out all you can about your Irish immigrant ancestor, especially the place of origin in Ireland. Once you pinpoint the parish or townland where your ancestor lived in Ireland, you are then ready to take the next step and search Irish records. Depending on the time period, you will begin with either birth, marriage, and death certificates; church parish registers; census records; or land and property records.

Birth, Marriage, and Death Certificates

6

In all of us there is a hunger, marrow deep, to know our heritage—to know who we are and where we came from. Without this enriching knowledge, there is a hollow yearning. No matter what our attainments in life, there is still a vacuum, an emptiness, and the most disquieting loneliness.

—Alex Haley

Birth, marriage, and death certificates are among the best sources of genealogical information in Ireland. The government required the registration of all births, marriages, and deaths in Ireland beginning in January of 1864. Registration of non-Catholic marriages started even earlier, in April of 1845. These civil registration records form the backbone of Irish genealogy from the mid-1800s to the present. Birth and marriage certificates are particularly useful for identifying all the children in a family and tracing lineages back to the early 1800s.

> → **Record Spotlight** ←
> Birth, marriage, and death certificates form the backbone of Irish genealogy from 1864 to the present.

Availability of Records

All Irish civil registration of births, marriages, and deaths has survived intact to our day. The General Register Office in Dublin holds statutory registers and indexes from 1864 to 1921 for all of Ireland as well as non-Catholic marriages from 1845 to 1863. Records for the Republic of Ireland from 1922 to present are also at the General Register Office. Records for the six counties of Northern Ireland—Counties Antrim, Derry (Londonderry), Down, Armagh, Fermanagh, and Tyrone—are available at the General Register Office in Belfast.

The Family History Library has microfilm copies of the following birth, marriage, and death records:
- For all Ireland (before 1922):
  - Birth indexes, 1864–1921
  - Birth registers, 1864–March 1881; 1900–13
  - Marriage indexes, 1845–1921 (only non-Catholic marriages from 1845 to 1863)

53

- Marriage registers, 1845–70 (only non-Catholic marriages from 1845 to 1863)
- Death indexes, 1864–1921
- Death registers, 1864–70
- For the Republic of Ireland:
  - Birth, marriage, and death indexes, 1922–58
  - Birth registers, 1930–55
- For Northern Ireland:
  - Birth, marriage, and death indexes, 1922–59
  - Birth, marriage, and death registers, 1922–59

You may order birth, marriage, and death certificates directly from the General Register Office in Dublin <www.groireland.ie> or the General Register Office in Belfast <www.groni.gov.uk>. To obtain current details on ordering options and prices, refer to these websites or the additional contact information listed in Chapter 19, "Archives and Libraries."

Birth Registers

Civil registration of births in Ireland began on 1 January 1864. The parents had primary responsibility for registering the birth of a child. The registration was supposed to occur within three months of birth, or a late registration fee was levied. Even so, there are known births that were not registered in the early years of the program. Each birth certificate contains these details:

- Full name of the child
- Birth date and birthplace
- Gender
- Father's full name and place of residence
- Father's rank, profession, or occupation
- Mother's full name, including maiden name
- Mother's place of residence
- Informant's name, place of residence, signature, and qualification (e.g., relationship to the child or "present at birth")
- Date of registration
- Registrar's signature
- Registrar's district, Superintendent Registrar's District (also referred to as the registration district or Poor Law Union), and county where birth was registered

Birth certificates are packed with information about the child and parents (figure 6-1). Parents' residences are stated, usually as a rural townland or city street address. As you collect the birth certificates for all the children in a family you will get a list of addresses where the family lived.

One note of caution about dates in Irish birth certificates: be careful about assuming that birth dates are always correct. In general, the younger the child was when registered, the more accurate the birth date written in the official register. Birth

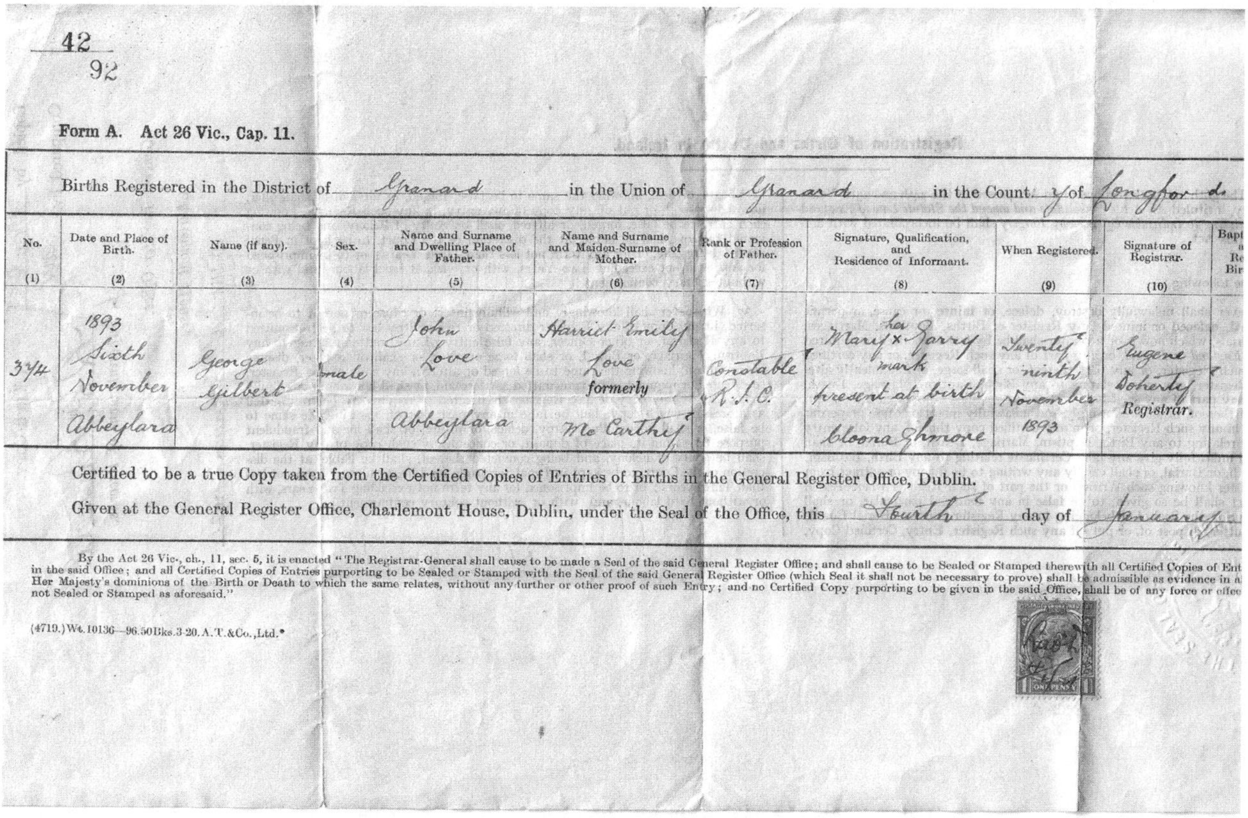

42
92

Form A. Act 26 Vic., Cap. 11.

Births Registered in the District of Granard in the Union of Granard in the County of Longford.

No. (1)	Date and Place of Birth. (2)	Name (if any). (3)	Sex. (4)	Name and Surname and Dwelling Place of Father. (5)	Name and Surname and Maiden-Surname of Mother. (6)	Rank or Profession of Father. (7)	Signature, Qualification, and Residence of Informant. (8)	When Registered. (9)	Signature of Registrar. (10)	Bapt...
374	1893 Sixth November Abbeylara	George Gilbert	male	John Love Abbeylara	Harriet Emily Love formerly Mc Carthy	Constable R.I.C.	Mary her x mark Garry present at birth Cloonaghmore	Twenty ninth November 1893	Eugene Doherty Registrar.	

Certified to be a true Copy taken from the Certified Copies of Entries of Births in the General Register Office, Dublin.

Given at the General Register Office, Charlemont House, Dublin, under the Seal of the Office, this Fourth day of January

By the Act 26 Vic., ch., 11, sec. 5, it is enacted "The Registrar-General shall cause to be made a Seal of the said General Register Office; and shall cause to be Sealed or Stamped therewith all Certified Copies of Ent[ries] in the said Office; and all Certified Copies of Entries purporting to be Sealed or Stamped with the Seal of the said General Register Office (which Seal it shall not be necessary to prove) shall be admissible as evidence in a[ll] Her Majesty's dominions of the Birth or Death to which the same relates, without any further or other proof of such Entry; and no Certified Copy purporting to be given in the said Office, shall be of any force or effec[t] not Sealed or Stamped as aforesaid."

(4719.) Wt. 10136—96.50Bks.3-20. A.T.&Co.,Ltd.*

ONE PENNY

Figure 6-1. Irish birth certificate.

registration in one of my Irish families demonstrates the need for caution. Each of the six children was baptized in the church, but only five of the births were registered with the government. The births were registered and the children baptized when they were weeks or months old. *None of the five birth dates in civil registration agrees with the corresponding birth date in the baptismal records*. Families did not always remember birthdays as well as we do nowadays. Also, if a child was more than three months old, some families "fudged" the birth date to avoid paying the late registration penalty.

A birth certificate provides the full birth names of the father and mother, making it easier to search for the parents' marriage certificate.

Marriage Registers

Civil registration of non-Catholic marriages began on 1 April 1845; this was expanded to include Catholic marriages on 1 January 1864. Although the bride and groom were responsible for registering their own marriage, the officiating priest or minister typically submitted the marriage certificate to the registrar. Marriage certificates had to be filed within three days of the marriage ceremony, so marriage dates are usually very accurate. Each marriage certificate (figure 6-2) contains these details:

- Full names of the bride and groom
- Marriage date and place, including the church or registrar's district

- Ages of the bride and groom
- Marital conditions of the bride and groom (e.g., "bachelor," "widower")
- Places of residence of the bride and groom
- Ranks or professions of the bride and groom
- The names and professions of the couple's fathers
- Signatures of the officiating authority, bride, groom, and two witnesses
- Whether the couple was married by license or banns
- Registrar's district, Superintendent Registrar's District (Poor Law Union), and county where marriage was registered

Marriage certificates are critical for family history research, as they indicate the creation of a new family and provide links to the previous generation. Irish marriage certificates supply the names and professions of the couple's fathers, often making it possible to trace one or both family lines back another generation.

As a general rule, marriages were commonly celebrated in the church that the bride's family attended, occasionally in the bride's home. Marriages were registered in the corresponding registrar's office. If one of the newlyweds lived in a different civil parish, the place of residence is usually stated as a townland and parish on the marriage certificate.

The ages of the bride and groom may simply be stated as "Full" or "Minor," with "Full" signifying that the individual was at least twenty-one years old. Many marriage certificates give these qualifiers rather than actual ages. The marital condition may be listed as "spinster," "bachelor," "widow," or "widower." A single woman was called a spinster and a single man was called a bachelor, regardless of age.

Remember to take note of the marriage witnesses for later reference. The witnesses were usually close relatives or good friends of the bride or groom.

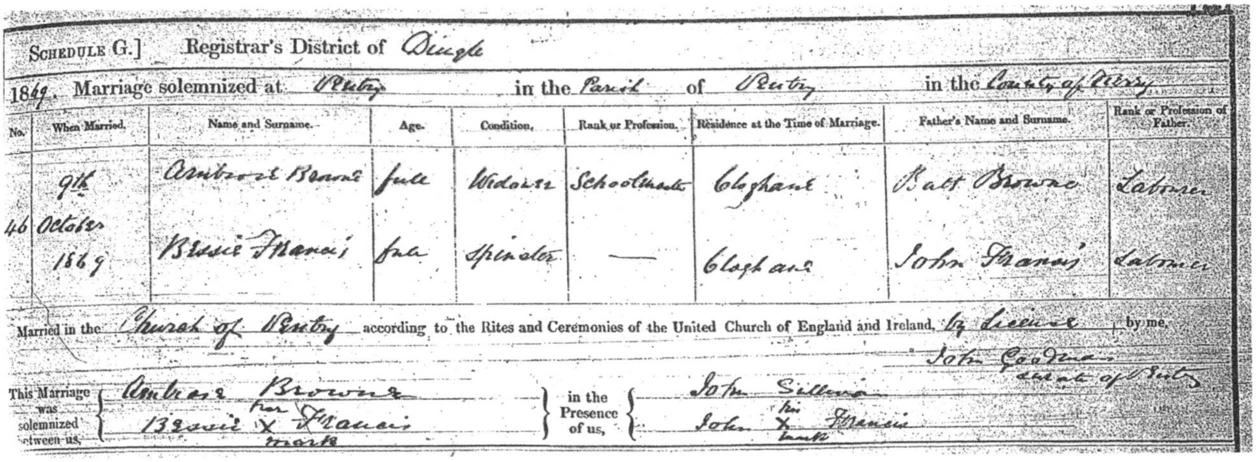
SCHEDULE G.] Registrar's District of Dingle

1869. Marriage solemnized at Ventry in the Parish of Ventry in the County of Kerry

No.	When Married.	Name and Surname.	Age.	Condition.	Rank or Profession.	Residence at the Time of Marriage.	Father's Name and Surname.	Rank or Profession of Father.
46	9th October 1869	Ambrose Browne	full	Widower	Schoolmaster	Cloghane	Batt Browne	Labourer
		Bessie Francis	full	Spinster	—	Cloghane	John Francis	Labourer

Married in the Church of Ventry according to the Rites and Ceremonies of the United Church of England and Ireland, by Licence by me, John Goodman curate of Ventry

This Marriage was solemnized between us, Ambrose Browne, Bessie X Francis her mark, in the Presence of us, John Sullivan, John X Francis his mark

Figure 6-2. Civil registration of marriage.

Death Registers

Civil registration of deaths began on 1 January 1864. The informant, often the surviving spouse or attending physician, was required to report the death to the civil registrar within two weeks. Each death certificate contains the following details:

- Full name of the deceased
- Death date and place
- Gender
- Marital condition
- Age at last birthday
- Occupation
- Certified cause of death
- Duration of final illness
- Informant's signature and place of residence
- Qualification of informant (relationship to the deceased may be mentioned)
- Date of registration
- Registrar's signature
- Registrar's district, Superintendent Registrar's District (Poor Law Union), and county where death was registered

Death registers (figure 6-3) provide relatively little information on the deceased, when compared with the rich content of birth and marriage records. Even the age at last birthday needs to be treated with suspicion. Far too many ages end in a zero, indicating that many were simply rounded to the nearest decade, or worse. If possible, ages on death certificates should be compared with age information from other sources (e.g., church burial register, tombstone inscription, or national census) to estimate birth dates.

For the death certificate of a child, the occupation field might indicate the father's profession.

Birth, Marriage, and Death Indexes

From April 1845 through December 1863, the only civil registration in Ireland was for non-Catholic marriages. The marriage index books are organized alphabetically by surname and then by given name (figure 6-4). Each entry provides a name, registration district, volume, and page number. One entry exists under the bride's name, another under the groom's name. These early marriage indexes are handwritten. While some pages are difficult to read, the handwriting is generally quite good throughout.

In January 1864, civil registration started for all births, marriages, and deaths in Ireland. From 1864 to 1877, separate annual indexes were published: one for births, one for marriages, and one for deaths. Each entry in the indexes includes a person's name, Superintendent Registrar's District (Poor Law Union), volume, and page number. Entries in the death indexes also note the age of the deceased. From 1878 through 1902, the indexes are further broken out by quarter year; the quarters end in March, June, September, and December each year. Beginning in 1903, the indexes

1868. DEATHS Registered in the District of Hollymount in the Union of Ballinrobe in the County of Mayo

No.	Date and Place of Death	Name and Surname	Sex	Condition	Age last Birthday	Rank, Profession, or Occupation	Certified Cause of Death and Duration of Illness	Signature, Qualification, and Residence of Informant	When Registered	Signature of Registrar
109	Twenty-first December 1867 Hollymount House	Thomas Spencer Lindsey	Male	Widower	77 years	Private Gentleman	Cardiac Debility 4 years No medical Certificate	J. Spencer Lindsay Hinds Present at Death Occupier Deceased Hollymount House	Twenty-third January 1868	Gerald E. Barron Registrar
110	Twenty-eighth December 1867 Carrowmaw	Bridget Henaghan	Female	Married	40 years	Farmer's Wife	Bronchitis Chronic several years Uncertified No medical Attendant	Mardax Henaghan Present at Death Carrowmacon	Fourth January 1868	Thomas Stafford Deputy Registrar
111	Second January 1868 Lisatava	Bridget McHugh	Female	Married	40 years	Farmer's Wife	Heart Disease 12 months Uncertified No medical Attendant	Michael McHugh Present at Death Lisatava	Eighth January 1868	Thomas Stafford Deputy Registrar
112	Thirty-first December 1867 Gruddoge	Michael O'Brien	Male	Widower	59 years	Farm Labourer	Liver Disease 12 months Uncertified No medical Attendant	Mary O'Brien Present at Death Gruddoge	Eleventh January 1868	Thomas Stafford Deputy Registrar
113	Fifth January 1868 Big Park	Thomas Willis	Male	Bachelor	24 years	Farmer's Son	Phthisis 3 weeks Uncertified Phthisis 9 Months Certified 3/1/68	Mark Willis Present at Death Big Park	Eleventh January 1868	Thomas Stafford Deputy Registrar
114	Fourth January 1868 Stone Park	Mary Biggins	Female	Spinster	20 years	Farmer's Daughter	Phthisis About 3 years Uncertified No medical Attendant	Patt. Biggins Present at Death Stone Park	Eleventh January 1868	Thomas Stafford Deputy Registrar

Figure 6-3. Civil registration of deaths.

INDEX to BIRTHS REGISTERED in IRELAND in 1866.

District.	Vol.	Page	Name and Registration District.	Vol.	Page	Name and Registrar
....	7	411	PELL, John Joseph. Dublin, North	12	584	PERCY, Robert Henry Car
....	13	328	PELLETT, Anna Maria. Dublin, South	12	656	—— William. Antrim ..
....	20	286	PELLICAN; John. Listowel	10	500	PERDUE, John. Callan ..
....	6	091	PELLY, Catherine. Ballinasloe..................	19	37	—— Mary Anne. Tipper
elin. Lisburn.	1	659	—— Catherine Evangiline. Dublin, South. ...	2	745	PERIU, Patrick. Gort ..
....	17	715	—— John Joseph. Dublin, South	2	737	PERKINS, Cornelius. Thu
....	11	893	—— Mary. Portumna	14	946	—— Joseph John. Dubl
th..............	7	572	PEMBERTON, Marian Sydney. Dublin, North .	17	527	—— Patrick. Naas .....
....	5	140	—— (female). Dublin, South	7	811	—— Robert Henry. Dul
....	11	222	PEMBROKE, Ellen. Tralee..................	20	627	—— Thomas. Oughtera
....	20	104	—— Ellen. Tralee.....................	15	596	—— (female). Ballina ..
....	11	782	—— Margaret. Kilkenny..	8	603	PERKINSON, Barkly. Abb
....	7	937	—— Mary. Dingle	15	207	PERKISSON, Briget. Thu
....	7	732	—— Mary Eliza. Kilkenny..............	3	609	PERNILL, Patrick. Clifde
....	3	447	—— Patrick. Listowel	10	501	PERRIN Ellen. Dublin, N
erick	20	432	PENDER, Anne. Enniscorthy	14	725	—— Henrietta. Rathdow
....	19	500	—— Bernard. Carrick-on-Shannon	18	65	—— William Alexander.
....	14	82	—— Bridget. Enniscorthy	4	814	—— (female). Cavan —
....	14	476	—— Bridget. Enniscorthy	9	753	PERROT, Catherine. Dubl
....	10	128	—— Daniel. Gorey	7	876	—— Sarah. Clonakilty...
....	6	178	—— Daniel. Gorey	7	877	PERROTT, Margaret. Ban
...h	7	540	Elizabeth Nenagh	2	651	Robert Cork

Figure 6-4. Civil registration birth index.

reverted back to their original annual format. The birth indexes were dramatically improved in 1903 by including the mother's maiden name for each entry. This makes it much easier to find birth records for all the children in a family.

Finding Your Ancestors in Indexes

Searching the civil registration indexes on microfilm is fairly straightforward. Go to the Family History Library Catalog on FamilySearch <www.familysearch.org>, click to search by Place, and type in *Ireland*. Select the topic *Civil Registration Indexes* and choose the birth, marriage, or death index you want to search. Find the film for the year (or quarter year) of your ancestor's birth, marriage, or death. If you don't know the exact date, start with your best estimate and extend your search before and after as needed.

It is especially easy to find marriage records using the indexes, even if you are not certain exactly which year the couple married. Just search the indexes year-by-year (or quarter-by-quarter) until you find a volume with both the bride's and groom's names in the index, referencing the same registration district, volume, and page number.

If you know which county your ancestor lived in, you will be looking for all entries under his name that mention a registration district within the right county. To find the names of registration districts for any county, consult the table of registration districts found in the Appendix.

If your ancestor's name was common and there are numerous matching entries in the index, you will need to know the precise registration district (Poor Law Union) he lived in. For example, if your ancestor Michael Murphy was born in County Galway, his birth could have been registered in any of these registration districts: Ballinasloe, Ballinrobe, Clifden, Galway, Glennamaddy, Gort, Loughrea, Mountbellew, Oughterard, Portumna, Scarriff, or Tuam. However, if you know he was actually from the townland of Gorteen, you could identify the Poor Law Union (registration district) as Loughrea and then narrow down your search to just those Michael Murphy's in the birth index with the registration district of Loughrea.

A number of geographical dictionaries and townland indexes can help you identify the registration district if you know the townland or civil parish where your ancestor lived. The most accessible of these books is the *General Alphabetical Index to the Townlands and Towns, Parish and Baronies of Ireland: Based on the Census of Ireland for the Year 1851*, originally published in 1861 and reprinted by Genealogical Publishing Company in 2000. This index is available on a number of websites, including Irish Origins <www.irishorigins.com>. See Chapter 4, "Place Names and Land Divisions," for more details.

> ↓
> **Research Tip**
>
> When searching for your ancestor in the civil registration indexes, remember to look for your ancestor's name under all possible spellings.

When searching for your ancestor in the civil registration indexes, remember to look for your ancestor's name under all possible spellings. If his name were Patrick O'Flaherty, you would search for Pat Flaherty, Patrick Flaherty, Pat O'Flaherty, and Patrick O'Flaherty. Surname prefixes like "Mac" and "O" were added and omitted routinely. Other spelling variations may also need to be checked.

If you don't find your ancestor in the year (or quarter) you expect, try the index for the next year. Some births were registered two or three months after birth and might appear in the index of the following year.

When you do find your ancestor in the index, write down the entire entry, including the name, registration district, volume, and page number. You will be using all the information to find the original certificate in the registers.

Finding Your Ancestors in Registers

Once you have found an ancestor in a civil registration index, it is easy to find the actual birth, marriage, or death certificate. Go to the Family History Library Catalog under the heading *Ireland—Civil Registration*, and choose the birth, marriage, or death register you want to search. Find or order the film for the year (or quarter year) and volume of your ancestor's birth, marriage, or death. When searching the microfilm, go directly to the page number you found in the index. Your ancestor's birth entry will be on that page of the register. Always photocopy the actual certificate—you will definitely want a copy for your records—and details you might overlook when you first read the certificate may become more meaningful later on.

The Family History Library's microfilm collection of actual birth, marriage, and death certificates is complete through 1958 except for the following gaps:

- For all Ireland (before 1922):
  - Birth registers, June 1881–99; 1914–21
  - Marriage registers, 1871–1921

- Death registers, 1871–1921
- For the Republic of Ireland:
  - Birth registers, 1922–29
  - Marriage registers, 1922–58
  - Death registers, 1922–58
- For the Northern Ireland:
  - No gaps

If your ancestor's birth, marriage, or death occurs during any of these time periods, you will need to order a copy of the certificate directly from the General Register Office in Dublin or Belfast (see Chapter 19, "Archives and Libraries," for contact information).

A number of births, marriages, and deaths have been indexed and abstracted over the last couple of decades. Some of these indexes are available online, others are published in books or on CD-ROM, while others are searchable through Irish Heritage Centres. One online example is the International Genealogical Index, a database of births and marriages on FamilySearch <www.familysearch.org>. This index contains entries from the early years of Irish civil registration, including most of the births registered from 1864 to 1866 and marriages registered from 1845 to 1846, as well as portions of subsequent years. The *British Isles Vital Records Index*, second edition, is a CD-ROM collection also available from FamilySearch <www.familysearch.org>. This 16-CD collection contains indexes to many birth and marriage records from the British Isles, including over one million births and almost one hundred thousand marriages from Ireland.

Completeness of Registers and Indexes

Although registration of births, marriages, and deaths was compulsory, not everyone obeyed the law. In the first few years of civil registration especially, perhaps 10–15 percent of births and marriages were never recorded, even though there were penalties for failure to register.

Even if your ancestors registered with the government, their names may not be listed in the indexes. For example, my great-grandparents Michael O'Connor and Mary Jane Browne are not listed in the national marriage index even though their marriage certificate is in the registers. This marriage was probably listed in the marriage index prepared by the Registration District but unintentionally omitted when the General Register Office in Dublin combined all the local indexes to create the national index.

> ✔
> ### Warning
> A small but significant percentage of births, marriages, and deaths were never recorded, particularly in the early years of civil registration.

Late Registrations

Most births, marriages, and deaths were registered, and these registrations were done within the prescribed time limits. Some events were reported late, with informants falsifying dates rather than paying the late registration fee. Other births, marriages, and deaths were accurately reported well after the deadline; these Late Registrations are published in the back of national indexes or handwritten on the appropriate page in the index. When the event does not appear in the index, remember to check the brief index of late registrations at the end of the book.

Other Irish Sources

Each of the major sources of Irish genealogy—civil registration, censuses, church registers, and land records—can be a springboard to help you find your ancestor in other sources. When you find your ancestors in one source, use the information to find them in all the major sources.

> ### ↓ Research Tip
> When you find your ancestors in one source, use the information to find them in all the major sources.

The 1901 and 1911 censuses provide ages for each member of the family. Form these you can calculate approximate birth years and then search for the birth certificates. The 1911 census also provides the number of years a couple was married. You can use this information to calculate the year of marriage and then search the marriage indexes beginning with that year.

Church baptismal registers can be used to find the civil registration of a child's birth. The marriage in a parish register can help you find the civil registration of marriage, which often includes details lacking in the ecclesiastical record. Church burial registers may help you find death certificates.

Land records often indicate a change in tenancy the same year or the year after the head of household dies. You can use land records to approximate the year of death and then more easily find the death certificate. Wills are another valuable source of information to help you obtain a death certificate.

In Summary

Birth, marriage, and death certificates document the vital events of your Irish ancestors and their descendants from 1864 to the present. Birth certificates state when and where a child was born, the names of the parents, and other family history details. Marriage certificates not only record the newlyweds' marriage date and place; they also document the couple's residences, occupations, and fathers' names. Death certificates mention the death date and place, the cause of death, and the age at time of death. These vital records can help you identify entire families and extend your family history back to the early nineteenth century.

References and Selected Reading

General Alphabetical Index to the Townlands and Towns, Parishes and Baronies of Ireland: Based on the Census of Ireland for the Year 1851. 1861. Reprint, Baltimore: Genealogical Publishing Company, 2000.

Handran, George B., CG. *Townlands in Poor Law Unions*. Salem, Mass.: Higginson Book, 1997.

Church Records

God the Father, God the Son, God the Holy Ghost,
Bless, preserve, and keep you;
The Lord mercifully with his favour look upon you;
And so fill you with all spiritual benediction and grace,
That ye may so live together in this life,
That in the world to come ye may have life everlasting.
Amen.

—Marriage blessing pronounced by the minister upon the newlyweds,
from the Book of Common Prayer *(1662)*

Ireland is a deeply religious country and has been throughout recorded history. Where the records still exist, Irish church registers preserve wonderful details about our ancestors and their families. Baptismal records help us connect the generations of our ancestry. Marriage records help us see a husband and wife begin a new family. Burial records provide a final mortal glimpse of each ancestor.

Church records are essential sources for tracing ancestors who were poor, tenant farmers. Very few records document the lives of those who owned no land, left no will, and appeared on no surviving census. This chapter describes the records kept by the three largest churches in Ireland (Roman Catholic, Church of Ireland, and Presbyterian) and suggests strategies to help you get the most out of these marvelous sources.

> **→ Record Spotlight ←**
> Church baptism, marriage, and burial registers are the best source of Irish family history prior to 1864.

Church Membership in Ireland

The Roman Catholic Church is the predominant church in Ireland and has been since the days of Saint Patrick. The church with the second largest membership in Ireland is the Church of Ireland, alternately known as the Protestant Church, the Episcopal Church, and the Anglican Church. From 1536 to 1870, the Church of Ireland was the official church of the state, the Established Church. After the Church of Ireland, the Presbyterian Church has the next largest membership, followed by the Methodist Church.

The 1861 census of Ireland revealed that 78% of the people in Ireland were Roman Catholic, 12% were Church of Ireland, 9% were Presbyterian, and 1% were Methodist. Less than 0.5% of the population was of other faiths (see table 7-1). Roman

Table 7-1: Religious Affiliations in Ireland

Province	Population	% Roman Catholic	% Church of Ireland	% Presby-terian	% Methodist	% Other
Connaught	913,135	94.8%	4.4%	0.3%	0.3%	0.1%
Leinster	1,457,635	85.9%	12.4%	0.8%	0.4%	0.4%
Munster	1,513,558	93.8%	5.3%	0.3%	0.3%	0.3%
Ulster	1,914,236	50.5%	20.4%	26.3%	1.7%	1.1%
All Provinces	5,798,564	77.7%	12.0%	9.0%	0.8%	0.5%

Information summarized from the 1861 census.

Catholics represented the largest percentage of the population in every county but two: Presbyterians accounted for the greatest number of people in Counties Antrim and Down. The following counties boasted the largest concentration of people for each major religion in 1861:

- County Clare was 98% Roman Catholic
- County Fermanagh was 38% Church of Ireland
- County Antrim was 48% Presbyterian
- County Fermanagh was 3% Methodist

Before the Great Famine of the late 1840s, an even higher percentage of the Irish population was Roman Catholic, notwithstanding the many centuries of persecution against the Catholic Church.

The Penal Laws

The Roman Catholic faith has flourished in Ireland for over fifteen hundred years, but not without opposition. In 1541, the English monarch, King Henry VIII, forced the Irish Parliament to declare him King of Ireland. In 1550, a proclamation was issued, banning Catholic religious ceremonies. Over the next century, many decrees were pronounced against the clergy and membership of the Catholic Church in Ireland. Beginning in the 1690s, a number of significant restrictions were placed on Catholics; these Penal Laws banned Catholics from holding public office, obtaining education, bearing arms, practicing law, and buying land. Catholic priests were forbidden to celebrate mass—those who did were to be exiled, with the threat of execution if they returned to Ireland. The main reason the government instituted the Penal Laws was to weaken the influence and power of the Catholic Church both politically and economically. By 1744, the Penal Laws were strictly enforced. The next few decades were especially difficult for the Catholic Church.

Beginning with the first Catholic Relief Act in 1772, the restrictions placed on Catholics were gradually lifted. In 1829, the Catholic Emancipation Act restored full rights to Irish Catholics.

Roman Catholic Records

Catholic parishes kept registers of baptisms and marriages; Catholic burial registers are rare. The majority of Catholic parish registers in rural Ireland began in the 1820s or later. Catholic parishes in the cities often date back to the mid-1700s. Some few parish registers survive from the late seventeenth century. Catholic parish records are especially helpful for tracing ancestors in the decades just before 1864, when civil registration began. In fact, even after 1864 not everyone registered their marriages or children's births with the government, although it was required by law. Parish registers may therefore provide the only record of these events even after civil registration began.

Catholic Baptismal Records

Catholic families generally had their children baptized soon after birth, so the baptism date is a good approximation of the birth date. A typical entry in a Catholic baptismal register (figure 7-1) contains at least this information:

- Child's full name
- Date of the baptism
- Father's full name
- Mother's full maiden name
- Godparents' (sponsors) names

Occasionally, the priest also recorded the place of residence, specifying the townland or street name as in the civil registration of a birth. Less frequently, the father's occupation was recorded in a baptismal entry.

Some priests kept their parish registers in English, especially in more urban, English-speaking areas. Others wrote in Latin, particularly in the more rural, Gaelic-speaking regions. When the priest kept Latin records, he translated the first names into Latin. Priests also tended to abbreviate a number of first names and repeated words, as in the following example from 1836, transcribed from the Killury baptismal register:

Rev^d D^{ns} O'Sullivan baptizant Joannem fil. legt. Barthol^{ai} Brown et Margarita Lyset de Clihane. Guliel^s Connor et Cath^a Clancy.

Expanding the abbreviations and translating words and given names to English, this record reads:

Reverend Dennis O'Sullivan baptized Johanna, legitimate daughter of Bartholomew Brown and Margaret Lyset [Lysaght] of Clihane [Cloghane]. [Godparents:] William Connor and Catherine Clancy.

The mother's maiden name is almost universally included in Catholic baptismal registers, an important detail typically missing from nineteenth-century Church of Ireland baptismal registers. Knowing the mother's maiden name, you have better information for correctly matching each of the children to the right family and a greater chance of tracing the ancestry of the mother.

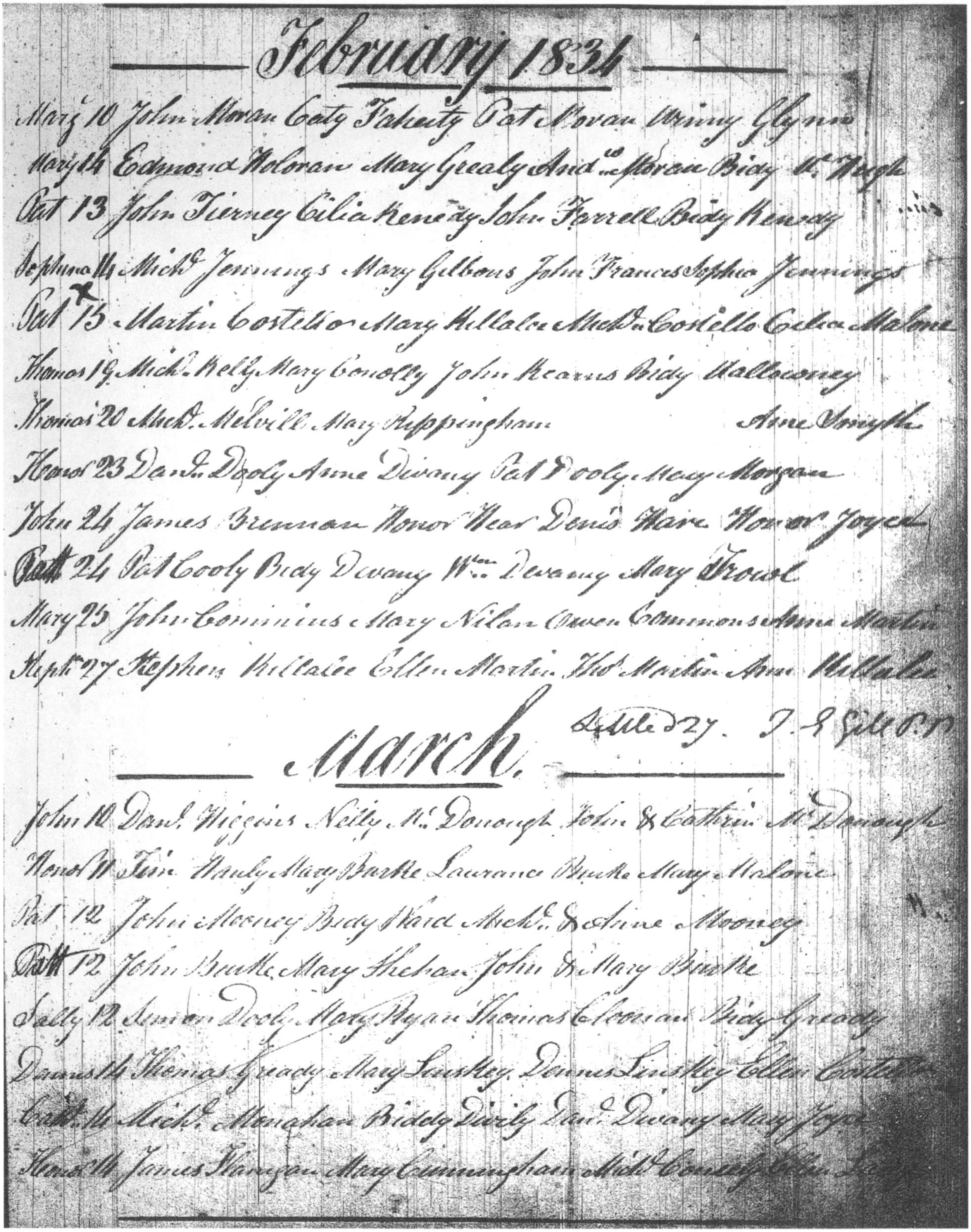

Figure 7-1. Catholic baptismal register, Oranmore Parish.

The parents often invited close family members to be the godparents, providing us with potential clues about the extended family.

Catholic Marriage Records

A typical entry in a Catholic marriage register (figure 7-2) contains this information:

- Full name of the groom
- Full maiden name of the bride
- Date of the marriage
- Names of the witnesses

The place of residence may also appear in a marriage register. In later years you may be fortunate to find the names of the fathers of the bride and groom recorded in the marriage book. Some registers even list the full names of the mothers of the bride and groom.

Table 7-2 shows an exceptional example of a Catholic marriage record taken from a page of the *Liber Matrimonium*, or Marriage Book, for the parish of Castleisland, in County Kerry (FHL 1279379). This example was the fifteenth marriage celebrated in the parish in 1899.

Catholic Burial Records

Few Catholic parishes kept burial records until well into the twentieth century. However, if you are fortunate enough to find burials registered in your ancestor's parish, you will typically find this information recorded for each entry:

- Full name of the deceased
- Date of the burial

Many Catholics were buried in Church of Ireland cemeteries, as the Church of Ireland was the state church. Always remember to check the burial register of the corresponding Church of Ireland parish just in case your Catholic ancestors were buried there.

Research Tip

Regardless of your ancestors' religion, always remember to check the registers of the local Church of Ireland parish for their burial records. Ministers of the state church often buried Catholics and nonconformists in Church of Ireland burial grounds.

Identifying Your Ancestor's Catholic Parish

Catholic parishes may have the same names as associated civil parishes, but they are generally larger and of earlier origin. If you know the townland or civil parish where

Table 7-2: Example of Information from a Catholic Marriage Record

Name	Surname	Residence	Parents	Residence	Date	Priest	Witnesses	Residence
Joannes	Hickey	Dromultin	Laurantis Hickey, Hanora Sullivan	Dromultin	Junii 15th 99	Joannes Foran	Laurentius Hickey	Dromultin
Hanora	Browne	Mullin	Edmundi Browne, Catherina Keefe	Mullin			Ellena Galvin	Adurhle[?]

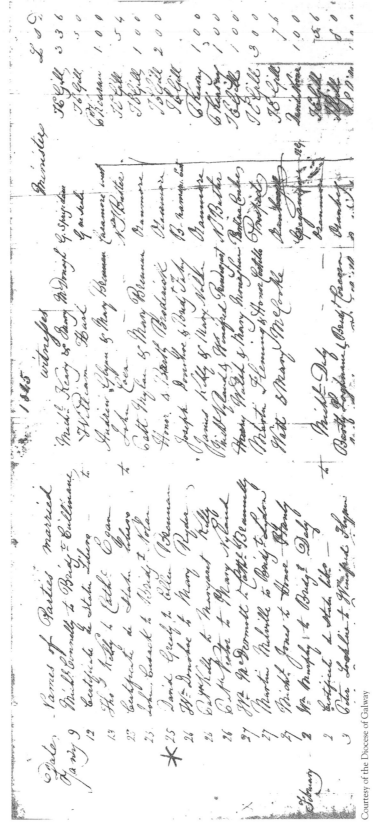

Figure 7-2. Catholic marriage register, Oranmore Parish.

your ancestor lived, there are a number of excellent sources to help you identify the Catholic parish of your ancestor. Brian Mitchell's *A New Genealogical Atlas of Ireland* has Catholic parish maps and civil parish maps for each county in Ireland. John Grenham's *Tracing Your Irish Ancestors*, also has Catholic parish maps for each county. Grenham's book has extensive tables of all Catholic parishes in each county. These tables list the date ranges of surviving baptism, marriage, and burial registers for each parish, including which libraries and archives have copies of each of these records.

Reading Latin Words in Catholic Parish Registers

If you need to read Catholic parishes registers written in Latin, don't worry. The Latin is usually less of an obstacle than the handwriting. Table 7-3 lists some common terms found in Catholic parish registers, in English and Latin.

Availability of Catholic Parish Registers

Most Catholic parish registers are available on microfilm at the National Library of Ireland in Dublin. These microfilms generally begin with the earliest registers of a parish and continue through 1880 or 1900. At the time of this writing, researchers may examine the registers for the dioceses of Kerry and Limerick on microfilm at the National Library only if they have written permission from the bishop. The easiest way to request permission is by e-mail. Contact

> ↓
> ### Library Tip
> Most Catholic parish registers are available on microfilm at the National Library of Ireland in Dublin through 1880 or 1900. About one-third of these microfilms are also available at the Family History Library.

Table 7-3: Latin Words Commonly Found in Catholic Parish Registers

English	Latin
and	*Et*
birth, born	*nati, natus*
burial, buried	*sepulti, sepultus*
christening, christened	*baptismi, baptizatus*
daughter	*Filia*
day	*Die*
death, deceased	*mortuus, defunctus*
father	*Pater*
godparents	*patrini*
given name	*Nomen*
husband	*maritus, sponsus, conjux*
marriage	*matrimonium, copulatio, copulati, conjuncti*
marriage banns	*banni, proclamationes, denuntiationes*
month	*Mense*
mother	*Mater*
parents	*Parentes*
son	*Filius*
surname	*Cognomen*
wife	*uxor, marita, conjux, sponsa*
witnesses	*Sponsores*
year	*Ano*

information for the Bishop of Kerry is available at <www.dioceseofkerry.ie>; contact information for the Bishop of Limerick is found at <www.limerickdiocese.org/Directory/Diocese/Bishop.htm>. At present, the Archbishop of Cashel and Emly does not allow researchers to examine the microfilmed registers of his diocese at the National Library. To commission a search of the parish registers of this diocese, contact Tipperary Family History Research (see Chapter 18, "Irish Heritage Centres," for contact information).

The Family History Library has copies of National Library microfilms for approximately one-third of the Catholic parishes. Many original parish registers are held in local custody. County Heritage Centres have indexed many of the Catholic parish registers for their respective counties. The Public Record Office of Northern Ireland has copies of most registers for Ulster.

Church of Ireland Records

Many surviving Church of Ireland parish registers begin between 1770 and 1820, somewhat earlier than most Catholic parish registers. Registers of a few dozen Church of Ireland parishes date back to the 1600s. Clergy of the Church of Ireland kept records of baptisms, marriages, marriage license bonds, burials, and vestry minutes.

Church of Ireland Baptismal Records

Church of Ireland baptisms, or christenings, were usually performed within a few days or weeks after birth. However, some infants weren't christened until they were several months old. A typical entry in a Church of Ireland baptismal register (figure 7-3) contains this information:

- Child's full name
- Date of the baptism
- Father's full name
- Mother's given name (but not her maiden name)
- Clergyman's name

Occasionally, the place of residence is recorded. In later records, the father's occupation is also listed, as is the date of birth.

Church of Ireland Marriage Records

A typical entry in a Church of Ireland marriage register contains at least this information:

- Full name of the groom
- Full maiden name of the bride
- Date of the marriage
- Name of the clergyman

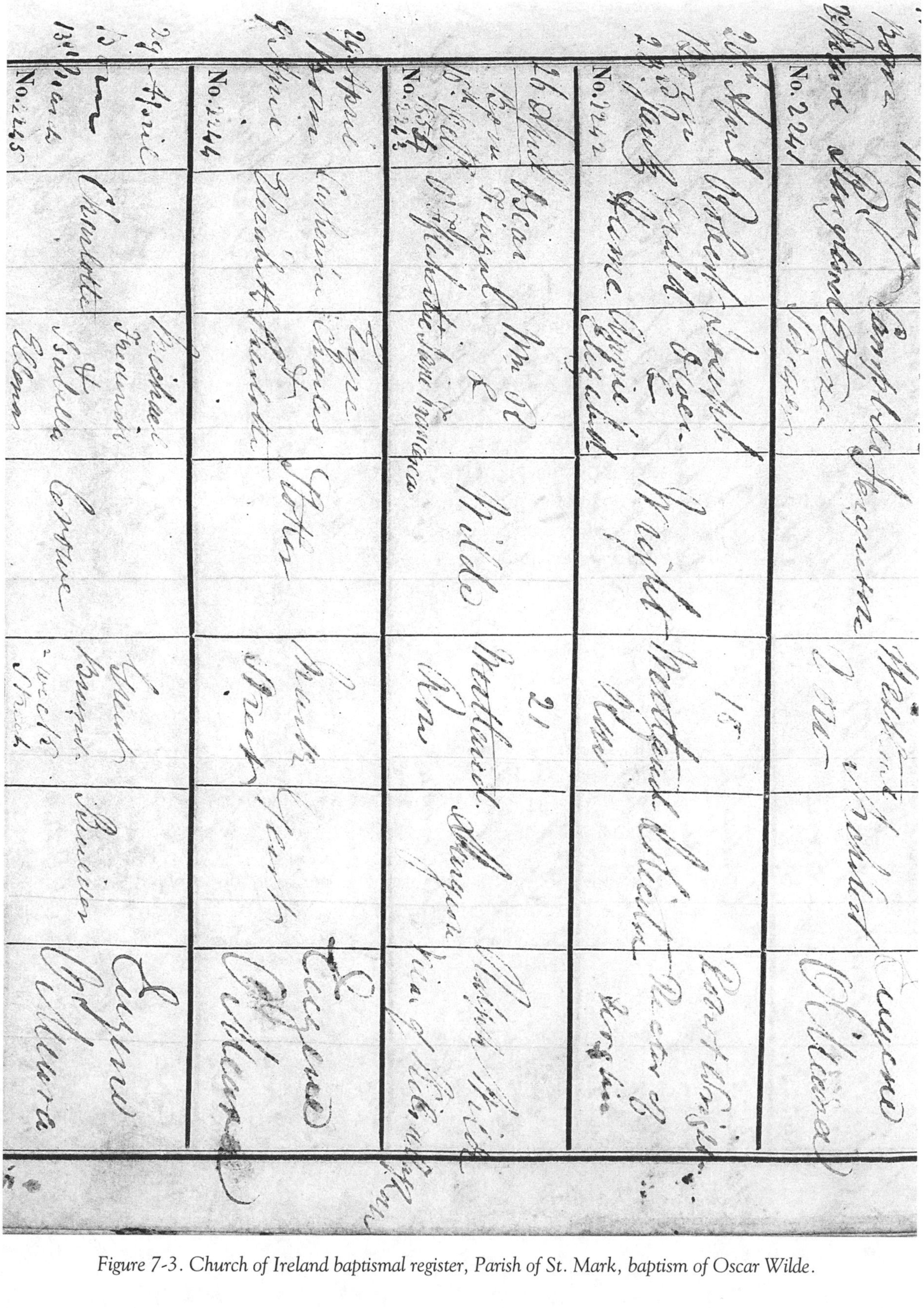

Figure 7-3. Church of Ireland baptismal register, Parish of St. Mark, baptism of Oscar Wilde.

Once civil registration of non-Catholic marriages began in 1845, the contents of most Church of Ireland marriage registers reflected the same information, including the ages, occupations, marital statuses, and residences of the bride and groom; the names and occupations of the fathers of the bride and groom; and the names of two witnesses. Take note of the witnesses names, as they might have been close family members.

The couple usually wed in the bride's parish. If the bride or groom were from another parish, a note to this effect might be recorded in the parish register. Catholics, Presbyterians, and Methodists were sometimes married in the Church of Ireland.

Marriage License Bonds

Couples intending to marry were required by law to either have their marriage announced in church for three consecutive Sundays (called "marriage banns") or to obtain a marriage license. Most couples chose to have marriage banns announced in church, as this practice cost no money. Couples desiring to avoid this custom could purchase a marriage license bond from the diocese. Although these bonds were destroyed in the June 1922 Civil War bombing of Four Courts, Dublin, the original indexes are intact and are housed in the National Archives in Dublin. The surviving indexes of marriage license bonds list the names of the intended bride and groom and the year they received their marriage license. These marriage license bond indexes are available on microfilm from the Family History Library.

Church of Ireland Burial Records

A typical entry in a Church of Ireland burial register (figure 7-4) contains this information:

- Full name of the deceased
- Date of the burial
- Age of deceased
- Townland of residence (sometimes omitted)

Even if your ancestors did not belong to the Church of Ireland, you may wish to examine the burial registers; many Catholics, Presbyterians, and others have their burials listed in Church of Ireland parish registers because the Church of Ireland was the state Church.

Church of Ireland Vestry Minutes

The minutes of parish vestry meetings contain additional information about individuals, couples, and families within the parish beyond the genealogical details found in parish registers. Vestry minutes may even list baptisms, marriages, and burials. Many of the surviving vestry books are available at either the Public Record Office of Northern Ireland or the Representative Church Body Library in Dublin. Some vestry minutes are still held by the local parishes.

BURIALS in the Parish of _Dingle_

in the County of _Kerry_ in the Year 18_61 & 1862_

Name.	Abode.	When Buried.	Age.	By whom the Ceremony was performed.
Jessica Marcum Son of Thomas & Margaret Marcum No. 14	Dingle	15th of September 1861 at Garfiny	seven years	Lewis Sam H Lewis
Mary Brown wife of Ambrose Brown No. 15	Ventry	6th of October 1861	25 years	Tho J Goodman
Margaret Marshall No. 16	Dingle	12th of November 1861	76 years	Tho J Goodman
Emma Loney daughter of James & Eliza No. 17	Dingle	17th of November 1861	6 months	Lewis Sam H Lewis
Mary Fitzgerald No. 18	Dingle	5th of December	17 years	Lewis S H Lewis
Johanna Keane daughter of James & Johanna No. 19	Dingle	15th of April	2 years	Tho J Goodman
Thomas West No. 20	Cloghane	7th of June 1862	70 years	Lewis S H Lewis
Eliza Leahy daughter of Darby & Johanna Buried at Garfiny No.	Dingle	12 of July 1862	11 years	Tho J Goodman

Figure 7-4. Church of Ireland burial register, Dingle Parish.

Availability of Church of Ireland Parish Records

After the Church of Ireland was disestablished as the state religion, legislation was enacted to deliver the parish registers to the government for safekeeping. All baptism and burial registers prior to 1871 and marriage registers prior to April 1845 were declared public records. Those parishes able to provide adequate storage of these records were permitted to retain custody of the registers. All other parishes were required to send at least a copy of their registers to the Public Record Office in Dublin. A large percentage of parishes sent the only copy of their registers to the Four Courts in Dublin. This was extremely unfortunate, as almost every one of these books was destroyed in the bombing of Four Courts in June 1922. Registers from over one thousand Church of Ireland parishes were destroyed. However, hundreds of parishes had not yet sent their registers to Four Courts before the bombing, so their records were spared. Other parishes only sent a copy of their registers, retaining the original registers in local custody.

Most surviving baptism, marriage, and burial registers date from the eighteenth and nineteenth centuries, but a very few exist from much earlier dates. The earliest surviving register is from the Dublin parish of St. John the Evangelist and dates from 1619.

The official archive for Church of Ireland parish registers is the Representative Church Body Library (RCBL) in Dublin. The RCBL currently holds registers for almost one thousand parishes, including transcriptions of some original registers destroyed in the Civil War bombing of Four Courts. More parishes offer their registers and vestry minutes to the RCBL each year for safekeeping.

The ProGenealogists website <www.progenealogists.com> offers a searchable database of parishes (not records), listing the available dates of baptisms, marriages, and burials for each parish, as contained in the RCBL. Vestry minutes are also inventoried. Go to <http://ireland.progenealogists.com/ParishRegisters.asp> to see which parish registers are held by the RCBL.

The RCBL is transcribing registers parish by parish and has already published a number of registers. The RCBL website lists the transcribed registers in its "Parish Register Series," found at <www.ireland.anglican.org/library/libresources.html>.

The National Archives of Ireland has microfilmed the registers of approximately 350 Church of Ireland parishes. The microfilms of these baptism, marriage, and burial registers are available to the public. The Public Record Office of Northern Ireland has microfilmed Church of Ireland parish registers for the following counties: Antrim, Armagh, Cavan, Derry (Londonderry), Donegal, Down, Fermanagh, Leitrim, Louth, Monaghan, and Tyrone.

Definition

The plantation of Ulster was an English and Scottish settlement that began in the early 1600s and forced many Irish-Catholic families from their lands.

Presbyterian Church Records

In the early seventeenth century, many Presbyterians emigrated from Scotland to Ireland with the plantation of Ulster. Many fled Scotland to escape religious persecution, but the Penal Laws in Ireland were also difficult to endure. Many emigrated from Ireland to America within a few years.

In 1782, the Penal Laws were relaxed to the point that Presbyterian ministers were allowed to solemnize marriages according to the rites of the Presbyterian Church. By 1845, Presbyterians were allowed to marry members of the Church of Ireland within the Presbyterian Church.

By 1861, 9% of the population of Ireland was Presbyterian. In fact, 26% of the population of Ulster was of the Presbyterian faith, with half of County Antrim confessing Presbyterianism. Over 96% of all Presbyterians in Ireland lived in the province of Ulster.

Presbyterian congregations did not have a parish and diocese organization like the Catholic and Anglican churches. To identify the Presbyterian congregations your ancestors might have attended, you will want to determine the locations of Presbyterian meetinghouses closest to your ancestors' homes. One of the best tools to use to locate Presbyterian congregations in Ireland is Brian Mitchell's book, *A New Genealogical Atlas of Ireland*, which has Presbyterian congregation maps for each of the nine counties of Ulster. The locations of Presbyterian congregations are identified within each civil parish for these counties.

Presbyterian Baptismal Records

Although the earliest surviving Presbyterian Church register in Ireland dates from 1674, ministers were not required to keep record of baptisms and marriages until 1819. By the 1830s, a number of Presbyterian ministers had started keeping baptism and marriage registers.

Presbyterian baptismal registers varied significantly in form and content, depending on the congregation. A nineteenth-century baptismal entry in a Presbyterian register would generally contain:

- Child's full name
- Father's full name
- Mother's maiden name
- Parent's townland of residence

Over time, ministers began to write more detailed baptismal entries. Eventually, many baptismal registers began to include additional details such as the date of birth and the names of sponsors.

Presbyterian Marriage Records

A typical entry in a Presbyterian marriage register contains at least the following information:

- The date and place of marriage
- The names of the bride and groom
- The name of the bride's father

Presbyterian Burial Records

The Penal Laws allowed no one but members of the Church of Ireland to maintain cemeteries. Even when the Penal Laws were retracted, the Presbyterian Church rarely kept burial records. Check the burial registers and graveyards of the Church of Ireland for your earlier Presbyterian ancestors; check for Presbyterian graveyards starting in the nineteenth century. See lists from Chapter 4, "Irish Presbyterian Records," in James Ryan's *Irish Church Records*.

Additional Records of the Presbyterian Church

Other records that survive beyond the baptism and marriage registers include kirk session minutes, committee minutes, communicants' roll, stipend payers' books, lists of new communicants, lists of elders, marriage notices, and other miscellaneous records, depending on the congregation. The session minutes often contain records of births, baptisms, and marriages, so these records should be consulted in addition to the baptismal and marriage registers. For instance, if the marriage register no longer exists, the kirk session minute book may have the only record of a couple's marriage. Check *An Irish Genealogical Source: Guide to Church Records* for details on holdings at the Public Record Office of Northern Ireland for individual churches.

Availability of Presbyterian Records

Most Presbyterian church records are still held in local custody by the minister of the congregation. The Public Record Office of Northern Ireland in Belfast holds the largest collection of Presbyterian church records.

In Summary

In Ireland, surviving church records document millions of baptisms, marriages, and burials from the eighteenth to the twenty-first centuries. Some few parish registers still exist from the early 1600s, but most begin between the late 1700s and early 1800s. Church records are the best source of Irish family history, especially before civil registration of births, marriages, and deaths began in 1864. In many areas of Ireland, parish registers predate all other significant genealogical records. Baptism and marriage registers are the best tools to extend your family history back through the generations.

References and Selected Reading

Grenham, John. *Tracing Your Irish Ancestors: The Complete Guide*. 2d ed. Baltimore: Genealogical Publishing Company, 1999.

An Irish Genealogical Source: Guide to Church Records. Belfast: Public Record Office of Northern Ireland, 1994.

Mitchell, Brian. *A Guide to Irish Churches and Graveyards*. Baltimore: Genealogical Publishing Company, 1995.

———. *A Guide to Irish Parish Registers*. Baltimore: Genealogical Publishing Company, 1995.

———. *A New Genealogical Atlas of Ireland.* 2d ed. Baltimore: Genealogical Publishing Company, 2002.

Reid, Noel, ed. *A Table of Church of Ireland Parochial Records and Copies.* Naas, County Kildare: Irish Family History Society, 1994.

Ryan, James G., ed. *Irish Church Records: Their History, Availability and Use in Family and Local History.* 2d ed. Glenageary, County Dublin: Flyleaf, 2001.

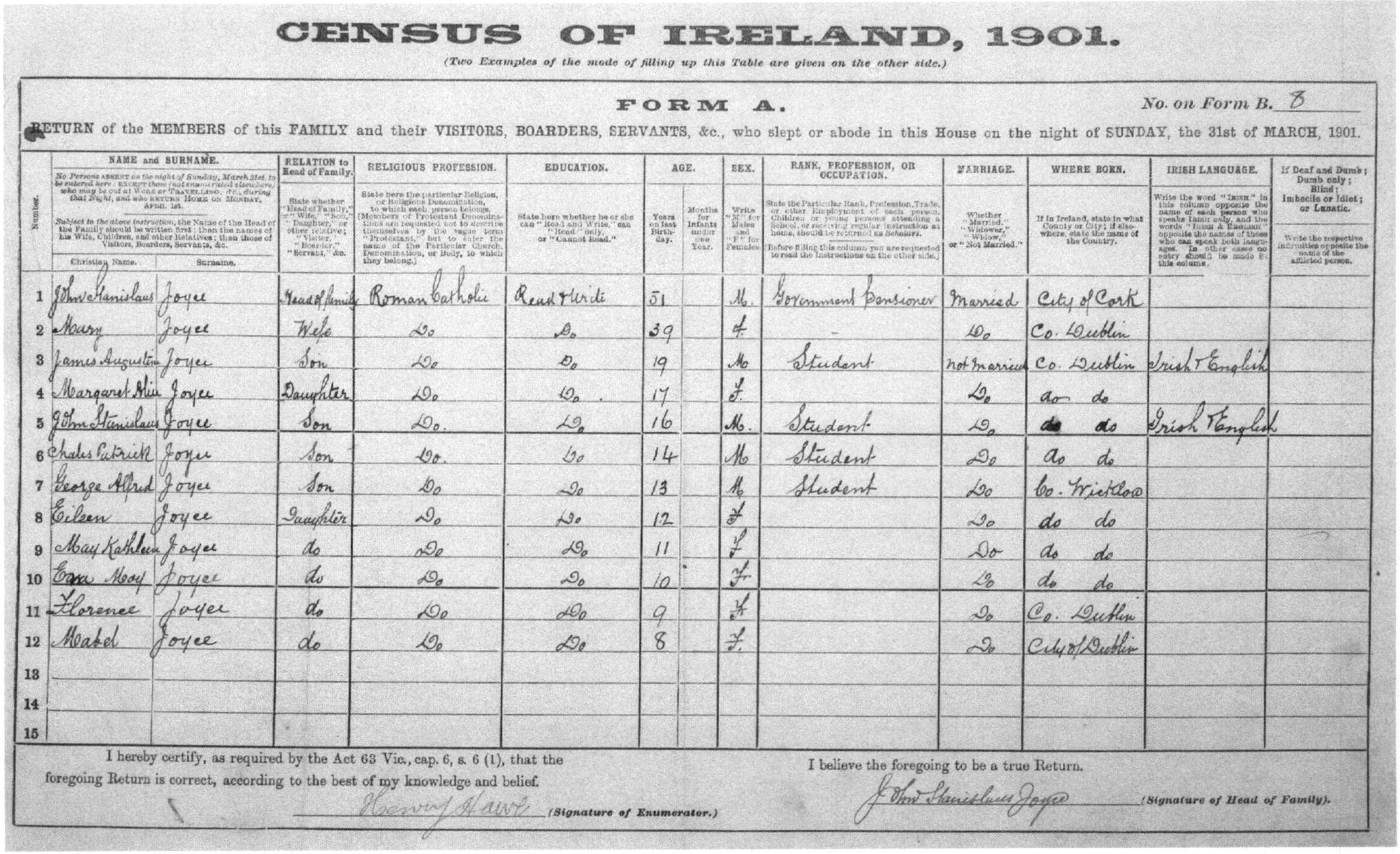

CENSUS OF IRELAND, 1901.

(Two Examples of the mode of filling up this Table are given on the other side.)

FORM A.

No. on Form B. 8

RETURN of the MEMBERS of this FAMILY and their VISITORS, BOARDERS, SERVANTS, &c., who slept or abode in this House on the night of SUNDAY, the 31st of MARCH, 1901.

Number.	NAME and SURNAME. No Persons ABSENT on the night of Sunday, March 31st, to be entered here: EXCEPT those (not enumerated elsewhere) who may be out at WORK or TRAVELLING, &c., during that Night, and who RETURN HOME ON MONDAY, APRIL 1st. Subject to the above instruction, the Name of the Head of the Family should be written first; then the names of his Wife, Children, and other Relatives; then those of Visitors, Boarders, Servants, &c. Christian Name.	Surname.	RELATION to Head of Family. State whether "Head of Family," "Wife," "Son," "Daughter," or other relative; "Visitor," "Boarder," "Servant," &c.	RELIGIOUS PROFESSION. State here the particular Religion, or Religious Denomination, to which each person belongs. [Members of Protestant Denominations are requested not to describe themselves by the vague term "Protestant," but to enter the name of the Particular Church, Denomination, or Body, to which they belong.]	EDUCATION. State here whether he or she can "Read and Write," can "Read" only, or "Cannot Read."	AGE. Years on last Birthday.	AGE. Months for Infants under one Year.	SEX. Write "M" for Males and "F" for Females.	RANK, PROFESSION, OR OCCUPATION. State the Particular Rank, Profession, Trade, or other Employment of each person. Children or young persons attending a School, or receiving regular instruction at home, should be returned as Scholars. [Before filling this column you are requested to read the Instructions on the other side.]	MARRIAGE. Whether "Married," "Widower," "Widow," or "Not Married."	WHERE BORN. If in Ireland, state in what County or City; if elsewhere, state the name of the Country.	IRISH LANGUAGE. Write the word "IRISH" in this column opposite the name of each person who speaks IRISH only, and the words "IRISH & ENGLISH" opposite the names of those who can speak both languages. In other cases no entry should be made in this column.	If Deaf and Dumb; Dumb only; Blind; Imbecile or Idiot; or Lunatic. Write the respective infirmities opposite the name of the afflicted person.
1	John Stanislaus	Joyce	Head of Family	Roman Catholic	Read & Write	51		M.	Government Pensioner	Married	City of Cork		
2	Mary	Joyce	Wife	Do	Do	39		F.	-	Do	Co. Dublin		
3	James Augustine	Joyce	Son	Do	Do	19		M	Student	not married	Co. Dublin	Irish & English	
4	Margaret Alice	Joyce	Daughter	Do	Do	17		F.		Do	do do		
5	John Stanislaus	Joyce	Son	Do.	Do	16		M.	Student	Do	do do	Irish & English	
6	Charles Patrick	Joyce	Son	Do.	Do	14		M	Student	Do	do do		
7	George Alfred	Joyce	Son	Do	Do	13		M	Student	Do	Co. Wicklow		
8	Eileen	Joyce	Daughter	Do	Do	12		F		Do	do do		
9	May Kathleen	Joyce	do	Do	Do	11		F		Do	do do		
10	Eva Mary	Joyce	do	Do	Do	10		F		Do	do do		
11	Florence	Joyce	do	Do	Do	9		F		Do	Co. Dublin		
12	Mabel	Joyce	do	Do	Do	8		F.		Do	City of Dublin		
13													
14													
15													

I hereby certify, as required by the Act 63 Vic., cap. 6, s. 6 (1), that the foregoing Return is correct, according to the best of my knowledge and belief.

Henry Hawe (Signature of Enumerator.)

I believe the foregoing to be a true Return.

John Stanislaus Joyce (Signature of Head of Family).

Courtesy of the National Archives of Ireland

Figure 8-1. 1901 census of Ireland, Dublin, household of James Joyce.

Censuses and Census Substitutes

We can have exciting experiences as we learn about our vibrant, dynamic ancestors. They were very real, living people with problems, hopes, and dreams like we have today. In many ways each of us is the sum total of what our ancestors were.

—James E. Faust

The ideal family history source for Ireland would name every single person in the country by family. That's precisely what a census does. Every ten years, a day was assigned as the day of the census in Ireland. On census day, constables throughout Ireland went door-to-door to fill out or collect forms for every household. Every person in the home needed to be properly listed by name, age, occupation, and relationship to the head of household.

The 1821 Irish census was the earliest census in the British Isles to name every man, woman, and child in an entire country. This census was taken two decades before the first every-name census in England and almost three decades before the first every-name census in the United States.

Censuses in Ireland were taken every decade from 1821 to 1911. No census was attempted in 1921, as the Irish people were fighting for independence from British rule. Although Irish censuses were taken in 1926, 1936, 1946, and every five or ten years thereafter, these more recent documents are sealed from public inspection for one hundred years from the date of creation under existing privacy laws.

Unfortunately, all nineteenth-century Irish censuses were destroyed, save a few fragments and transcriptions for individual parishes or counties (described in detail later in this chapter). During World War I, the Irish government intentionally destroyed the original 1861–91 census forms, presumably pulping them for paper. Transcriptions of one parish from 1861 and two parishes from 1871 are all that remain. The explosion and subsequent fire that gutted Four Courts in June of 1922 destroyed most of the 1821–51 census returns. Some fragments and transcriptions survive, including most of the 1831 returns for County Derry (Londonderry).

Because virtually all government census records from nineteenth-century Ireland were destroyed, family historians must rely heavily on other genealogical sources for

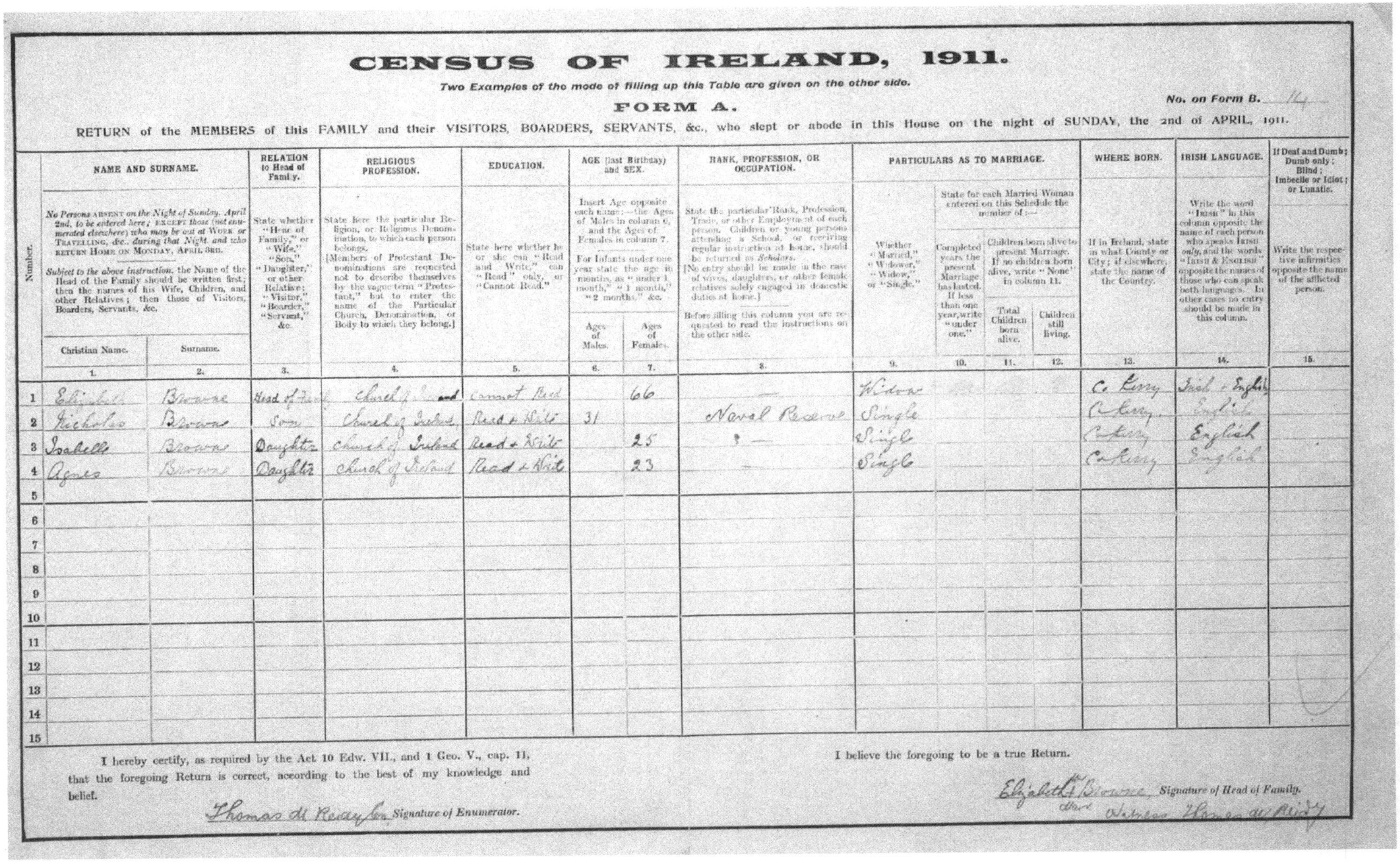

CENSUS OF IRELAND, 1911.

Two Examples of the mode of filling up this Table are given on the other side.

FORM A.

No. on Form B. 14

RETURN of the MEMBERS of this FAMILY and their VISITORS, BOARDERS, SERVANTS, &c., who slept or abode in this House on the night of SUNDAY, the 2nd of APRIL, 1911.

NAME AND SURNAME		RELATION to Head of Family.	RELIGIOUS PROFESSION.	EDUCATION.	AGE (last Birthday) and SEX		RANK, PROFESSION, OR OCCUPATION.	PARTICULARS AS TO MARRIAGE.				WHERE BORN.	IRISH LANGUAGE.	If Deaf and Dumb; Dumb only; Blind; Imbecile or Idiot; or Lunatic.
Christian Name.	Surname.				Ages of Males.	Ages of Females.		Whether "Married," "Widower," "Widow," or "Single."	Completed years the present Marriage has lasted.	Total Children born alive.	Children still living.			
1.	2.	3.	4.	5.	6.	7.	8.	9.	10.	11.	12.	13.	14.	15.
Elizabeth	Brown	Head of Family	Church of Ireland	Cannot Read		60		Widow				Co. Cork	Read English	
Gerald	Brown	Son	Church of Ireland	Read & Write	31		Naval Reserve	Single				Cork	English	
Isabell	Brown	Daughter	Church of Ireland	Read & Write		25	—	Single				Kerry	English	
Agnes	Brown	Daughter	Church of Ireland	Read & Write		23	—	Single				Cork	English	
5														
6														
7														
8														
9														
10														
11														
12														
13														
14														
15														

I hereby certify, as required by the Act 10 Edw. VII., and 1 Geo. V., cap. 11, that the foregoing Return is correct, according to the best of my knowledge and belief.

Thomas M. Keary/ea, Signature of Enumerator.

I believe the foregoing to be a true Return.

Elizabeth Brown, Signature of Head of Family.

Figure 8-2. 1911 census of Ireland, Dingle, County Kerry.

this century. For example, other name lists, or census substitutes, do exist for Irish genealogy. For the 1800s and early 1900s, the best census substitutes include land records, tax lists, school registers, religious censuses, government pension applications, and other miscellaneous name lists.

The 1901 and 1911 censuses are the only complete censuses of Ireland now available for researchers.

1901 and 1911 Censuses of Ireland

These census records are of inestimable value to family historians. In fact, the Irish government waived the one-hundred-year privacy clause for census records and released the 1901 and 1911 censuses (figures 8-1 and 8-2) early.

The 1901 and 1911 censuses enumerated the entire population of Ireland, naming 4,458,775 and 4,390,219 people, respectively. The census returns for each year were organized by county, district electoral division, and townland. A "House and Building Return" form listed all families in the townland. For each family, this form listed a detailed description of the house and its quality, the name of the head of family, the number of rooms occupied by the family, and the name of the landholder. You can see at a glance the names of all heads of family in the neighborhood. In essence, this form serves as a brief index to the families in the neighborhood. Since close relatives were often neighbors, you might see a related family on the "House and Building Return" form.

A detailed census enumeration form was repeated for each family and listed all family members individually. This form was entitled "RETURN of the MEMBERS of this FAMILY and their VISITORS, BOARDERS, SERVANTS, &c., who slept or abode in this House on the night of SUNDAY, the 31st of MARCH, 1901" (or "SUNDAY, the 2nd of APRIL, 1911.") The following details were included for each family member:

- Christian name
- Surname
- Relation to the head of family
- Religious profession
- Education (whether able to read and write)
- Age at last birthday (often inaccurate)
- Sex
- Rank, profession, or occupation
- Whether married, widower, widowed, or single
- For each married woman, the following information was recorded *only in the 1911 census*:
  - Completed years in the present marriage
  - Total number of children born alive
  - Number of children still living
- Birthplace (county or city if born in Ireland, else country of birth)

> **Record Spotlight**
>
> The 1901 and 1911 censuses are the only complete censuses of Ireland now available for researchers.

- Whether able to speak Irish (Gaelic) only, or whether able to speak both Irish and English
- Whether deaf, dumb, blind, imbecile, idiot, or lunatic

The census enumerator, typically the local constable, signed his name to each of these family pages, as did the head of family.

The 1901 and 1911 censuses are a springboard to many other Irish records. Once you find a family in one of these censuses, you will automatically feel compelled to search the other census. The age of each family member can lead you to the baptismal record and the civil registration of birth. The number of years married can lead you to the church marriage and the civil registration of marriage. The total number of children born alive compared with the number of children still living may lead you to search for additional children who died young.

Even if your ancestors left Ireland in the late 1800s, these census records may still be of value. Perhaps parents, brothers, sisters, or other relatives stayed behind in Ireland. You might find them on the census.

Whenever you find a family in the 1901 or 1911 census, remember to photocopy the townland summary pages as well as the family sheet for your ancestors. Also remember to examine the list of other families in the townland to see whether other relatives were living nearby.

Finding Your Ancestors in the 1901 and 1911 Censuses

The 1901 and 1911 censuses have been microfilmed and are available for researchers at the National Archives of Ireland, the Family History Library, and a few other libraries around the world. The Public Record Office of Northern Ireland has microfilm copies of the 1901 census for the six counties of Northern Ireland: Antrim, Armagh, Down, Fermanagh, Derry (Londonderry), and Tyrone. Many Heritage Centres in Ireland have created computer indexes of censuses for their respective counties and will search them for a fee (see Chapter 18, "Irish Heritage Centres").

To use the 1901 and 1911 censuses at the Family History Library, you will need to identify the district electoral division (DED) for your ancestor's townland. The easiest way to do this is to look up the DED name and number for the townland in the *General Alphabetical Index to the Townlands and Towns of Ireland* for the 1901 census (FHL 865092). You will then do a Place search in the Family History Library Catalog for your ancestor's civil parish. Under *Ireland, [County], [Civil Parish]* you will select either the 1901 or 1911 census and choose the film with the right DED name or number. The Family History Library has also compiled an index to guide genealogists researching their urban ancestors: *Ireland 1901 Census Street Index*. This street index shows which microfilms of the 1901 census cover which streets in Belfast, Dublin, Cork, Limerick, Londonderry, and Waterford.

Significant portions of the 1901 and 1911 censuses have been abstracted and posted on the Internet. The largest Irish census database on the Web at the time of printing is an every-name index to the 1901 census for Counties Leitrim and Roscommon. This

---

✦

Internet

Significant portions of the 1901 and 1911 censuses have been abstracted and posted on the Internet. Many Irish Heritage Centres have also indexed 1901 and 1911 census returns for their respective counties.

database is complete for these two counties, with name indexes under construction for a number of other counties, including Galway, Mayo, Sligo, Wexford, and Westmeath. The main Web page describing this project is <www.leitrim-roscommon. com/1901census>. You can search the 1901 census by going to <www.leitrim-roscommon.com/1901census/census.shtml>. Other websites host census indexes for other counties—an excellent example is the 1901 census index for County Clare available on the County Clare Library website <www.clarelibrary.ie>.

Nineteenth-Century Censuses of Ireland

Very little now remains of the original censuses from the 1800s, and few copies were made. The most significant surviving fragments and copies of these earlier censuses are:

- Fragments of the original 1821 (figure 8-3) census for Counties Cavan (sixteen parishes, almost half the county), Fermanagh (two parishes), Galway (seven parishes), Meath (eighteen parishes), and Offaly (nine parishes).
- A transcription of parts of the 1821 census for Counties Kilkenny (seven parishes) and Waterford (partial).
- Most of the original 1831 census for County Derry (Londonderry)—all but the parishes of Carrick, Formoyle, and Learmount survive. The County Derry Genealogy Centre has created a database of this 1831 Derry census.
- A small fragment of the original 1841 census for Killeshandra, County Cavan.
- Fragments of the original 1851 census for small portions of Counties Antrim and Fermanagh.
- A name index of the 1851 census for the city of Dublin, listing the names and addresses of all heads of household, over sixty thousand individuals. The entire index is available on a CD-ROM recently published by Eneclann, entitled *The 1851 Dublin City Census*.
- A transcription of the 1851 census for Aglish and Portnascully, County Kilkenny.
- A transcription of the 1861 census for Enniscorthy, County Wexford.
- A transcription of the 1871 census for Drumcondra and Loughbraclen, County Meath.

Most of these census fragments and transcriptions are available on microfilm at the Family History Library. Go to the Family History Library Catalog, search by Place, and enter *Ireland*. You will see a number of census years listed. Some of the surviving nineteenth-century census fragments have been indexed and posted on the Internet.

Old Age Pension Claims

The Old Age Pension Act of 1908 initiated a pension program for senior citizens in Ireland. To receive a pension, the applicant needed to supply proof that he or she was at least seventy years old. Government registration of births did not begin until

Col. 1. No. of House.	Col. 2. No. of Stories.	Column 3. NAMES OF INHABITANTS.	Col. 4. AGE.	Column 5. OCCUPATION.
17	1	John Pole	60	Farmer
		Catty Pole his Wife	38	
		John Pole his Son	22	Labourer & Kelpmaker
		Mich¹ Pole his Son	19	Kelpmaker & fisherman
		Mary Pole Daughter	12	at School
		Jacob Pole Son	5	
		Ned Pole Son under	1	
		Michael Folan Nephew	12	at School
		Bridget Flaherty his Mother in Law	68	
18	1	Ned Pole	56	Farmer & Fisherman
		Margaret Pole his Wife	39	
		Bridget Pole their Daughter	18	Wool Spinner
		Mathias Pole Son	17	Labourer & Kelpmaker
		Jacob Pole Son	9	at School
		Mary Pole Daughter	7	
		Onnor Pole Daughter	5	
		Mich¹ Pole Son	2	
		John Pole Son under	1	
19	1	Denis Hogan	60	Farmer
		Pat Hogan his Son	27	Labourer
		Mary Hogan his Wife	25	Flaxspinner
		Denis Hogan their Son	2	
		Mary Hassett	21	House Servant
		Kate Mulconry	50	Visitor
		Michael Mulconry her Son	20	Fisherman & Kelpmaker

Figure 8-3. 1821 census of Ireland, Innisheer, County Galway.

1864, so older pension applicants did not have birth certificates to supply proof of age. Those applicants who could not provide evidence of their age needed help from the government to substantiate their claim. Between 1908 and 1922, the Public Record Office in Dublin provided support to local Pensions Offices by searching the 1841 and 1851 census returns. They were doing basic genealogical research, searching for pension applicants listed as children or young adults in the 1841 and 1851 censuses.

Old Age Pension applications may include letters or documents verifying the age of the applicant, including government responses with extractions of the family from the 1841 and 1851 censuses. The Family History Library has microfilm copies of Old Age Pension records (figure 8-4) for all nine counties of Ulster: Antrim, Armagh, Cavan, Derry (Londonderry), Donegal, Down, Fermanagh, Monaghan, and Tyrone.

Josephine Masterson has indexed Old Age Pension claims from the original records in the Public Record Office of Northern Ireland. Her work is published in two books, *Ireland: 1841/1851 Census Abstracts (Northern Ireland)* and *Ireland: 1841/1851 Census Abstracts (Republic of Ireland)*.

Nineteenth-Century Census Substitutes

The loss of most nineteenth-century Irish censuses has increased the value of other name lists. A number of miscellaneous sources serve as substitutes for the destroyed Irish censuses, including land records, religious censuses, directories, school registers, regional censuses, and a variety of local name lists.

Land and property records are the best census substitutes for all Ireland in the 1800s. No other record provides coverage for the whole country. These records, listed below, are described in detail in Chapter 9, "Land and Property Records":

- Tithe Applotment Books, 1823–38, serve as a substantial substitute for rural Ireland in lieu of the 1821, 1831, and 1841 censuses.
- Griffith's Valuation, 1848–64, serves as a heads-of-household census for all of Ireland, helping to compensate for the loss of the 1851 and 1861 censuses.
- Canceled Land Books are good census substitutes for the years 1861, 1871, 1881, and 1891. These land valuation records begin in the 1850s and 1860s and continue through the twentieth century, listing the heads of household for each property.

All other census substitutes provide partial coverage of the populace, listing only people of a particular social status, economic station, religious affiliation, profession, or locality.

Commercial and social directories are census substitutes for urban areas. They contain name lists of merchants, wealthy landowners, professionals, teachers, clergy, and government officials in cities and smaller towns. Directories exist for most of the 1800s in the largest cities. By the late 1800s many small towns were also covered. More and more people of the middle class were listed by the end of the century. This census substitute is covered in Chapter 12, "Commercial and Social Directories."

National school registers are a unique census substitute, listing children rather than heads of families. Some national schools have records beginning as early as

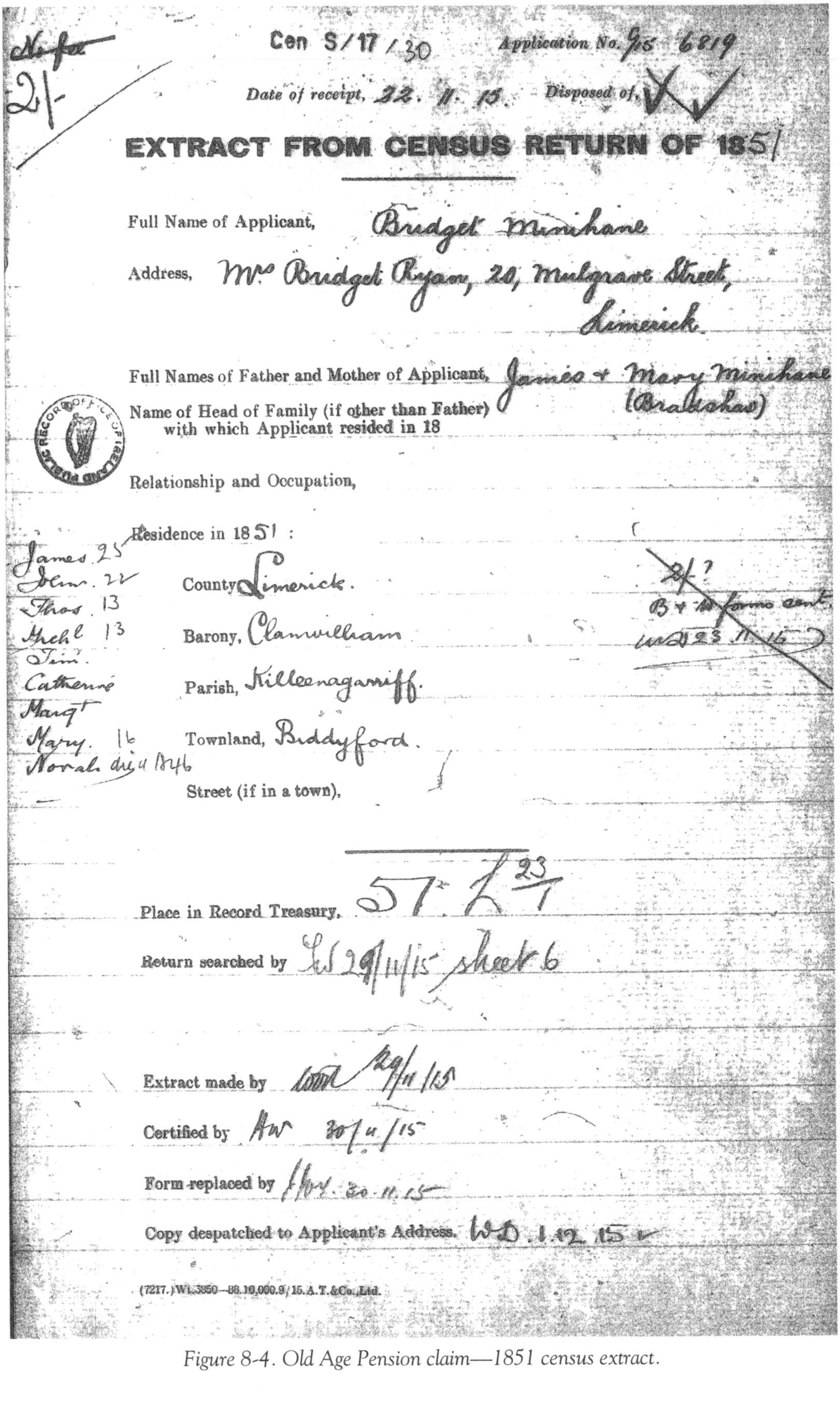

Nifer 21/-

Cen S/17/30 Application No. 95 6819

Date of receipt, 22. 11. 15. Disposed of,

EXTRACT FROM CENSUS RETURN OF 1851

Full Name of Applicant, Bridget Minihane

Address, Mrs Bridget Ryan, 20, Mulgrave Street, Limerick

Full Names of Father and Mother of Applicant, James + Mary Minihane (Bradshaw)

Name of Head of Family (if other than Father) with which Applicant resided in 18

Relationship and Occupation,

Residence in 1851 :

County Limerick.

Barony, Clanwilliam

Parish, Killeenagarriff.

Townland, Biddyford.

Street (if in a town),

James 25
Denis 22
Thos 13
Mchl 13
Tim.
Catherine
Margt
Mary 16
Norah died 1846

2/? B + 10 forms sent WD 23.11.15

Place in Record Treasury, 57. L 23/1

Return searched by LW 29/11/15 sheet 6

Extract made by 29/11/15

Certified by AW 30/11/15

Form replaced by AW 30.11.15

Copy despatched to Applicant's Address. WD. 1.12.15

(7217.) Wt. 3850—88. 10,000. 9/15. A.T.&Co., Ltd.

Courtesy of the National Archives of Ireland

Figure 8-4. Old Age Pension claim—1851 census extract.

1831. A school register lists each student's name, religion, father's occupation, date of enrollment, and other details such as the occasional mention of the family's migration or emigration. These records are most readily available for the six counties of Northern Ireland. This census substitute is the subject of Chapter 14, "National School Registers."

A number of name lists exist for various professions. These census substitutes are described in Chapter 15, "Occupation Records."

In 1796, the Irish government subsidized the linen industry by awarding spinning wheels or looms to those families who met specific quotas for growing flax. The list of flax growers who received awards has survived in part. Some fifty-six thousand people are listed by name, county, and parish. Ancestry.com offers an online index of this census substitute under the title "Irish Flax Growers List, 1796" <www.ancestry.com/search/rectype/inddbs/3732.htm>.

To learn more about local census substitutes for specific counties in Ireland, consult the guides to local family history sources listed below.

Guides to County Family History Sources in Ireland

All Counties

Helferty, Seamus, and Raymond Refaussé. *Directory of Irish Archives.* 3d ed. Dublin: Four Courts Press, 1999.

Maxwell, Ian. *Tracing Your Ancestors in Northern Ireland: A Guide to Ancestry Research in the Public Record Office of Northern Ireland.* Edinburgh: Stationery Office, 1997.

O'Neill, Robert K. *Irish Libraries: Archives, Museums and Genealogical Centres.* Belfast: Ulster Historical Foundation, 2002.

Ryan, James G. *Irish Records: Sources for Family and Local History.* Salt Lake City: Ancestry, 1997.

Smith, Frank. *Smith's Inventory of Genealogical Sources: Ireland.* Salt Lake City: Corporation of the President, The Church of Jesus Christ of Latter-day Saints, 1994.

Armagh

Guide to County Sources: Armagh. Belfast: Public Record Office of Northern Ireland, 1996.

Maxwell, Ian. *Researching Armagh Ancestors.* Belfast: Ulster Historical Foundation, 2000.

Cork

McCarthy, Tony, and Tim Cadogan. *Tracing Your Cork Ancestors.* Glenageary, County Dublin: Flyleaf Press, 1998.

Derry (Londonderry)

Mitchell, Brian. *County Londonderry: Sources for Family History.* Derry: Genealogy Centre, 1992.

Donegal

Duffy, Godfrey F. *Tracing Your Donegal Ancestors.* Glenageary, County Dublin: Flyleaf Press, 1996.

Dublin

Ryan, James G., and Brian Smith. *Tracing Your Dublin Ancestors.* 2d ed. Glenageary, County Dublin: Flyleaf Press, 1988.

Fermanagh
Guide to County Sources: Fermanagh. Belfast: Public Record Office of Northern Ireland, 1994.

Kerry
O'Connor, Michael H. *Tracing Your Kerry Ancestors*. 2d ed. Glenageary, County Dublin: Flyleaf Press, 1994.

Kildare
Kiely, Karel, Mary Newman, and Jacinta Ruddy. *Tracing Your Ancestors in Co. Kildare*. Naas, County Kildare: Kildare County Library, 1992.

Limerick
Franklin, Margaret. *Tracing Your Limerick Ancestors*. Glenageary, County Dublin: Flyleaf Press, 2003.

Longford
Leahy, David. *County Longford and Its People—An Index to the 1901 Census of Co. Longford*. Glenageary, County Dublin: Flyleaf Press, 1990.

Mayo
Smith, Brian. *Tracing Your Mayo Ancestors*. Glenageary, County Dublin: Flyleaf Press, 1997.

Roscommon
Farrell, Noel. *Exploring Family Origins in Old Roscommon Town*. Longford: Noel Farrell, 1998.

Tyrone
Campbell, Tim, and Ian Rice. *Guide to County Sources: Tyrone*. Belfast: Public Record Office of Northern Ireland, 1998.

In Summary

Irish censuses name all family members residing in the same household on the day of the census. Although most nineteenth-century census returns were destroyed, the 1901 and 1911 censuses have survived intact, preserving two complete enumerations of the Irish people. These census records not only name all family members; they also state family relationships, religious preference, education, age, gender, occupation, marital status, and birth county. Where census records have not been preserved, other name lists, or census substitutes, may be consulted to identify families. Censuses and census substitutes work best when used with other major sources of Irish family history, including birth, marriage, and death records; church parish registers; and land and property records.

References and Selected Reading
General Alphabetical Index to the Townlands and Towns, Parishes and Baronies of Ireland: Based on the Census of Ireland for the Year 1851. 1861. Reprint, Baltimore: Genealogical Publishing Company, 2000.

Masterson, Josephine. *Ireland: 1841/1851 Census Abstracts (Northern Ireland)*. Baltimore: Genealogical Publishing Company, 1999.

———. *Ireland: 1841/1851 Census Abstracts (Republic of Ireland)*. Baltimore Genealogical Publishing Company, 1999.

Land and Property Records

"Do you mean to tell me, Katie Scarlett O'Hara, that Tara—that land doesn't mean anything to you? Why, land's the only thing in the world worth working for, worth fighting for, worth dying for, because it's the only thing that lasts."
Scarlett replies, "Oh, Pa. You talk like an Irishman."
"It's proud I am that I'm Irish, and don't you be forgetting, Missy, that you're half-Irish, too. And, to anyone with a drop of Irish blood in them; why, the land they live on is like their mother. Oh, but there, there now, you're just a child. It'll come to you, this love of the land. There's no getting away from it if you're Irish."
—Gone with the Wind, *1939*

Historically, most Irishmen were tenant farmers who sowed and reaped someone else's land. They owned no land themselves, but leased or rented from a landlord. Six days a week they labored from dawn to dusk in the fields. On the seventh day they rested. Very few events in their lives were documented, perhaps their baptisms, marriages, and burials. But they had to pay rent on the land they farmed and the house they occupied. Many land and property records still survive from centuries ago. These records show us where our ancestors lived, the size and value of the property they rented, and sometimes the transfer of property to the next generation.

Land ownership and occupancy has been thoroughly and meticulously documented in all Ireland since the mid-1800s. Land records serve as excellent sources of family history from the time of the Great Famine to the present. This chapter introduces the major land records of Ireland, including the Tithe Applotment Books, Griffith's Primary Valuation of Tenements, the Canceled Land Books, and the Registry of Deeds.

Tithe Applotment Books

The earliest surviving record to name common tenant farmers across all Ireland was the Tithe Applotment Survey, recorded between 1823 and 1838. The tithe was a tax levied to support the clergy of the Church of Ireland, the state church. People of all religious denominations were tithed one-tenth of their annual produce. The tithe applied to everyone living on agricultural land other than church property. Originally, the tithe was paid in kind. The Tithe Composition Act of 1823 required that tithes be paid in cash to the Church of Ireland, and the government undertook a valuation of every tithable landholding in Ireland. Many of the poorest people appeared in the resulting Tithe Surveys. The Tithe Applotment Books list most families in rural Ireland in the decades just before the Great Famine of the 1840s (figure 9-1).

The National Library of Ireland prepared a comprehensive surname index to the Tithe Applotment Survey (and Griffith's Valuation). This index, commonly referred to as the Householders Index, allows you to search the civil parishes where your ancestors lived to see whether their surnames appear in the original records.

Genealogy.com has an online database called *Tithe Applotment Books of Ireland, 1823–38*. This database is a name index for the six counties of Northern Ireland: Antrim, Armagh, Down, Fermanagh, Derry (Londonderry), and Tyrone. This database is also available on CD-ROM.

The Tithe Applotment Books are only helpful for locating families occupying agricultural land subject to the tithe. Landless laborers, people living in cities and towns, and families occupying land exempt from the tithe were not listed in the Tithe Applotment Books. They may, however, appear in a later, more comprehensive land valuation record, Griffith's Valuation.

Griffith's Valuation

The only nineteenth-century sources listing all households in Ireland are land valuation records dating from the mid-1800s. Griffith's Primary Valuation of Tenements, published between 1848 and 1864, is the earliest surviving list of all householders and landholders in Ireland (figure 9-2). Subsequent updates to Griffith's Valuation, called "Canceled Land Books" and "Current Land Books," list property holders for all of Ireland from the mid-nineteenth century to the present.

Richard Griffith, director of the Valuation Office in the mid-1800s, published his monumental valuation of all land and buildings in Ireland under the official title *General Valuation of Rateable Property in Ireland*. Each property holder and landlord is listed, providing researchers with the equivalent of a heads-of-household census of Ireland for the years just after the Great Famine.

Griffith's Valuation is arranged by county, barony, civil parish, and townland. Each occupier (i.e., rent payer) is listed with the immediate lessor (i.e., landlord). A description of the property, the acreage, and the ratable annual valuation of the land and buildings are also reported. Each property holding has a reference number, and each townland has a map number indicating which Ordnance Survey map pertains to the area.

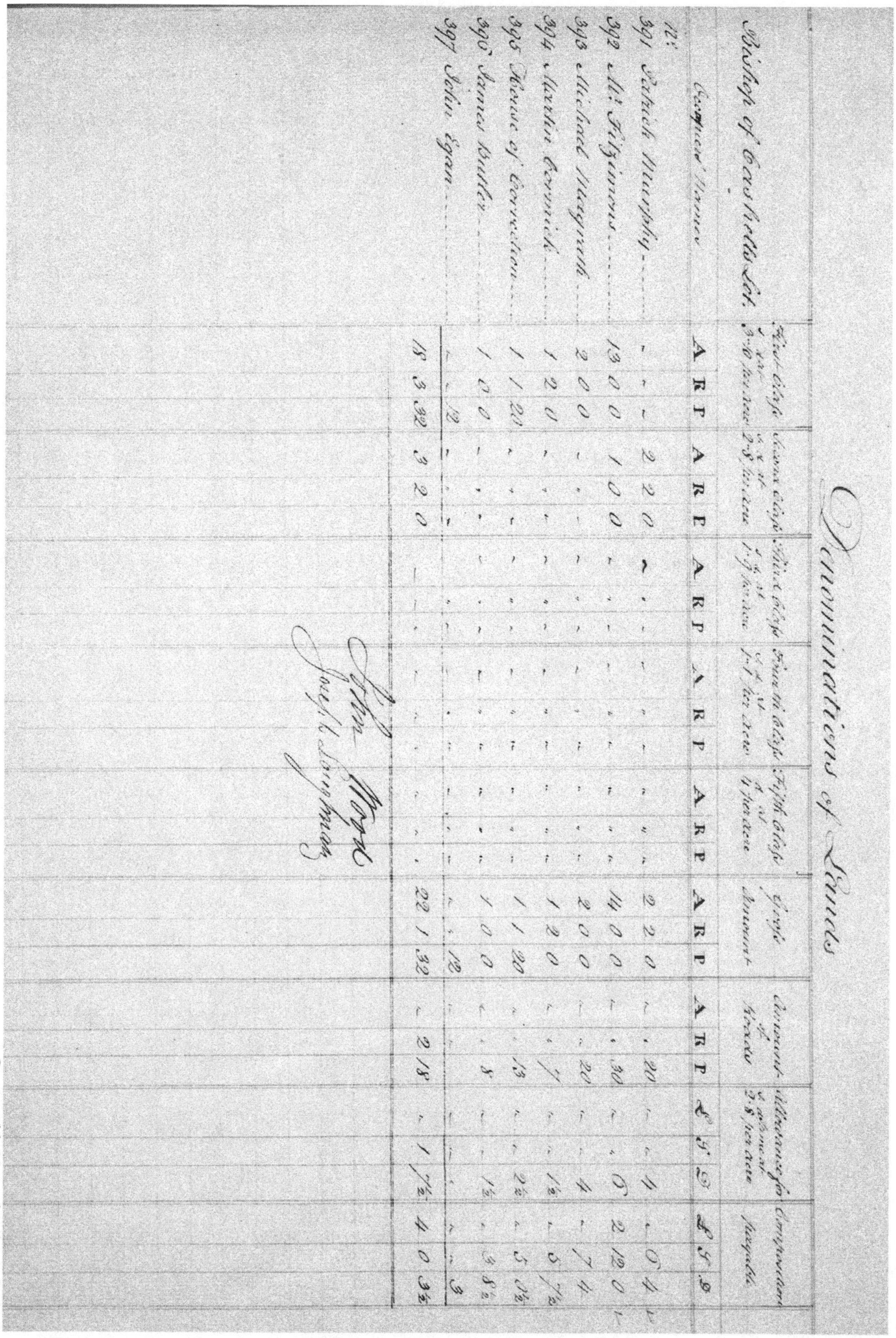

Denominations of Lands

Bishop of Cashel's Lot.

No.	Occupiers' Names	First Class (A R P)	Second Class (A R P)	Third Class (A R P)	Fourth Class (A R P)	Fifth Class (A R P)	Gross Amount (A R P)	Amount of Waste (A R P)	Allowance for ... (£ S D)	Composition Payable (£ S D)
391	Patrick Murphy	- - -	2 2 0	- - -	- - -	- - -	2 2 0	- - 20	- - 11	- 6 4
392	Mr Fitzgimons	13 0 0	1 0 0	- - -	- - -	- - -	14 0 0	- - 30	- - 6	2 12 0
393	Michael Magrath	2 0 0	- - -	- - -	- - -	- - -	2 0 0	- - 20	- - 4	- 7 4
394	Martin Cormick	1 2 0	- - -	- - -	- - -	- - -	1 2 0	- - 7	- - 1½	- 5 7½
395	House of Correction	1 1 20	- - -	- - -	- - -	- - -	1 1 20	- - 13	- - 2½	- 5 0½
396	James Butler	1 0 0	- - -	- - -	- - -	- - -	1 0 0	- - 8	- - 1½	- 3 8½
397	John Egan	- - 12	- - -	- - -	- - -	- - -	- - 12	- - -	- - -	- - 3
		18 3 32	3 2 0				22 1 32	- 2 18	- 1 7½	4 0 3½

Figure 9-1. Tithe Applotment Book.

PARISH OF CLONMANY.

No. and Letters of Reference to Map		Names. Townlands and Occupiers.	Immediate Lessors.	Description of Tenement.	Area. A. R. P.	Rateable Annual Valuation. Land. £ s. d.	Buildings. £ s. d.	Total Annual Valuation of Rateable Property. £ s. d.
		BALLYLIFFIN. (Ord. S. 3 & 10.)						
1		James Doherty, .	John Harvey, .	Land, . .	6 1 34	4 0 0	—	4 0 0
2		Denis Doherty (Smith) / John M'Geoghegan,	Same, .	Land, . .	8 1 19	{ 2 5 0 / 3 0 0	—	2 5 0 / 3 0 0
3		Denis Doherty (Pat), / Pk. Doherty (Carpenter)	Same, .	Land, . .	7 2 24	{ 3 0 0 / 1 10 0	—	3 0 0 / 1 10 0
4	a	Anne Doherty (Pat), .	Same, .	House, offices, and land,	11 2 33	6 15 0	2 10 0	9 5 0
5		William Tolan, .	Same, .	House, offices, and land,	10 0 13	6 10 0	2 10 0	9 0 0
6		Hugh Quigley, . / Charles Doherty,	Same, .	Land, . .	6 3 19	{ 3 0 0 / 1 10 0	—	3 0 0 / 1 10 0
7		Bryan Quigley, .	Same, .	Land, . .	8 1 9	5 10 0	—	5 10 0
8		William Granny,	Same, .	Land, . .	13 0 8	6 15 0	—	6 15 0
—	a	Neal Doherty, .	William Granny,	Offices, . .			0 10 0	0 10 0
9		Charles Doherty,	John Harvey, .	Land, . .	8 0 4	4 15 0	—	4 15 0
10	{ a / b	Patk. Doherty (Dan), / John Doherty (Dan),	Same, .	{ House, offices, & land, / House, office, & land,	13 1 28	{ 3 5 0 / 3 5 0	1 10 0 / 0 15 0	4 15 0 / 4 0 0
11		Owen Quigley. . / Anne M'Gonigle,	Same, .	Land, . .	13 2 8	5 10 0	—	5 10 0
12		Margaret Harken (Owen)	Same, .	Land, . .	6 3 0	3 5 0	—	3 5 0
13		Neal Doherty, .	Same, .	Land, . .	6 2 34	3 5 0	—	3 5 0
14		Wm. & Patrick Tolan,	Same, .	Land, . .	5 1 14	3 5 0	—	3 5 0
15		Bryan M'Colgan, .	Same, .	Land, . .	5 1 19	3 5 0	—	3 5 0
16		John M'Gonigle, / Owen Doherty, .	Same, .	Land, . .	6 1 39	{ 2 0 0 / 2 0 0	—	2 0 0 / 2 0 0
17		James M'Colgan,	Same, .	Land, . .	5 0 0	3 10 0	—	3 10 0
18	4 b	John Doherty (James),	Same, .	Land, . .	17 3 36 / 0 2 0	2 5 0 / 0 10 0	—	} 2 15 0
19		James & Cors. Doherty (Neal), . .	Same, .	Land, . .	17 0 6	2 5 0	—	2 5 0
—	a	Michael M'Colgan,	Free, . .	House & small garden,			0 5 0	0 5 0
20		Hugh Quigley, .	John Harvey, .	Land, . .	11 1 8	3 0 0	—	3 0 0
21		Owen Quigley (Bryan) / Mchl. Quigley (Bryan)	Same, .	Land, . .	7 1 39	{ 2 5 0 / 2 5 0	—	2 5 0 / 2 5 0
		VILLAGE OF BALLYLIFFIN.						
22	1	James Doherty (Neal),	John Harvey, .	House, office, & garden,	0 0 35	0 5 0	0 15 0	1 0 0
—	2 a	Owen Quigley, .	Same, .	Garden, . .	0 0 35	0 5 0		0 5 0
—	b	Unoccupied,	Owen Quigley. .	House, . .	—	—	0 15 0	0 15 0
—	3	Margaret Harken, .	John Harvey, .	House, office, & garden,	0 0 25	0 2 0	2 0 0	2 2 0
—	4	Margaret Quigley,	Same, .	House & small garden,			1 10 0	1 10 0
—	5	James Doherty,	Same, .	House, offices, & garden,	0 0 20	0 2 0	0 13 0	0 15 0
—	6	William Granny,	Same, .	House, offices, & garden,	0 1 5	0 5 0	2 0 0	2 5 0
—	a	John M'Colgan, .	Same, .	House, . .	—		0 15 0	0 15 0
—	7	Denis Doherty (Smith),	Same, .	House, offices, & garden,	0 0 30	0 5 0	2 10 0	2 15 0
—	8	Patrick Quigley,	Same, .	House, office, & garden,	0 0 30	0 5 0	1 0 0	1 5 0
—	9	Hugh Quigley, .	Same, .	House, office, & garden,	0 2 0	0 10 0	1 5 0	1 15 0
—	10	John M'Geoghegan, .	Same, .	Office and garden, .	0 0 20	0 2 0	0 6 0	0 8 0
—	11	Charles Doherty,	Same, .	House, office, & garden,	0 0 20	0 2 0	2 3 0	2 5 0
—	12	Pat Doherty (Carpenter)	Same, .	House, office, & garden,	0 1 0	0 5 0	1 0 0	1 5 0
—	13	Edward M'Ilhenny, .	Same, .	Garden, . .	0 3 10	0 10 0	—	0 10 0
—	14	Patrick Doherty,	Same, .	House and garden, .	0 0 30	0 5 0	0 15 0	1 0 0
—	15	Owen Quigley (Bryan)	Same, .	House, office, & garden,	0 0 20	0 2 0	0 18 0	1 0 0
—	16	Michael Quigley (Bryan)	Same, .	House, office, & garden,	0 0 35	0 5 0	1 0 0	1 5 0
—	17	Ann M'Gonigle, .	Same, .	House and garden, .	0 0 20	0 2 0	0 13 0	0 15 0
—	18	John M'Geoghegan, .	Same, .	House, office, & garden,	0 0 30	0 5 0	1 0 0	1 5 0
—	19	Bryan Quigley, .	Same, .	House and garden, .	0 0 30	0 5 0	1 5 0	1 10 0
—	20	Denis Doherty (Pat),	Same, .	House and garden, .	0 0 15	0 2 0	0 18 0	1 0 0
—	21	James M'Colgan, .	Same, .	House, office, & garden,	0 0 35	0 5 0	1 5 0	1 10 0
—	22	John Doherty (James),	Same, .	House & small garden,	—	—	0 10 0	0 10 0
				Waste under houses, streets, and small gardens, . .	4 3 13	—	—	—
23		John Harvey, .	In fee, . .	Mountain, . .	44 1 6	1 5 0	—	1 5 0
[A	1	Charles Doherty,		House, office, & land,			0 12 0	2 10 0
—	2	Patrick M'Gonigle,		House, office, & land,			0 15 0	4 15 0
—	3	James Doherty,		House, offices, & land,			1 0 0	7 0 0
—	4	Patrick Houton,		House, office, & land,			0 10 0	4 10 0
—	4	Anne Doherty, .		House, office, & land,			0 12 0	2 10 0

Figure 9-2. Griffith's Valuation.

Ordnance Survey maps are scaled at six inches per mile, displaying houses, churches, cemeteries, schools, boundaries, roads, and many other details. These maps can help you find the physical location of the land holding and help you pinpoint the site of the house your ancestors occupied.

Identifying information beyond the tenant's name is sometimes recorded in Griffith's Valuation. Some names have appellations known as "agnomens" parenthetically appended. If two people of the same name occupied property in the same townland, the valuator distinguished between the two by adding fathers' names, occupations, "jun." or "sen." (meaning "younger" or "older," not implying a relationship), maiden names, or some other differentiating characteristic in parentheses. For example, in Carrigeenwood, Brosna, County Kerry, there are nine tenants listed in Griffith's Valuation, two of them with the surname Connor. The valuator chose to distinguish between the two by recording their names as "Denis Connor (*Philip*)" and "John Connor (*Darby*)." These names may be interpreted as Denis, son of Philip Connor, and John, son of Darby Connor.

Some names are written with the qualification "Reps. of" or "Representatives of," as in the example "Reps of Ambrose Browne." This means that the individual has died and his or her interest in the property is temporarily represented by someone else, typically a spouse, adult child, or estate administrator. These entries are helpful for approximating when an ancestor died.

The acreage of the property gives an indication of the social and economic standing of the tenant. A laborer or cottier typically occupied a half dozen acres of land or less, maybe occupying only a house with no land. A small farmer might have occupied twenty or thirty acres. Larger properties were occupied by the primary farmers of the townland or by owners of livestock herds.

The valuation of a tenant's house gives an indication of the relative quality of the structure. Many poor families in Ireland paid only five shillings per year to rent their houses; some paid even less.

Not every head of family is listed as a householder or landholder in Griffith's Valuation. Perhaps two families lived in the same tenement, or multiple generations of the same family lived together. In either case, it is possible that only one individual was listed as the occupier in Griffith's Valuation.

Griffith's Valuation is available at many libraries in the United States and Ireland in book format and on microfilm. You may order copies of the microfilms from the Family History Library; these microfilms will be sent to your local Family History Center. Digital images of Griffith's Valuation are also available online by paid subscription on the websites Irish Origins <www.irishorigins.com> and Otherdays.com.

Manuscript copies of earlier valuations do exist for many localities, and the original hand-written field books, house books, and tenure books used to compile Griffith's Valuation are available for the Republic of Ireland at the Valuation Office in Dublin. Early manuscripts of land valuation records for Northern Ireland are available at the Public Record Office of Northern Ireland in Belfast.

Digital Indexes of Griffith's Valuation

Recognizing the significance of Griffith's Valuation for genealogists, a number of organizations have created national and county indexes to this collection. Three national indexes are readily searchable from your home, one on CD-ROM and the other two on the Internet. Brøderbund Software, in connection with Heritage World and the Genealogical Publishing Company, published an index on CD-ROM entitled *Index to Griffith's Valuation of Ireland, 1848–1864*. This CD-ROM index lets you search on the names of tenants; you may also search by location. The two Internet indexes to Griffith's Valuation are available by subscription at Irish Origins <www.irishorigins.com> and Otherdays.com.

The Otherdays.com index to Griffith's Valuation lets you search on the names of tenants and landlords; you may also search by location, organization (e.g., societies, police), and building (e.g., churches, graveyards, schools). Each resulting match is linked to a digital image of the corresponding page in Griffith's Valuation. As an added bonus, the associated Ordnance Survey map is also just one click away. If you plan on traveling to Ireland, you may be able to visit your ancestor's property using these maps in conjunction with modern-day maps.

The Irish Origins index to Griffith's Valuation is the most comprehensive index to date, including details gleaned from the various preliminary editions of Griffith's Valuation and the final published edition now available in many libraries. This index was transcribed and prepared from original documents by Eneclann, a genealogy research firm in Dublin. The index links to digital images of Griffith's Valuation.

You can use these name indexes to help you pinpoint where your ancestors lived in Ireland, especially when an ancestor's name is uncommon. Let's say you are searching for "Michael Abberton of Ireland"—you have no specific information on where he lived in Ireland, but you know that he was in Ireland in the mid-1800s. You check the index to Griffith's Valuation on CD-ROM and find that there are fourteen Abberton families listed, two under the name Michael Abberton. All fourteen of these Abberton families lived in Ballynakill Parish, County Galway, during the mid-1850s. Now you may check local church records, civil registration, Canceled Land Books, and other sources in Ballynakill Parish to determine whether your ancestor Michael Abberton is one of those listed in Griffith's Valuation.

Canceled and Current Land Books

Since the publication of Griffith's Primary Valuation, updates to each property valuation have been maintained in Canceled Land Books (figure 9-3), also known as Revision Books. Griffith's Valuation was hand copied into new books, property by property, with large gaps between each entry. Any changes in tenants, landlords, acreage, buildings, or valuations were recorded by crossing out the old information and inserting an update. Revisions were made with different colors of ink so that any comments (e.g., the year the change was recorded) would be easily identified with the

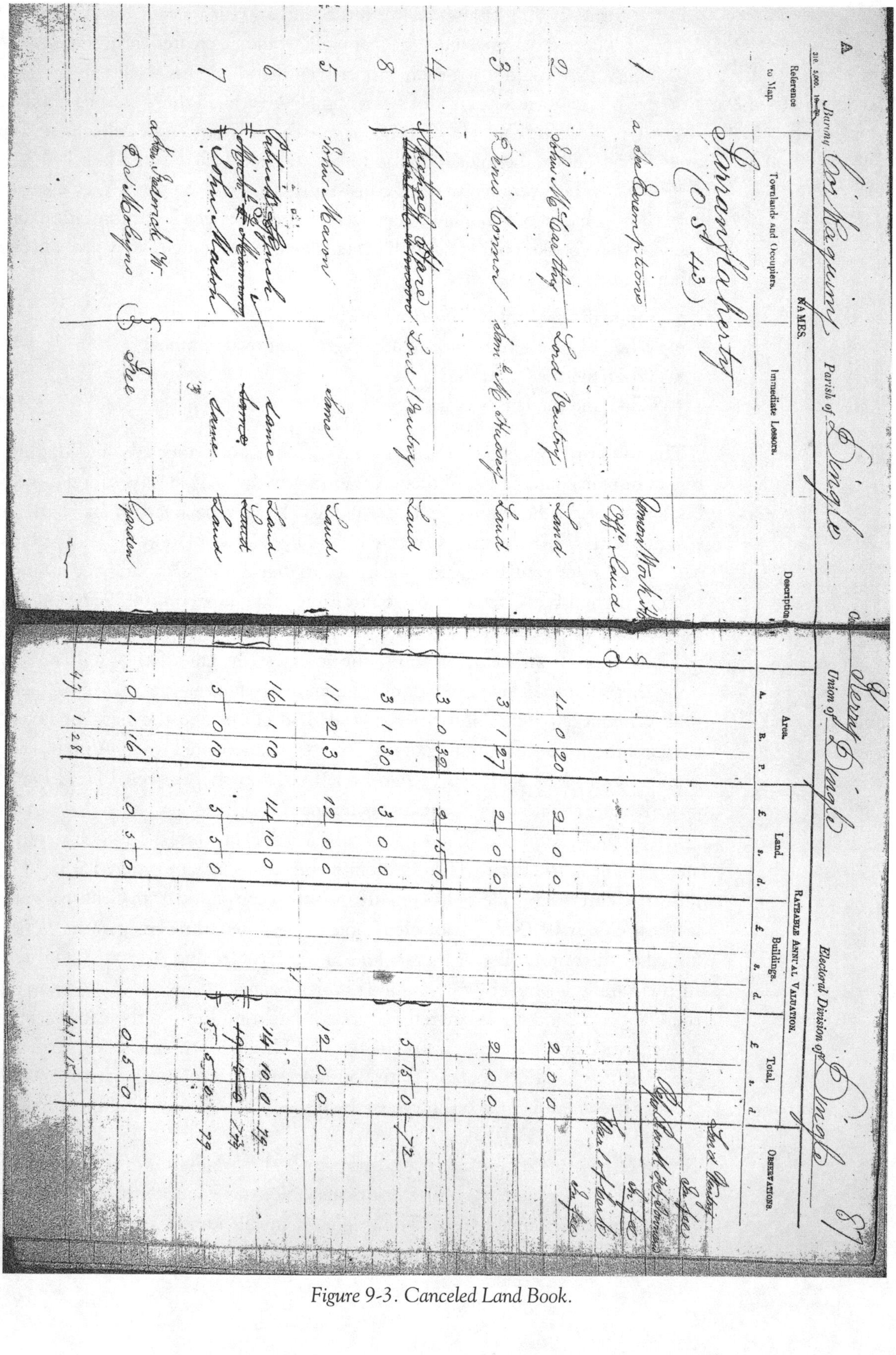

Courtesy of the National Archives of Ireland

Figure 9-3. Canceled Land Book.

corresponding change. After ten to fifteen years, a revision book would fill up and be canceled. Another book would be created from the most recent information for each property, and the process would start over. The most recent copy of a revision book is called the Current Land Book.

The Canceled Land Books are the only genealogy collection spanning all households in Ireland from the mid-1800s to the late 1900s. Since they were maintained consistently through the years, they can provide clues about your ancestors over a number of decades. Information found in these books, combined with other genealogical sources, may provide answers to questions like:

- When did the family move into the area?
- When did the sons move out and begin their own families?
- When did the father die?
- When did the family emigrate?

The following case study illustrates the usefulness of Canceled Land Books: I was researching my grandfather William O'Connor with the goal of learning more about his family before he immigrated to America. I knew he lived in Ballyard, Tralee, County Kerry. I searched the Canceled Land Books and found that William's father, Michael Connor, rented a gate house from Colonel William Rowan. According to the Canceled Land Book, tenancy passed to John, the oldest son, in 1907. This change in occupancy suggests that the father may have died in or about 1907. In 1913 the property passed from the oldest son to the youngest, my grandfather William Connor. Soon thereafter the land passed from William to his mother, Mary Connor, suggesting that William left home and his widowed mother became the head of household. Researching American immigration records I discovered that William actually immigrated to Massachusetts in August 1913. Thus, the Canceled Land Books can provide clues about major events in your ancestors' life.

Microfilms of Canceled Land Books for most localities in the Republic of Ireland are available at the Family History Library and copies may be ordered at local Family History Centers. The microfilms usually span the time period from Griffith's Valuation to the 1920s or 1930s, but Canceled Land Books dated as recently as the 1970s were filmed by the Family History Library for some parts of Ireland. You can find these films in the Family History Library Catalog under *Ireland, [County]—Land and property*; the Canceled Land Books are referred to as "Valuation lists" in the catalog, and they are organized by registration district (Poor Law Union). The easiest way to determine the Poor Law Union associated with your ancestor's townland or parish is to search the 1851 townland index online (see Chapter 4, "Place Names and Land Divisions," for details).

While these microfilms are black and white, the originals are in color. Although the various colors are not easily distinguishable, the majority of the revisions can be interpreted reasonably well. The original Canceled and Current Land Books for the Republic of Ireland are available at the Valuation Office in Dublin, where you can purchase color copies of the original pages. The books for Northern Ireland are available exclusively at the Public Record Office of Northern Ireland in Belfast.

Land Ownership and the Registry of Deeds

Another collection of land records predates the Tithe Applotment Books and Griffith's Valuation. In 1708, the Irish Parliament established the Registry of Deeds to document the Protestant ownership of land resulting from the transfer of property out of the hands of the Catholic majority. Registration was voluntary, but many chose to establish evidence of land ownership in the registry. If your ancestors were wealthy landholders, you may find them listed in the Registry of Deeds. This source may help you trace property-owning families back into the 1700s.

When original documents were registered, copies or abstracts were made and deposited in the Registry of Deeds. These records, known as memorials, were copied and bound into Transcript Books. There are name indexes and land indexes for the memorials in the Registry of Deeds.

Transcripts of memorials of deeds, conveyances, and wills are housed in the Registry of Deeds in Dublin. These documents have been microfilmed for the time period 1708–1929. Microfilm copies may be searched at the Public Record Office of Northern Ireland and the Family History Library.

In Summary

Griffith's Valuation and the Canceled Land Books are great tools for finding where ancestors lived in Ireland during the last century and a half. The Tithe Applotment Books are helpful for the pre-Famine generation, from the 1820s through the 1830s. The Registry of Deeds may help you trace wealthy landowners back to the 1700s. When used with church records, civil registration, census records, gravestone inscriptions, and other sources, these land records can help you successfully trace many Irish families.

References and Selected Reading

Land Owners in Ireland: Return of Owners of Land of One Acre and Upwards. 1876. Reprint, Baltimore: Genealogical Publishing Company, 1998.

Reilly, James R., CGRS. *Richard Griffith and His Valuations of Ireland.* Baltimore: Genealogical Publishing Company, 2002.

St. Patrick's Cathedral in Dublin, Ireland

Gravestone Inscriptions

Earth to earth, ashes to ashes, dust to dust.
　　　—Burial of the Dead, from the Book of Common Prayer *(1662)*

I will ransom them from the power of the grave; I will redeem them from death.
　　　　　　　—Hosea 13:14

There is something wonderful about walking through an old cemetery, finding your ancestor's grave, touching the cold, weathered headstone, and reading the inscription. You feel somehow much closer to your ancestor while standing at the grave site, where the family gathered years ago to witness the burial.

In Ireland, the custom of erecting grave markers was well established by the seventeenth century (figure 10-1). Often, many generations of a family were buried in the same plot, with only a few names carved in the gravestone. Many of the poor in Ireland were buried in unmarked graves or were not named on the headstones of the family plot. Nevertheless, gravestone inscriptions may be a significant source of information for your family history. In many parish churches there were no burial registers, or the registers no longer exist. Gravestone inscriptions might be the best source of birth, marriage, and death information, especially before 1864, when the government began keeping registers of this information.

Inscription Examples

The most common gravestone inscriptions are brief, merely stating the name, residence, and death date of the deceased. Here is one such gravestone, from County Kerry:

In memory of Mary O'Connor of Ballyard, Tralee, died 10 Feb. 1963. A Faithful Friend. RIP. (*O'Kief, Coshe Mang, Slieve Lougher and Upper*

Figure 10-1. Gravestones in Sligo City Cemetery.

99

Figure 10-2. Gravestone inscription.

Blackwater in Ireland, vol. 8, p. 1838, from Tralee Old Cemetery, Barony of Trughanacmy, County Kerry.)

Family headstones are also fairly common, with the father, mother, and children all mentioned (figure 10-2). Here is an impressive example from County Cork, erected by three immigrant sons living in America:

Sacred to the memory of Geoffrey O'Connell, Dromkeen, who died Feb. 22, 1858, aged 64 years, of his wife Ellen O'Connell who departed Mar. 30, 1860, aged 55 yrs. & of their children, Rev. Chas. O'Connell, Jeremiah, Barth, Daniel Geoffrey, Jeremiah Timothy, Daniel and Julia. This tribute of filial esteem was erected by their sons Rev. Andrew O'Connell, Brooklyn, William & John O'Connell New York, America. (*O'Kief, Coshe Mang, Slieve Lougher and Upper Blackwater in Ireland*, vol. 8, p. 1837, from Macloneigh Cemetery, Barony of Muskerry West, County Cork.)

Some gravestones pre-date civil registration and the local parish registers. These gravestones are a major find. The inscriptions may contain birth, marriage, and death details unavailable from other sources, as in this example from County Down:

QUIN. Erected by James Quin of Ballygela in memory of his wife Margt. Quin alias MACNAMARA who died 5th July 1843 aged 50 years. Also his son James who died at sea 12th Febr. 1848 aged 26 years. Also his daughter Margt. who died 24th March 1849 aged 34 years. And his daughter Jane who died 26th Decr. 1847 aged 17 years. Also his sister Margt. who died 17th Decr. 1808 aged 60 years. The above named James Quin died the 30th April 1861 aged 90 years. (Lisbane Roman Catholic Graveyard, Roman Catholic parish of Ardkeen, County Down, as transcribed and published in *Gravestone Inscriptions*, Volume 13, County Down, compiled by R. S. J. Clarke, published by the Ulster-Scot Historical Foundation, Belfast, 1975, p. 94)

A few gravestone inscriptions even name family members who died abroad, such as this memorial from County Down:

CARSON. In loving memory of Thomas Carson, Sycamore Lodge, Ballylig, who died 25th November 1862. Also his wife Matilda Carson who died 13th January 1911. Also their son Thomas Macafee Carson who died in Brooklyn, U.S.A., 11th Feb.

1896. Also their son Joseph Carson who died 25th April 1924 aged 74 years. Also their daughter Annie Carson who died 13th February 1932. And their eldest daughter Martha Knox Carson who died 6th June 1936. "In God's keeping." (Rathmullan Graveyard, County Down, as transcribed and published in *Gravestone Inscriptions*, Volume 9, County Down, compiled by R. S. J. Clarke, published by the Ulster-Scot Historical Foundation, Belfast, 1972, p. 70.)

Locating Your Ancestor's Cemetery

Your Irish ancestors were most likely buried in a graveyard close to their home. Once you know where your ancestors lived and died, you will want to find the local graveyard and check to see whether the family was buried there. Many graveyards or burial grounds are often located adjacent to church buildings. Some graveyards are shared by various denominations and are located within cities or towns. Other graveyards are found in rather isolated locations.

Three key sources can help you identify the cemetery where your ancestors were buried: church burial registers, land records, and maps.

Search the church burial registers before searching for a gravestone, especially if you have ready access to the church records. If you find your ancestors listed in the parish burial register, you should then search for the graves in the parish cemetery to learn all the additional information inscribed on the gravestone. This may be done in person or by finding a transcript of gravestone inscriptions for the cemetery.

If your ancestor's church did not keep a burial register, you may want to check other local churches. For example, most Catholic and Presbyterian churches did not keep burial records in the nineteenth century. Many Catholics and Presbyterians were buried in the local Church of Ireland cemeteries and may appear in the Church of Ireland burial registers as well.

Land records list many of the cemeteries in Ireland. If your ancestors were buried in the early to mid-1800s, you should find the cemetery listed in Griffith's Valuation (see Chapter 9, "Land and Property Records"). Brian Mitchell's *A Guide to Irish Churches and Graveyards*, identifies the addresses of all cemeteries mentioned in Griffith's Valuation. Mitchell's book lists the cemeteries by county, parish, and townland and indicates the religious denomination of each cemetery.

Historical maps may help you pinpoint the cemetery where your ancestor was buried. In the 1830s and 1840s the Ordnance Survey mapped all of Ireland, noting many physical features and man-made structures (see Chapter 4, "Place Names and Land Divisions," for more details about Ordnance Survey maps). All cemeteries then in existence were included in the Ordnance Survey maps. These maps are extremely detailed, with a scale of one-sixth of a mile per inch. Even if your ancestor's cemetery has fallen into disuse or no longer exists, you may still find it on these old Ordnance Survey maps. Microfiche copies of the Ordnance Survey maps are available at many libraries, including the Family History Library.

Research Tip

Three key sources can help you identify the cemetery where your ancestors were buried: church burial registers, land records, and maps.

Modern maps may also help you locate your ancestor's cemetery. The best modern maps to consult are the Discovery Series maps, compiled and published by the Ordnance Survey for all of Ireland and Northern Ireland. These topographic maps are very detailed, with a 1:50,000 scale, or about three-quarters of a mile per inch. The Discovery Series maps list many graveyards and burial grounds, as well as the modern roads you would take to get there. You can buy these maps at many bookstores in the United States, or you can purchase them on the Internet.

Transcribed Gravestone Inscriptions

Wind, rain, heat, cold, lichen, dew, and the passage of time gradually erase the writing on all but the most durable tombstones. To preserve this vanishing information, many organizations in Ireland have spent years traveling from cemetery to cemetery copying gravestone inscriptions. One group began recording memorial inscriptions over one hundred years ago in a work entitled *Journal of the Association for the Preservation of the Memorials of the Dead* (FHL 1279252-54, 1279285). Published between 1888 and 1934, this journal contains many thousands of transcriptions from memorials and gravestones across Ireland. The selection of tombstones was not complete for a given cemetery, but often focused on the oldest or most curious stones, the more notable inscriptions, or gravestones of the most prominent people buried in the cemetery.

It is not uncommon to find that gravestone inscriptions from a hundred or more cemeteries have been transcribed for any given county. A number of Irish Heritage Centres have gathered significant collections of gravestone inscriptions, and some of these have name indexes searchable on the Internet (see Chapter 18, "Irish Heritage Centres," for details).

Some historical societies have transcribed gravestone inscriptions and published them in journals. An excellent source of this type is the collection of volumes entitled *Gravestone Inscriptions*, published by the Ulster-Scot Historical Foundation and cited earlier in this chapter. Another outstanding example is the collection of cemetery transcriptions published in Albert Casey's fifteen-volume series of genealogical records from Counties Kerry and Cork, *O'Kief, Coshe Mang, Slieve Lougher and Upper Blackwater in Ireland.*

Eneclann has published a CD-ROM of gravestone inscriptions under the title, *Irish Memorial Inscriptions, Volume 1, Memorials of the Dead, Counties Galway and Mayo (Western Seaboard)*. This CD-ROM, compiled and edited by Ian Cantwell, includes transcripts of memorials from 128 graveyards near the west coast of Counties Galway and Mayo. There are over three thousand memorials up to 1901 on this CD-ROM—these gravestones list over eight thousand names and frequent additional details such as family relationships, addresses, and occupations.

The county family history guides listed in Chapter 8, "Censuses and Census Substitutes," can help you find cemetery sources for your ancestor's county. Two sources have detailed information for all counties: James Ryan's comprehensive *Irish Records: Sources for Family and Local History*, and a book on Irish sources prepared by the staff of the Family History Library under the title *Smith's Inventory of Genealogical Sources: Ireland.*

Preparing to Visit the Cemetery

If you have the good fortune to visit your ancestor's home in Ireland, you will want to prepare to visit the local cemetery (see Chapter 20, "Visiting Ireland"). Find out ahead of time which cemeteries are closest and whether the gravestone inscriptions have been transcribed.

What do you need to do to prepare for a trip to the cemetery? What will you do when you arrive? Proper planning makes all the difference. Remember that an old graveyard might be untended, with tall wet grass and mud. Dress for the outdoors and bring boots and an umbrella, just in case.

Bring a good camera and take lots of pictures. Photograph any gravestone of a potential relative. If you find your ancestor's grave, take enough pictures from different angles to make sure you have captured the inscription clearly. Old tombstones have delicate surfaces that may flake or chip off, so you should not rub them with chalk or any other material. To draw out the lettering on a difficult-to-read inscription, try shining a mirror at a sharp angle to the surface. Spraying water on the stone may also help make the writing more legible, especially if dirt trickles off the flat surface and into the carved letters. As an extra precaution, you may want to draw a picture of the tombstone, including all writing and artwork, in case your photographs don't turn out.

The type of stone, the depth of the carvings, and the deterioration caused by weather, lichen, and man, all affect the readability of gravestone inscriptions. Some gravestones have eroded so much that the inscriptions are now impossible to read. Hopefully you will find a legible stone for your family.

The later the date of death, the more likely you will find a gravestone. However, remember that multiple generations may be buried in a family plot; the headstone might list a few family members while leaving no indication of the many others who went before. Even if you do not find the grave of your ancestor, it is still a moving experience to visit the cemetery where he or she was buried long ago.

In Summary

How do cemetery records fit in with the rest of your Irish family history research? Gravestone inscriptions may be the only source of birth, marriage, and death information before church records and civil registration. You might also discover siblings and other relatives undetected in other sources. Although gravestone inscriptions do not exist for all our Irish ancestors, when they do, they offer a moving expression of life, death, sorrow, and affection etched in stone.

References and Selected Reading

Casey, Albert E., and Eugene P. Thomas. *O'Kief, Coshe Mang, Slieve Lougher and Upper Blackwater in Ireland.* 15 vols. Birmingham, Ala.: Amite and Knockagree Historical Fund, 1952–71.

Journal of the Association for the Preservation of the Memorials of the Dead in Ireland. 7 vols. Dublin: The Association, 1895–1917.

Mitchell, Brian. *A Guide to Irish Churches and Graveyards.* Baltimore: Genealogical Publishing Company, 1995.

Ryan, James G. *Irish Records: Sources for Family and Local History.* Salt Lake City: Ancestry, 1997.

Smith, Frank. *Smith's Inventory of Genealogical Sources: Ireland.* Salt Lake City: Corporation of the President, The Church of Jesus Christ of Latter-day Saints, 1994.

Newspapers

You should always believe what you read in the newspapers, for that makes them more interesting.

—Rose Macauley

Irish newspapers contain many articles of genealogical value. Perhaps the most significant are birth, marriage, and death announcements, but business advertisements, bankruptcy notices, crime reports, accidents, military desertions, passenger arrivals, and court reports may feature your ancestors as well. Combined, these newspaper stories paint a picture of your ancestors' community and time.

The earliest Irish newspapers were published in the mid- to late-1600s. Big cities like Dublin, Belfast, and Cork were publishing many newspapers by the mid-1700s. Even the smaller market towns were publishing multiple newspapers by the 1800s. Newspapers were published weekly in the early 1700s. Later, newspapers were published bi-weekly or daily. In towns boasting two or three newspapers, each would publish on different days of the week to offer daily coverage of news without competing directly.

By the mid-1700s it became stylish to advertise biographical notices in the newspaper. These advertisements accompanied other news of the day, such as goods arriving by ship, court session reports, and ads for services. Here is a column transcribed (with original spelling and punctuation) from a Dublin newspaper, the *Freeman Journal*, dated Saturday, 10 September 1763:

A few Days ago died, in Christ-Church-lane, Mr. Peter Brett, formerly Parish-clerk of Castleknock.

The Quarter Sessions for the County of Dublin will be held at Kilmainham, on Tuesday the 6th of October next.

Tuesday was married, Mr. Bryan Reilly of the Town of Monaghan, an aminent Distiller, to Miss Mary Ford of Smithfield, an agreeable young Lady with a handsome Fortune.

Sept. 8.] Arrived the Young George of Dantzick, Martin Saun, thence Timber, &c. One Collier with Coals, and one Coaster with Linen Cloth. Sailed two Colliers home, Ballast.

Sptember 9. This Day the Quarter Sessions was held at the Tholsel, pursuant to Adjournment, when Mr. Mark Thomas, seizing Officer was tried for assaulting Mr. Peck Grocer, and acquitted. Catherine Stubbs, for Felony, to be transported for seven Years; Mary Moran, for petty Larcenary to be privately corrected, and eight others for Felony acquitted.—The Court adjourned to Monday Morning.

LOTTERY TICKETS in all the Schemes sold, (and register'd gratis) by W. Willamson, Wholesale-Stationer in Bride-street.

Before the mid-1800s most of these biographical notices pertained to wealthier families including nobility, merchants, professionals, and the farming gentry. Early newspapers rarely contained personal family history details aside from occasional marriage and death announcements of the wealthy. You would be more likely to find the marriage of one of the social elite than that of a poor farmer's daughter. Fortunately, by the 1840s and 1850s a broader spectrum of social classes began to announce births, marriages, and deaths in Irish newspapers.

A typical birth announcement would name only the father of the child, as in this example from the *Kerry Evening Post* in 1880: "On 19 May at Rathpeacon House, Cork, wife of Jackson D. Bogue, of a daughter."

Death announcements were often quite terse, as seen in this example from the *Hibernian Chronicle*, published in Cork on Monday, 20 November 1786: "Died last week the Rev. Mark West, late of this city." Occasionally, a glowing obituary might be printed rather than a brief death notice.

Marriage announcements were usually more detailed than birth and death notices. My great-grandaunt's marriage is one such example. Here is her marriage notice, found in the Saturday, 17 November 1894, edition of the *Kerry Evening Post*:

TALBOT-BROWN-On Wednesday, the 14th instant, at St. Mary's Church, Dingle, by the Rev. G. B. Anderson, rector, Andrew Talbot, Mount Kennedy Cottage, Dingle, third son of the late Andrew Talbot, Aghadoe House, Killarney, to Lizzie, second daughter of the late Ambrose Brown, Ventry, Dingle.

Why search newspapers to learn about your ancestor's birth, marriage, or death? Newspapers reported events soon after they happened, when the information was fresh. Some announcements also provide extra information lacking in civil and church records. You may even find biographical information published in a newspaper before civil registration or the local church records began.

Other articles of genealogical significance include elopements, business announcements, estate auctions, bankruptcies, legal notices, social events of prominent citizens, accidents, scandals, and passenger arrivals and departures. People clearly wanted to keep abreast of court proceedings, so the more notorious cases were usually printed in the newspaper.

Availability of Newspapers

The British Library in London houses the largest collection of Irish newspapers in the world. The National Library of Ireland in Dublin and the Linen Hall Library in Belfast have the second and third largest collections of Irish newspapers, respectively. Many smaller libraries in Ireland have their own collections of local newspapers, and a few historical newspapers in these libraries are unique.

The best reference aid for finding all known Irish newspapers is the NEWSPLAN database, available on the National Library website at <www.nli.ie/newsplan>. You can search NEWSPLAN by county to see a listing of historical newspapers. Under each newspaper title is a detailed listing of the dates and issues that still exist, where the originals are housed, what has been microfilmed, and where the microfilm copies may be found. For example, the database lists 532 newspapers for County Dublin; four began publication in the 1600s, 188 in the 1700s, and 185 in the 1800s.

Another helpful finding aid for Irish newspapers is John North's book, *The Waterloo Directory of Irish Newspapers and Periodicals, 1800–1900*. This directory is "an alphabetical listing and description of publications in Ireland in all fields, including the arts, sciences, professions, trades, labour, agriculture, industry, entertainment, sport, church and home." Each newspaper or periodical is covered, with such details as publication dates, proprietors and printers, frequency of publication, subjects covered, guiding principles or philosophies, and holdings of current repositories.

Irish Newspapers on the Internet

A few organizations have started posting digitized images and every-word indexes of Irish newspapers on the Internet. Ancestry.com has posted images and indexes for portions of one Dublin newspaper (*Freeman's Journal*, 1763–65). Otherdays.com has posted images and indexes for parts of two Dublin newspapers (*Freeman's Journal*, 1775–76, and the *Dublin Penny Journal*, 1832–36) and one Belfast newspaper (*Belfast Newsletter*, 1801). A word index for the *Belfast Newsletter*, 1737–1800, is also searchable online at <www.ucs.louisiana.edu/bnl>.

As more historical Irish newspapers are digitally imaged and indexed on the Internet, many more family historians will find valuable information about their ancestors.

Abstracts of Births, Marriages, and Deaths

Although newspapers contain wonderful genealogical information, their sheer volume makes newspapers difficult to search. Fortunately, many indexes and abstracts have been created for biographical notices, particularly births, marriages, and deaths. For example, the marriage of Andrew Talbot to Lizzie Brown mentioned above was abstracted in volume 11 of Albert E. Casey's monumental work, *O'Kief, Coshe Mang, Slieve Lougher and Upper Blackwater in Ireland*. The abstract reads:

m. On 14 Nov. at St. Marys Ch. Dingle Andrew TALBOT Mount Kennedy Cottage Dingle 3 s.o.l. Andrew Talbot Aghadoe Ho. Killarney to Lizzie 2 d.o.l. Ambrose BROWNE Ventry Dingle.

Biographical notices have been abstracted from many historical Irish newspapers. Another example is Rosemary ffolliott's *Biographical Notices Primarily Related to Counties Cork and Kerry: Collection from Newspapers, 1756–1827, with a Few References, 1749–1755* (figure 11-1). For details on newspaper indexes for individual counties, consult the county family history guides listed in Chapter 8, "Censuses and Census Substitutes."

Use Modern Newspapers to Find Living Relatives

With the help of modern newspapers, you might be able to find cousins living in Ireland today. You could even submit a classified advertisement to the newspaper in your ancestor's hometown. In the ad, you might talk about your ancestor, introduce yourself, and explain your interest in finding living relatives. Another possibility would be to write a letter to the editor, providing the same information; letters to the editor are free.

> ↓
> ### Research Tip
> By placing an ad in modern newspapers, you might be able to find cousins living in Ireland.

If you are planning a trip to Ireland and can specify the time frame of your visit and contact information during your stay, you might improve your chances of being published in the paper and actually getting in touch with living relatives. The excitement of meeting Irish cousins makes this a very worthwhile activity. The family history information you learn may surprise you as well.

In Summary

Historical newspapers often contain information of genealogical value found nowhere else. Newspapers provide insights into the local and national culture of the time. Although it is rather time-consuming work searching newspapers for family history details, a number of indexing projects have abstracted birth, marriage, and death notices from certain Irish newspapers. Modern newspapers are also useful, as they may help you connect with living relatives.

References and Selected Reading

Casey, Albert E., and Eugene P. Thomas. *O'Kief, Coshe Mang, Slieve Lougher and Upper Blackwater in Ireland.* 15 vols. Birmingham, Ala.: Amite and Knockagree Historical Fund, 1952–71.

ffolliott, Rosemary. *Biographical Notices Primarily Related to Counties Cork and Kerry Collection from Newspapers, 1756–1827, with a Few References, 1749–1755.* Privately Published. Available at the Family History Library of The Church of Jesus Christ of Latter-day Saints, Salt Lake City.

ffolliott, Rosemary. *Index to Biographical Notices in the Newspapers of Limerick, Ennis, Clonmel and Waterford, 1758–1821.* Privately Published. Available at the Family History Library.

North, John S. *The Waterloo Directory of Irish Newspapers and Periodicals, 1800–1900.* Waterloo, Ontario: North Waterloo Academic Press, 1986.

LYSAGHT   (see also LISLE)

CEP Th 11 Apl 1805   4th inst, Andrew Lysaght Esq of Ballyvorven

CMC F 13 Jly 1804   on Sunday at Ballykeal House, John Creaghe Esq
                      barrister at law, to Miss Lysaght, dau of George
                      Lysaght of Ballykeal, co Clare Esq
                      (MLB Charlotte Lysaght)

CA Tu 26 Apl 1803   on Tuesday last, Christopher Lysaght Esq, High
                      Sheriff of the co Clare to Miss Fitzgibbon dau of
                      the late Gibbon Fitzgibbon of the city of Limerick
                      Esq

HC M 20 Apl 1772   died a few days ago at the Right Hon. Lord Lisle's
                      in Dawson street, Dublin, of a lingering illness
                      the Hon. Mr Edward Moore Lysaght, a youth...

CEP M 6 Mch 1797   a few days ago at Kildimo church near Limerick, by
                      the Rev. Mountiford Longfield, Edward Lysaght Esq
                      to Miss Newson dau of the late Henry Newson of this
                      city Esq

SR Th 21 May 1818   on Saturday at Mallow, Edward Lysaght Esq, late
                      Clerk of the Crown for the co of Limerick

HC Th 26 May 1774   married last Saturday at Castle Harrison, Edward
                      Sayers Esq M.D. to Miss Lysaght, dau of William
                      Lysaght Esq
                      (MLB Elizabeth Lysaght)

Figure 11-1. Extract from Biographical Notices Primarily Related to Counties Cork and Kerry *by Rosemary ffolliott.*

Cork, Ireland.

Commercial and Social Directories

12

Every man should endeavour to know all he can about his family history....It is, or should be, a matter of interest to everyone to know something of those who have borne his name before him—no matter whether they have been earls or blacksmiths.
> —Edward Marion Chadwick, Ontarian Families: Genealogies of United Empire
> Loyalist and Other Pioneer Families

Long before the telephone, our ancestors consulted commercial and social directories to find people, goods, and services. To a modern reader, an early Irish directory would appear to be a mixture of white pages and yellow pages without phone numbers. Just as you would consult a phone book to quickly find a modern acquaintance, you should consult historical directories to find your Irish ancestors.

Was Your Ancestor Listed in Any Directories?

Nineteenth-century Irish directories are excellent sources of information about the urban middle and upper classes. If your ancestors were gentry, wealthy landowners, professionals, merchants, public officials, or teachers, you may discover important details about them by consulting commercial and social directories. The more wealthy or influential your ancestor, the more likely he will appear in numerous directories.

The best city directories tended to list heads of household, street-by-street, except for tenements. A number of Dublin city directories were organized like this, with some republished annually. If your ancestor wasn't prosperous but lived in Dublin or Belfast, you might still find a listing in the city directories.

While early directories focused exclusively on large cities, later directories expanded their coverage to include many towns in rural districts. Nobility, clergy, major landholders, merchants, and professionals were listed, as usual. In addition, schoolmasters, constables, butchers, and other prominent citizens also appeared in later Irish commercial directories, even in small market towns in rural areas.

Poor tenant farmers, cottiers, landless laborers, servants, and people in remote rural locations are simply not going to appear in these books. Nevertheless, directories can provide many specific details about the places where your ancestors lived.

111

What Can You Learn from Directories?

Directories list people and their businesses (figure 12-1). Directories provide a view of the economic, social, and political climate in Ireland. You can get a fairly clear picture of what life must have been like for your ancestors by reading about their hometown or the nearest city in contemporary directories.

Commercial and social directories provide numerous details about cities and small towns. Often many centuries of local history are recounted for each market town in a directory, with a description of the geography, the major industries, churches, and public services available. Businesses are advertised, academies and schools are listed, and newspaper and post services are described. In some directories, the exact street addresses are given for each household. You can almost picture the town when your family lived there with history, geography, occupations, and other interesting details contained in historical directories.

Directories may be the only documentation on your ancestor's specific profession, especially if your ancestor was a merchant. All sorts of now-obscure professions and trades are mentioned in Irish directories in the 1800s. For instance, *Slater's National Commercial Directory of Ireland*, published in 1846, lists these professions for the market town and seaport of Tralee: apothecary, brazier, butter merchant, coach maker, colourman, cooper, dyer, feather merchant, gentry, glover, ironmonger, leather cutter, livery stable keeper, milliner, nail maker, rag dealer, saddler, skinner, spinning wheel maker, straw bonnet maker, tallow chandler, turner, whip maker, wool comber, and woolen draper.

Directories often fill in important details other records miss. Consider how useful annual city directories can be for tracing ancestors. These directories are like annual census records. If you find an ancestor in one of these directories you can trace him year by year. You might see when his sons appear in their own households, when the family moves, when the family emigrates, or when the husband retires or dies. These clues may lead you to marriage and death records, immigration records, and more.

What Kinds of Directories Are There?

A number of publishers in Dublin, London, Belfast, and Cork produced directories in the 1800s. Some directories covered the entire United Kingdom of Great Britain and Ireland, while others included just Ireland. Some Irish directories were national and some provincial, while others focused on a particular region, county, or city. Many varieties of directories were published, including business, commercial, professional, postal, and social directories.

National Directories

James Pigot, Alexander Thom, and J. Slater published the three best series of national directories of Ireland for the 1800s:

1820   James Pigot, *Commercial Directory of Ireland*
1824   James Pigot and Co., *City of Dublin and Hibernian Provincial Directory*

1844   A. Thom, *Irish Almanac and Official Directory* (issued annually from 1844 to the present)

1846   J. Slater, *National Commercial Directory of Ireland* (figure 12-1)

1856   J. Slater, *Royal National Commercial Directory of Ireland*

1870   J. Slater, *Directory of Ireland*

1881   J. Slater, *Royal National Commercial Directory of Ireland*

1894   J. Slater, *Royal National Commercial Directory of Ireland*

These directories cover all four provinces of Ireland, with the later directories tending to have more information on more people and places.

Also valuable is W. Holden's 1811 publication, *Holden's Annual London and Country Directory of the United Kingdom and Wales*. Ancestry.com has published this directory on the Internet in the form of digital images and a searchable index of every word in the directory.

Local Directories

Many commercial and social directories covered single provinces, counties, regions, or cities. Smaller towns were often listed in these directories. In Connaught, some of the most valuable historical directories are:

1839   *Directory of the Towns of Sligo, Enniskillen, Ballyshannon, Donegal, etc.*

1865   *Sligo Independent Almanac*

1889   *Sligo Independent Directory*

In the province of Leinster, a number of county and city directories were published:

1751   Peter Wilson, *An Alphabetical List of Names and Places of Abode of the Merchants and Traders of the City of Dublin*

1830   McCabe, *Drogheda Directory*

1834   Pettigrew and Oulton, *Dublin Almanack and General Register of Ireland*

1839   T. Shearman, *New Commercial Directory for the Cities of Waterford and Kilkenny, Towns of Clonmel, Carrick-on-Suir, New Ross and Carlow*

1840   *New Trienniel Commercial Directory for 1840, 1841, 1842*

1850   Henry Shaw, *New City Pictoral Directory of Dublin City*

1872   George Griffith, *County Wexford Almanac*

1884   George Henry Bassett, *Kilkenny City and County Guide and Directory*

1885   George Henry Bassett, *Wexford County Guide and Directory*

1886   George Henry Bassett, *Louth County Guide and Directory*

In Munster, the best provincial and regional directories from the nineteenth century are:

1866   George Henry Bassett, *Directory of the City and County of Limerick, and of the Principle Towns in the Counties of Tipperary and Clare*

1886   Francis Guy, *Postal Directory of Munster* (figure 12-2)

POST OFFICE, Bridge street, TRALEE, Mr. William Mason, *Post Master*.—Letters from DUBLIN, and the NORTH OF IRELAND, also from ENGLAND, arrive every afternoon at half-past four, and are despatched every morning at eight.—Letters from CORK and the SOUTH OF IRELAND, arrive every afternoon at five, and are despatched every morning at six.

Letters from CAHERCIVEEN and MILLTOWN, arrive every evening at nine, and are despatched every afternoon at half-past five.—Letters from DINGLE arrive every morning at seven, and are despatched every afternoon at five.—Letters from LISTOWEL and TARBERT arrive every morning at twenty minutes before eleven, and are despatched every afternoon at three.—Letters from KILLARNEY and CASTLE ISLAND arrive every morning at twenty minutes before eleven, and are despatched every afternoon at twenty minutes before two.

POST OFFICE, BLENNERVILLE, Ellen Daughton, *Post Mistress*.—Letters from all parts arrive (from TRALEE) every evening at six, and are despatched every morning at seven.

GENTRY AND CLERGY.

Allen Mr. William, Ballymullen
Bateman William, Esq. (poor law guardian), Prince's quay & Fibough Lodge
Blackhall Mrs. C. Upper Castle st
Blennerhassett Frederick, Esq. Blennerville [Day place
Blennerhassett John Hurly, Esq. 3
Blennerhassett Rowland, Esq. 6 Day place
Busteed John, Esq. 8 Day place
Busteed Mrs. William, Strand st
Casey John, Esq. the Spa [ville
Chambers Mrs. Elizabeth, Blenner-
Chute Arthur, Esq. Upper Castle st
Chute Caleb, Esq. Prince's quay
Chute Pierce, Esq. Nelson st
Chute Richard, Esq. J.P. Blennerville House
Collis Samuel, Esq. the Spa
Collis Samuel, Esq. the Spa
Connor Miss, 12 Denny st
Day Miss Agnes, Nelson st [st
Denny Rev. Anthony, Rectory, Nelson
Denny William, Esq. 1 Day place
Drummond John, Esq. (stipendiary magistrate), the Mall
Eagar James, Esq. Prince's quay
Eagar John Frederick, Esq. Ballymullen House [race
Eagar Rowland Tallis, Esq. the Ter-
Fairfield Capt. Chas. Geo. 2 Day place
Fitzgerald Robert, Esq. Strand st
Foley Miss Mary Ann, Denny st
Foley Rev. Patrick, c. c. Castle st
Gun George, Esq. Plover Hill, and Drummond Cottage, Ballybunion
Gun Wilson, Esq. Oak Park
Hay Mr. Richard, Nelson st
Hickson Mrs. Sarah, Nelson st
Hilliard George, Esq. Day place
Hilliard John, Esq. Denny st
Hilliard William, Esq. the Terrace
Huggard John, Esq. Prospect Lodge
Hurly John, Esq. Bridge place
Hurly Rev. Robt. Conway, Bridge pl
Hussey Walter, Esq. 5 Day place
King Jeremiah, Esq. 14 Denny st
Lauder Miss Bridget, 8 Denny st
Lawlor Mrs. Catherine, Nelson st
Lynch Mrs. —, the Spa
M'Can Henry, Esq. (secretary to the Grand Jury of the county of Kerry) Prince's quay
M'Carthy John, Esq. the Spa
M'Enery Very Rev. John Gerald, Castle st [Day place
M'Gillicuddy Daniel DeCourcy, Esq. 4
Mathews Mr. Benjamin, Nelson st
Mawe Rev. John, c.c. Castle st
Morris Mrs. Eleanor, Strand st
Morris Mrs. Sarah, Nelson st
Montgomery Martin, Esq. the Spa
Murphy Mrs. Barbara, Strand st
Murphy Richard, Esq. Lohercannon
Neligan Mrs. John, 17 Denny st
O'Connor Major Gerald Fitzgerald, the Spa [st
O'Flaherty Rev. Edmund, c.c. Castle
Ponsouby Mrs. Honoria, 7 Day Place
Quill Mrs. Catherine, Nelson st
Quill M. Esq. Caherina House

Rowan Rev. Arthur Blennerhassett, Rectory, Blennerville
Stephens Henry, Esq. Blennerville
Stephens Mr. Samuel, Ballymullen
Stokes Geo. Day, Esq. Prince's quay
Stokes Col. John Day, the Spa
Stokes Capt. Oliver Day, 15 Denny st
Stokes Captain Patrick D. Nelson st
Thompson Peter, Esq. Prince's quay
Tidmarsh Mrs. Margaret, Nelson st
Wade Rev. Robert, Nelson st
Weeks John, Esq. Strand st
Williams Mrs. Margaret, Blenneville

ACADEMIES AND SCHOOLS.

Allman John (classical), Nelson st
Brosnan Maurice, Blackpool
Carter Benjamin (day), Nelson st
CATHOLIC SCHOOL, Upper Castle street—John Griffin & Jeremiah O'Connor, masters
Harman Ann, Nelson st
Horan Timothy (classical), Nelson st
INFANTS' SCHOOL, Church lane— Margaret Brennan, mistress
M'Carthy Jno. (classical), Strand st
Martin Fanny & Margaret (ladies'), Nelson st
Mason Charles, Nelson st
NATIONAL SCHOOL, Blennerville— Denis Ready, master; Catherine Kerby, mistress
PAROCHIAL SCHOOL, Church lane —Benjamin Carter, master; Eliz. Carter, mistress
Slattery Catherine (boarding & day), Strand street [Well lane
Sullivan Jeremiah (day), Moyder

AGENTS.

D'Alton Power (mail coach), Upper Castle st [Castle street
Fitzgerald Michael (flour), Upper
Ruttle William (flour), Bridge st
Sheehy Robert (flour), the Mall

APOTHECARIES.

Donovan Franklin, the Mall
Eagan John, the Mall
Lawlor Michael & Robt. the Square
O'Sullivan & Roche, the Mall
Poyntz John, the Mall

ARCHITECTS.

Bourke James (and civil engineer), Day place
English James, Denny st
Payne Thomas, the Mall

ATTORNEYS.

Benner Arthur, 2 Denny st
Connor James Edward, Nelson st
Flynn Jeremiah, Nelson st
Huggard & Magill, 23 Denny st
Hurly Thomas Barry, Nelson st
Lawlor Edward, Nelson st
Lynch Daniel, Nelson st
Lynch George Dwyer, Nelson street, and 8 Langrishe place, *Dublin*
Lynch John (and poor law guardian and town commissioner), Bridge place, and 47 Jervis st, *Dublin*
Mawe James Harvey, Nelson st
Morphy Edward, the Mall; house Prince's quay
Neligan William John, 18 Denny st

O'Connor William, Nelson street, & Langrishe place, *Dublin*
Palmer & Chute, Godfrey place
Ruttle Michael John, Nelson st
Stokes Edward Day, Castle street, & at 3 Upper Gloucester st, *Dublin*
Supple Daniel, jun. Upper Castle st, and at 72 Chapel street, *Dublin*
Supple Justin, Nelson street, & 105 Upper Dorset street, *Dublin*

AUCTIONEERS.

Barrett James, Nelson st
Morris John, Lower Castle st
Walsh Jno. Stephen & Co. the Square

BAKERS.

Flynn Anthony, Upper Castle st
Hallinan Patrick, the Mall*
Harrington Maurice, the Mall
Healey Michael, Bridge st
Huggard Stephen, Upper Castle st
Leahy John & Son, the Mall
M'Carthy John, the Mall
M'Gillycuddy Patrick, Upper Castle st
O'Sullivan Patrick, Upper Castle st
Parker John, Upper Castle st
Tuomy John, Bridge st

BANKS.

BANK OF IRELAND (Branch of), Denny street—(draws on the Bank of England and the Parent Bank of Dublin)—Mr. Charles K. M'Grath, agent; Mr. Wm. Allen, sub-agent
NATIONAL BANK OF IRELAND (Branch of), Denny st—(draws on Barnetts', Hoare & Co. London) —Mr. Thomas Quill, manager
PROVINCIAL BANK OF IRELAND (Branch of), Denny st—(draws on Spooner, Attwoods' & Co. London) —Mr. Thomas Stewart, manager
SAVINGS' BANK, Bridge place—Mr. John Lynch, treasurer

BLACKSMITHS.

Cournane John, Russell st
Dunn Thomas, Rock st
Galivan Michael, Abbey st
Galivan Thomas, Moyderwell lane
Lawler Michael, Upper Castle st
M'Carthy Denis, Moyderwell lane

BOOKSELLERS & STATIONERS.

Coggin Jas. D. (& printer), the Mall
Higgins Jane, Nelson st
M'Auliff William (& binder), Lower Abbey street
Purcell Jane, the Mall

BOOT AND SHOE MAKERS.

Brown Michael, Russell st
Eaton John, Russell st
Falvey Charles, Russell st
Harman James, Nelson st
Hill Thomas, Upper Castle st
M'Carthy Daniel, the Mall
Magrath Marquis, the Mall
Mansfield John, Moyderwell lane
O'Brien John, Nelson st
O'Neill Cornelius, Upper Castle st
Shea James, Nelson st
Stack Eugene, Strand st
Thompson Thomas, Pye lane
Williams Robert, Bridge st
Wright William (military), the Mall, and 1 Denmark st, *Limerick*

Figure 12-1. Slater's National Commercial Directory of Ireland, *1846.*

1889   Francis Guy, *Postal Directory of Munster* (issued annually from 1889)

1893   Francis Guy, *Directory of Munster*

In Ulster, most directories focus on the city of Belfast, with a few others concentrating on individual counties:

1788   Richard Lucas, *General Directory of the Kingdom of Ireland*

1807/8 Joseph Smith, *Belfast Directories*

1820   *Belfast Almanack*

1820   Joseph Smyth, *Directory of Belfast and Its Vicinity*

1839   Mathew Martin, *Belfast Directory*

1841   Mathew Martin, *Belfast Directory*

1842   Mathew Martin, *Belfast Directory*

1835   William T. Matier, *Belfast Directory*

1852   James A. Henderson, *Belfast and Province of Ulster Directory* (sixteen issues from 1852 to 1900)

1860   Hugh Adair, *Belfast Directory*

1865   R. Wynne, *Business Directory of Belfast*

1887   *Derry Almanac and Directory*

1888   George Henry Bassett, *The Book of Antrim*

Availability of Directories

The Family History Library has copies of a number of commercial and social directories in Ireland, including Pigot's, Slater's, and Thom's directories for select years. The library has a number of city directories for Belfast and Dublin. Many regional directories are also available at the Family History Library, such as Francis Guy's directory of Munster.

Irish repositories with the largest collections of directories are the National Library of Ireland, the National Archives of Ireland, Trinity College in Dublin, and the Linen Hall Library in Belfast. The Public Record Office of Northern Ireland has a large collection of commercial and social directories for Belfast.

A few Irish directories are now available on the Internet, particularly on the websites Ancestry.com and Otherdays.com.

In Summary

Commercial and social directories list people and businesses much like modern phone books. While a few Irish directories were published in the 1700s, it was not until the early 1800s that a large number of directories were published. Throughout the nineteenth century, directories gradually covered a larger percentage of the population in cities and remote rural areas. You might find your ancestors listed in some of these directories and learn their occupations or residences. Directories also preserve a sense of what life must have been like in or near your ancestors' town or city many years ago.

SHANID CASTLE.

Conveyances.— Foynes 6½ m. (Limerick, Foynes and Newcastle ry.) nearest station.

Poor Law—Union of Glin ; Dispensary and Registration district of Tarbert No. 2.

Petty Sessions district of Glin.
Civil bill officer—John Martin

Schools.

National, Ballyhahill. Head teachers— Male, Patrick O'Connor ; Female, Mrs Madden.

National, Cloonlahard. Head teachers— Male, John Kenneally ; Female, Mrs Kenneally.

Drapers.

Clancy Margaret   Fitzgerald Joseph

Grocers.

Clancy Margaret   O'Connor Patrick
Fitzgerald Joseph   Walsh Bridget

Shopkeepers.

Fitzgerald Joseph, hardware, etc.
Scollard Catherine

Trades.

Madigan John, cooper
O'Connor Patrick, cooper
Scanlan Timothy, smith
Walsh William, cooper

Vintners.

O'Connor Patrick   Walsh Mrs
Scollard Richard

Principal Farmers.

PARISH KILMOYLAN.

Barrett William, Knocknagornagh
Bridgeman Patrick, Finnoo
Connors Edward, Finnoo
Connor Thomas, Cloonlahard
Cregan Denis, Ballyhahill
Cregan John, Ballyhahill
Cummane Mary, Ballyhahill
Cummane Mrs D, Cloonlahard

Cummane Mrs J, Cloonlahard
Cummane Patrick, Cloonlahard
Enright Edmond, Cloonlahard
Enright James, Finnoo
Enright John J, Cloonlahard
Enright Patrick M, Cloonlahard
Enright Patrick P, Cloonlahard
Fitzmaurice John, Ballyhahill
Griffin Patrick, Finnoo
Guiry Michael, Finnoo
Hanley Cornelius, Finnoo
Kennedy Patrick, Ballyhahill
Liston John, Knocknagornagh
Madigan Mrs, Cloonlahard
Martin John, Finnoo
Mulcare Patrick, Cloonlahard
Naughton Patrick, Finnoo
Nolan James, Finnoo
O'Brien Patrick, Ballyhahill
O'Connor James, Ballyhahill
O'Connell J, Knocknagornagh
Riedy Patrick, Cloonlahard
Scollard Patrick, Ballyhahill

PARISH KILFERGUS.

Ambrose Jeremiah, Flean
Houlihan John, Flean
Houlihan Mrs T, Flean
O'Brien Patrick, Flean
Riordan John, Flean
Stanley Joseph, Flean

Ballyheige

(CO. KERRY.)

Post office and parish, 11¼ m. from Tralee and 6 m. from Ardfert. The parish has a population of 2,735, the village 201. It is situated on a bay of the same name on the western coast, and includes within its limits the promontory of Kerry head. There is a large extent of mountain, bog and waste, and from its exposed situation to the Atlantic timber acquires little growth. Several of the low boggy tracts are defended only by sandhills from the eruptions of the sea. Brownstone for building is found near the shore. The strand is about five miles in extent, and when the tide is out from the water's edge to the sand hills is over half-a-mile. The district was formerly in the possession of the ancient clan of the De Cantillons.

Postal address.—**Ballyheige, Tralee.** Ardfert 6 m. nearest money order and telegraph office.

Postmistress—Mary Warren
Conveyances.—Ardfert 6 m. (Limerick and Tralee ry.) nearest station.

Poor Law—Union of Tralee, and Dispensary and Registration district of Ardfert.

Petty Sessions district of Causeway.

Constabulary district of Tralee. In charge of Ballyheige station—
Sergeant Bartholomew Feehan

Coastguards—Division of Ballyheige.
Divisional officer—George Robertson

Gentry, Clergy, etc.

Crosbie Lieut-Col James, D L, J P, Ballyheige castle
Griffin John (agent Col Crosbie)
McCarthy Rev Florence, P P, St Mary's
Pope William, Maulin cottage
Raymond Rev Wm, A B, rector, The Glebe
Robertson George, R N, coastguard officer

Figure 12-2. Guy's Postal Directory of Munster, 1886.

References and Selected Reading

Begley, Donal F., ed. *Irish Genealogy: A Record Finder*. Minneapolis: Irish Books and Media, 1987.

———. *Handbook on Irish Genealogy*. Dublin: Heraldic Artists, 1987.

Grenham, John. *Tracing Your Irish Ancestors: The Complete Guide*. 2d ed. Baltimore: Genealogical Publishing Company, 1999.

Ryan, James G. *Irish Records: Sources for Family and Local History*. Salt Lake City: Ancestry, 1997.

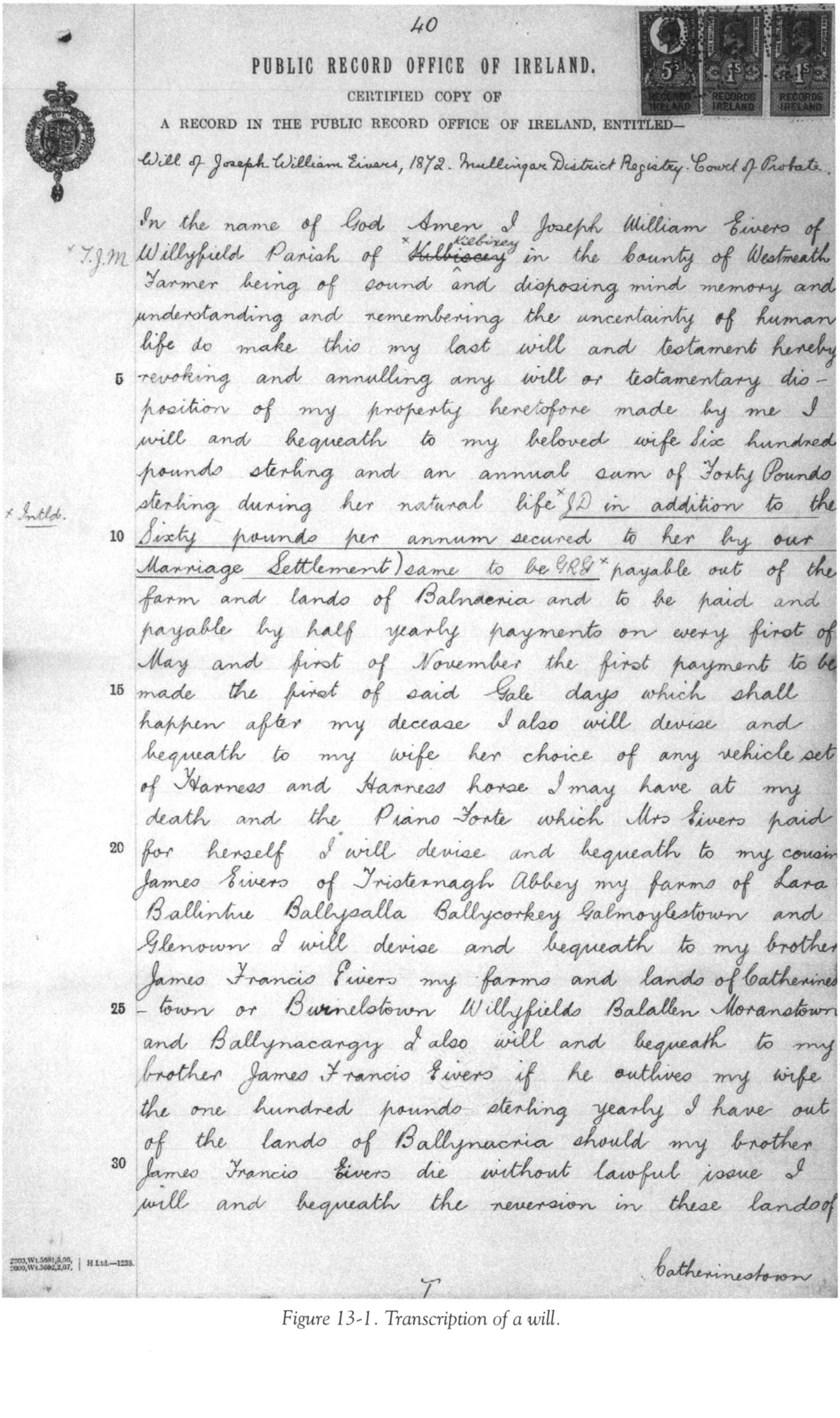

40

PUBLIC RECORD OFFICE OF IRELAND.

CERTIFIED COPY OF

A RECORD IN THE PUBLIC RECORD OFFICE OF IRELAND, ENTITLED—

Will of Joseph William Eivers, 1872. Mullingar District Registry. Court of Probate.

In the name of God Amen I Joseph William Eivers of Willyfield Parish of ~~Kilbiscey~~ ×Kilbixey in the County of Westmeath Farmer being of sound and disposing mind memory and understanding and remembering the uncertainty of human life do make this my last will and testament hereby revoking and annulling any will or testamentary disposition of my property heretofore made by me I will and bequeath to my beloved wife Six hundred pounds sterling and an annual sum of Forty Pounds sterling during her natural life× (J.D in addition to the Sixty pounds per annum secured to her by our Marriage Settlement) same to be GRS× payable out of the farm and lands of Balnacria and to be paid and payable by half yearly payments on every first of May and first of November the first payment to be made the first of said Gale days which shall happen after my decease I also will devise and bequeath to my wife her choice of any vehicle set of Harness and Harness horse I may have at my death and the Piano Forte which Mrs Eivers paid for herself I will devise and bequeath to my cousin James Eivers of Tristernagh Abbey my farms of Lara Ballintue Ballysalla Ballycorkey Galmoylestown and Glenown I will devise and bequeath to my brother James Francis Eivers my farms and lands of Catherines-town or Burnelstown Willyfields Balallen Moranstown and Ballynacargy I also will and bequeath to my brother James Francis Eivers if he outlives my wife the one hundred pounds sterling yearly I have out of the lands of Ballynacria should my brother James Francis Eivers die without lawful issue I will and bequeath the reversion in these lands of

× T.J.M

× Intld.

2200,Wt.5681,3,06, 2000,Wt.5692,2,07, | H Ltd.—1233.

Catherinestown

7

Figure 13-1. Transcription of a will.

13

Wills and Administrations

*But you have gone now, all of you that were so beautiful when you were quick with life.
Yet not gone, for you are still a living truth inside my mind. So how are you dead, my
brothers and sisters, and all of you, when you live with me as surely as I live with myself?*
—Richard Llewellyn, How Green Was My Valley

Wills are a rich source of family history information on individuals who left property
to their heirs (figure 13-1). Most wills name three generations of the family, beginning
with the deceased and naming the surviving spouse, children, and grandchildren.
Many wills convey property to nephews, nieces, and other relatives. The precise legal
language of a will helps ensure that relationships of heirs are clearly stated. Wills may
also mention friends, business associates, and members of the local clergy. Even the
witnesses and executors named in wills are often close relatives.

Did Your Irish Ancestor Leave a Will?

Before the twentieth century most people in Ireland, whether Catholic or Protestant,
were too poor to leave a will. The majority of Irish families rented their house and
property and farmed someone else's land. Nonetheless, your poorer ancestors may be
named in someone else's will. It is worth taking the time to search for any wills or
administrations left by your ancestor's family.

The small percentage of the population who left wills in Ireland were property
owners, usually male members of the upper and middle classes of Irish society. They
were not always wealthy—even if your ancestor had a net worth of just a few pounds
sterling, he might have drawn up a will.

Few married women left wills, as their husbands typically held the property.
However, a widow might have left a substantial estate and listed many family
members in her will.

If your Irish ancestor owned property but died intestate (i.e., without leaving a will),
his estate was handled through Letters of Administration. Administrations named the
next of kin, providing valuable information on family relationships.

If you know when your ancestor died, you can search for a will or letters of administration. Even if you have only a rough idea when your ancestor died, you can search for a will to help identify the date of death. If you find a will or administration, you will learn the date the will was created and the date it was probated (i.e., proven valid in court). Your ancestor will have died between these two dates. Wills were usually probated within a year of death.

The Church of Ireland had responsibility for probating wills and administrations prior to 1858. After 1858, all matters of probate were handled by the government in district registries.

> ## Definitions
> A testator is one who leaves a will. A person who died without leaving a will is said to have died intestate.

Wills Destroyed in the Irish Civil War

The Probate Act of 1857 transferred probate authority from the Church of Ireland to newly established government probate districts. Over the course of time, the Church of Ireland courts transferred their wills and administrations to Dublin, where they were deposited in the Public Record Office. The Public Record Office transcribed these wills and administrations into Will and Grant Books. In 1922, when the Public Record Office was bombed, all the original pre-1858 wills and administrations were destroyed, as were most of the transcribed copies in the Will and Grant Books.

Fortunately, will indexes and administration indexes survived the destruction. Even better, copies of most wills after 1858 were preserved. In addition, tens of thousands of wills probated prior to 1858 have since been collected by the National Archives of Ireland and the Public Record Office of Northern Ireland. Almost all of these wills and indexes are available on microfilm at the Family History Library. You can find these records in the Family History Library Catalog under the headings, *Ireland—Probate Records* and *Ireland—Probate Records—Inventories, Registers, and Catalogs.*

Pre-1858 Wills and Administrations

Between 1536 and 1858, the Church of Ireland was responsible for all wills and administrations in Ireland. Catholics, Anglicans, Presbyterians, and others all had their wills probated in Church of Ireland courts. Each Church of Ireland diocese had its own probate court, called a Consistorial Court. Wills were probated in these Consistorial Courts unless the individual had property worth more than 5 in a second diocese; in this case, the will was probated in the Prerogative Court of Armagh, the highest probate court in Ireland.

To identify the right Consistorial Court, you need to know the Church of Ireland diocese where your ancestor lived. Brian Mitchell's *A New Genealogical Atlas of Ireland* has county maps that associate civil parishes with Church of Ireland dioceses. Use the maps in this book to identify the diocese where your ancestor lived. Once you know your ancestor's diocese, you can search the indexes of the corresponding court to see whether a will was probated or an administration drawn up.

Although most original wills probated before 1858 have been destroyed, some originals, copies, or abstracts do survive. Even the will and administration indexes contain valuable information and should not be overlooked. These probate indexes list the name of the deceased, place of residence, and the year of the will or administration (figure 13-2).

Here are the recommended steps to follow when searching for an Irish will before 1858:

1. Identify or estimate the year your ancestor died before 1858.
2. Find the Church of Ireland diocese (and Consistorial Court) corresponding to your ancestor's civil parish. Brian Mitchell's *A New Genealogical Atlas of Ireland* can help you find the right diocese.
3. Search the Eneclann CD-ROM, *Indexes to Irish Wills, 1484–1858* (which may be purchased online at Ancestry.com or at <www.eneclann.ie>. This CD-ROM indexes over seventy thousand surviving original wills, administrations, transcriptions, and abstracts from this early time period; each of these records has information beyond an entry in a will index.
4. Search for your ancestor's name in the will index of the Consistorial Court, beginning with the year of death and a few subsequent years if necessary.
5. Search the administration index in the same manner.
6. If you suspect your ancestor held property in two dioceses, search the will and administration indexes of the Prerogative Court of Armagh.
7. If you find your ancestor's will or administration in the indexes, look for a copy or abstract on microfilm at the Family History Library.

Post-1858 Wills and Administrations

From 1858 to the present, the government courts have had jurisdiction of wills and administrations. Twelve probate registries were created at this time, the Principle Registry in Dublin and eleven District Registries in Armagh, Ballina, Belfast, Cavan, Cork, Kilkenny, Limerick, Londonderry, Mullingar, Tuam, and Waterford. If your ancestor had a will or administration after 1858, the probate papers would have been filed in the court having jurisdiction where he lived.

All original wills and administrations probated between 1858 and 1900 were destroyed, but transcribed copies exist for the eleven District Registries (even the transcribed copies for the Principle Probate Registry were lost in the fire). All wills since 1904 still exist for all twelve registries. Copies of surviving wills and administrations for the eleven District Registries are available on microfilm at the Family History Library.

Post-1858 Calendars of Wills and Administrations

The Irish government began publishing will calendars annually beginning in 1858. These Irish Will Calendars contain abstracts of all wills and administrations probated

PUBLIC RECORD OFFICE OF IRELAND.

Class.—TESTAMENTARY. *Diocese Ardfert and Aghadoe* Sub-Class.—WILLS

District Registry Cork Bay. Tray.

TESTATOR'S NAME.		RESIDENCE.	YEAR OF PROBATE.	NUMBER.	
Sanders	Robert	Briaghigg, Kerry. Gent.	1729		
Sandes	Fitzmaurice (Rev)	Carrunakilla	1847		
"	Henry	Chanter of Ardfert Cathedral	1714		
"	William	Sallowglin, Kerry	D. 1811		
Saunders	"	Breahig, Kerry	1832, 1844		
Savage	Darby	Castle Island, Kerry. Shopkeeper	1833		
"	Thomas	Tralee. Painter and Glazier	1833		
Savane	Cornelius	Abbeyfeale(?)	1731		
Scanlan	Edmond	Pollough, Kerry. Farmer	1835		
"	Jeremiah	Sronebeg. Farmer	1838		
"	John	Ballinorigg, Kerry	1805		
"	"	Killarney, Kerry. Gent.	1824		
"	"	East Gloura, Galey. Kerry. Lodged	1855	Dated 1840	
"	Maurice	Groumlowrigh, Kerry. Gent.	1839		
"	Michael	Tullyhevell, Kerry. Farmer	1837		

Figure 13-2. Consistorial Court will index.

in the various registries throughout the year (figure 13-3). These abstracts are listed alphabetically by the name of the deceased, with the following information:

- Name of the deceased
- Address
- Occupation
- Date of death
- Date of probate
- Whether a will or administration was filed
- Names and relationships of next of kin
- Value of the estate
- The registry in which the will was proven

Finding an entry in a will calendar clearly provides much genealogical information. If the will was probated in any of the eleven district registries, you may be able to obtain a transcribed copy of the entire will. The will calendars make it very easy to find wills and administrations after 1858. You can search the annual will calendars year-by-year looking for a will or administration. However, a general index exists for the years 1858 through 1877, expediting the search for these decades. Annual will calendars and the general index are available on microfilm at the Family History Library. The Ulster Historical Foundation has also created a consolidated index for the years 1878 through 1900.

In Summary

Wills are an extremely valuable source of genealogical information about families who left estates to their heirs. Will calendars and indexes provide many details about the deceased and next of kin. The wills themselves often yield enough information on families to construct pedigree charts showing relationships for three generations. Your ancestor's will might also shed light on his character and how he regarded those closest to him at the end of his life.

References and Selected Reading

Mitchell, Brian. *A New Genealogical Atlas of Ireland.* 2d ed. Baltimore: Genealogical Publishing Company, 2002.

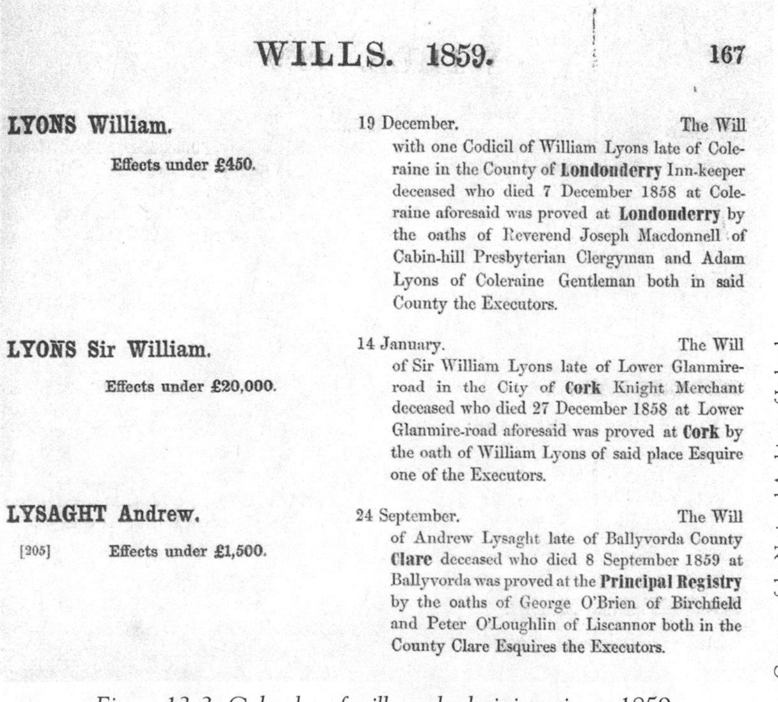

WILLS. 1859. 167

LYONS William.
Effects under £450.

19 December. The Will with one Codicil of William Lyons late of Coleraine in the County of **Londonderry** Inn-keeper deceased who died 7 December 1858 at Coleraine aforesaid was proved at **Londonderry** by the oaths of Reverend Joseph Macdonnell of Cabin-hill Presbyterian Clergyman and Adam Lyons of Coleraine Gentleman both in said County the Executors.

LYONS Sir William.
Effects under £20,000.

14 January. The Will of Sir William Lyons late of Lower Glanmire-road in the City of **Cork** Knight Merchant deceased who died 27 December 1858 at Lower Glanmire-road aforesaid was proved at **Cork** by the oath of William Lyons of said place Esquire one of the Executors.

LYSAGHT Andrew.
[205] Effects under £1,500.

24 September. The Will of Andrew Lysaght late of Ballyvorda County **Clare** deceased who died 8 September 1859 at Ballyvorda was proved at the **Principal Registry** by the oaths of George O'Brien of Birchfield and Peter O'Loughlin of Liscannor both in the County Clare Esquires the Executors.

Figure 13-3. Calendar of wills and administrations, 1859.

Courtesy of the National Archives of Ireland

REGISTER OF INFANTS IN *Ballybough* NATIONAL SCHOOL.

Date of Entrance, 18 72.	Register Number.	Pupils' Names.	Age of Pupil last Birth Day.	Religious Denomination.	Residence.	Occupation or Means of Living of Parents.	Annual Examination.						Page of Register to which Transferred.
							First.		Second.		Third.		
							No. of Days Present.	Result.	No. of Days Present.	Result.	No. of Days Present.	Result.	
18.11.'72	56												
1.3.'73	58								118	X	130	X	13
21.4.'73	59												
21.4.'73	60												
21.4.'73	61												
21.4.'73	62												
5.5.'73	63												
12.5.'73	64										183	X	14
19.5.'73	65												17
19.5.'73	66												
19.5.'73	67												
19.5.'73	68												
9.6.'73	69						114	X	193	X			
9.6.'73	70												

Figure 14-1. Register from Ballybough National School.

National School Registers

I have never let my schooling interfere with my education.
—Mark Twain

Education is not the filling of a pail, but the lighting of a fire.
—William Butler Yeats

Irish schools often kept detailed records of their students—some of these records even predate civil registration. You can use school registers to identify precise places of residence, establish the birth dates of schoolchildren, and learn the occupations of their fathers. You may even learn how well your ancestors did in school!

In 1831 the Irish national school system was organized, built on principles and practices of the Kildare Place Society, an organization devoted to educating the poor in Ireland. Thousands of national schools were established in the 1830s, with hundreds of thousands of students in attendance. By the early twentieth century, almost one million students ages three to nineteen were enrolled in national schools. These national schools were designed to allow students of all religious backgrounds to attend.

Genealogical Details in National School Registers

Most national school registers provided an alphabetical index of pupils and a detailed register (figure 14-1). The register typically contained, as a minimum, each pupil's full name, date of entrance, age, residence, parents' occupation, and the date the pupil left the school. The registers also describe the pupil's attendance, subjects studied, and performance on examinations.

Some national school registers also indicate the pupil's month and year of birth, religious denomination, character, previous school attended, cause of removal, and destination. Under the column entitled "Character of pupil, cause of withdrawal, and destination" typical comments range from "rather dull, working in a foundry" to "a very smart boy, left to learn classics." Sometimes the school register indicates that the family moved to another part of Ireland, as in "removed to Cavan with the family" or "appointed P. teacher in Belfast." Some entries provide emigration information, as in "removed to England" or "gone to New Zealand." Each of these entries also provides the date the pupil's name was "struck off" the register, indicating a date and destination of emigration from Ireland.

Other national school registers have three parts: an index, a summary register, and a detailed register. The detailed register lists five pupils per page. The top section of the page shows each pupil's date of entrance, full name, age at last birthday, religious denomination, residence, occupation of parents, and the school previously attended. This last item can help you trace a family to their previous residence. The bottom section of the page shows many details of each pupil's academic progress, year by year, including grades for the following subjects: reading, spelling, writing, arithmetic, grammar, geography, and needlework. These academic progress reports also mention whether the students received scholarships for excellence in their studies. This kind of extra information adds flesh to the bones of your family history.

Availability of National School Registers

The Public Record Office of Northern Ireland has collected and microfilmed the registers of about fifteen hundred national schools in Northern Ireland. Records for some schools begin as early as the 1840s and 1850s, with many extending into the 1920s and later. Copies of these school registers are also available on microfilm at the Family History Library for three of the five school districts. The Public Record Office of Northern Ireland <www.proni.gov.uk> has published an excellent handbook for these records, entitled *Guide to Educational Records*. This book is also available at the Family History Library.

While many national school registers also exist in the Republic of Ireland, most of them remain in local custody. Some schools currently in operation still have their old registers from the 1800s. Parish priests hold some national school registers. Dozens of national school registers have been submitted to the National Archives of Ireland by the Department of Education or by private donation. Some of these national school registers have been microfilmed and are available at the Family History Library. To view a current list of national school registers by county for the Republic of Ireland, visit the National Archives website at <www.nationalarchives.ie/topics/Nat_Schools/ns.html>.

In Summary

National school registers offer details on each of the schoolchildren in the family from the early to mid-1800s onward. The occasional mention of a child's graduation and occupation or the family's removal or emigration, makes these school records an invaluable source for Irish family history.

References and Selected Reading

Maxwell, Ian. *Tracing Your Ancestors in Northern Ireland: A Guide to Ancestry Research in the Public Record Office of Northern Ireland*. Edinburgh: Stationery Office, 1997.

Public Record Office of Northern Ireland. *Guide to Educational Records*. Belfast: Public Record Office of Northern Ireland, 1993.

Occupation Records

No man is an Ireland.
    —Chicago Mayor Richard Daley

A number of records of genealogical value exist for certain occupations in Ireland. Among the most well-documented ranks, professions, and occupations are constables, aristocracy and gentry, clergy, doctors, flax weavers, merchants, postal workers, railway workers, seamen, and teachers. If your ancestor was a craftsman or merchant, especially in a large city, he may have been a member of a craft or trade guild. Guilds often kept records of their membership. Some professions maintained fairly detailed records of their members, supplying genealogists with birth and marriage information, details on spouses and children, and more.

What Was Your Ancestor's Occupation?

You can learn what your ancestor did for a living by finding his marriage and death certificates in civil registration. The birth and marriage certificates of his children will also tell you his profession. Beyond civil registration, censuses also identify the occupations of everyone in the family. You should check each of these sources—sometimes different occupations appear on different records for the same person.

To learn more about your ancestor's occupation, consult commercial and social directories. These sources are especially useful if you know your ancestor was a merchant or tradesman and if you would like to know more specific details about the nature of his profession and where he worked. Many Irish directories list people by occupation and address, especially in the larger cities. See Chapter 12, "Commercial and Social Directories," for more details.

Once you know your ancestor's occupation, you can search for records that might have been kept describing him and his employment. Depending on your ancestor's profession, you may find employment records, service records, pension papers, guild memberships, or other documents of value. To illustrate the genealogical richness of occupation records, a few professions with excellent records are listed below, including constables, teachers, and tradesmen.

Royal Irish Constabulary

Service records for constables begin as early as 1816, when the police force was known as the Peace Preservation Force. Twenty years later, this organization was dubbed the Irish Constabulary, receiving its Royal status somewhat later. The service records of each constable have recently been indexed, making these records very easy to search. The original service records are available at the National Archives in Kew, England, while microfilm copies are available at the Family History Library. An online index to the Royal Irish Constabulary service records, from 1816 to 1921, is available at Ancestry.com.

These details are listed in each constable's service record with the Royal Irish Constabulary (figure 15-1):

- Full name
- Age (at least in years, often with quarters or months specified)
- Height (very specific, to the quarter inch, as there was a height requirement for service)
- Religion
- Native county (could not serve in same county as relatives)
- Trade or profession before joining
- Marital status (often the exact date of marriage is provided)
- Native county of wife (could not serve in same county as relatives)
- Date of appointment
- Details on each term of service (usually the county and transfer date are listed, with rank)
- Promotions, penalties, decorations
- Date of retirement
- Date of pension (the pensions are available at the National Archives in Kew, England)
- Date of death

There is an incredible amount of genealogy in these service records, from the constable's age, birthplace, and marriage date to the list of places where his family lived over the years.

I have a personal example to show how useful these service records can be. From family papers and military papers I learned that my great-grandfather John Love was a constable. I searched the Royal Irish Constabulary index on Ancestry.com and found two entries for John Love. Both men were born around the right time period to be my great-grandfather. This database gave me the Family History Library microfilm number (FHL 856067) and page number for each entry. I looked up the two service records and immediately identified one as my great-grandfather.

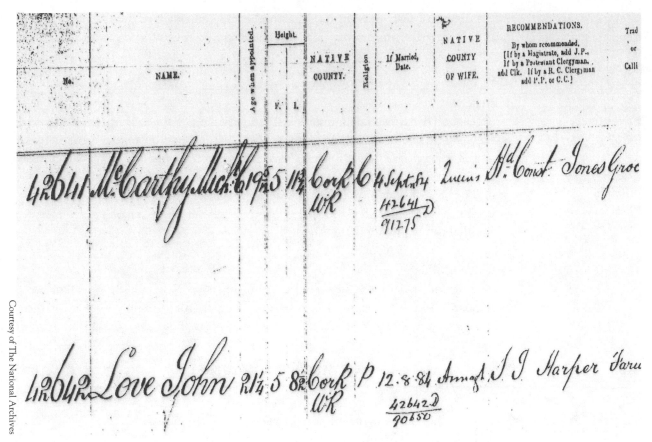

Courtesy of The National Archives

Figure 15-1. Royal Irish Constabulary service record.

I found his marriage date, approximate birth date, county of birth, wife's county of birth, and the locations where the family lived for over a decade. This single document led me to birth certificates, a marriage certificate, parish registers, and a pension record.

For more information on the Royal Irish Constabulary, I recommend Jim Herlihy's *The Royal Irish Constabulary: A Short History and Geographical Guide*.

Teachers

School records furnish valuable details about teachers. For example, if your ancestor was either a schoolmaster or schoolmistress in the early 1800s, check the 1826 publication entitled "Second Report of the Commissioners of Irish Education Inquiry" (figure 15-2). All teachers are listed by county, barony, and civil parish, with such details as:

- County, barony, civil parish, and townland at which the school is held
- Name of master or mistress of the school
- Religion of master or mistress
- Free or pay school
- Total annual income of master or mistress, arising in all ways from the school

- Physical description of the schoolhouse and probable cost thereof
- Number of pupils in attendance, enumerated by religion and gender
- Societies, associations, churches, and patrons connected with the school

Many of these details are useful even if your ancestor attended the school as a student.

Teachers had to attend training courses and teach under supervision for a time before they could receive a teaching certificate authorizing them to teach in the national school system. The Public Record Office of Northern Ireland has compiled an index to records of qualified teachers spanning two decades, under the title "An Index of Teachers Qualified to Teach at Training Colleges (1893–1907) and of Teachers Qualified to Teach Irish (1895–1912)." You can search this index on microfilm at the Family History Library (FHL 993558).

Trade Guilds

Craft and trade guilds supported their membership by establishing workmanship standards, enrolling apprentices, and providing training. Guilds were created for many crafts and trades. Apothecaries, barber surgeons, butchers, goldsmiths, masons,

Appendix, N° 22.—PAROCHIAL RETURNS:

24. COUNTY OF KERRY—continued. BARONY and PARISH.	DIOCESE.	NAME of Townland or Place, at which the School is held.	NAME of MASTER or MISTRESS.	RELIGION of Master or Mistress.	FREE or PAY SCHOOL.	TOTAL Annual INCOME of Master or Mistress, arising in all ways from the School.	DESCRIPTION of the SCHOOL-HOUSE, and probable COST thereof.
CORCAGUINNY—continued.							
Dingle	Ardfert	Dingle	James Parker	protestant	pay	about 10l.	clay mortar and stone; about 10l.
		—	Thomas Fitzgerald	R. catholic	pay	uncertain	stone and mud mortar; about 18l.
		—	Honora O'Keeffe	protestant	pay	7/7 p' quarter for each pupil.	stone and mud mortar; about 20l.
Donquin		Ballyikeen	James Russell	Wesleyan methodist.	free	21 l.	stone and mud; about 8l.
Dunartin		Boulteen	Maurice Fitzgerald	R. catholic	pay	about 15l.	stone and mud mortar; 8l. or 9l.
Kilgobbin		Knockglass	Michael Brennan	R. catholic	pay	about 9 l.	stone and mud mortar, thatched; about 6l.
		Garrahees	Morty O'Connell	R. catholic	pay	about 10l.	stone and mud mortar, thatched; from 6l. to 10l.

Figure 15-2. 1826 census of National School teachers.

merchants, stationers, shipwrights, tailors, and weavers all had their own guilds to strengthen their professions. There were also military and religious guilds. The majority of guild members were Protestant, although some Catholics did join guilds. Most guilds in Ireland were established in Dublin, with craft or trade guilds being the most numerous. Guilds often kept meticulous records of their membership, supplying the modern genealogist with family history details about early ancestors.

What kinds of guild records would you expect to find on your craftsman or merchant ancestor? Guilds kept membership records, minute books, and account books. You may find your ancestor in these records, along with his professional associates, business partners, and competitors. You may learn about how he became a member of his guild, whether it was because his father, grandfather, or father-in-law practiced the same craft or trade.

You can learn about the daily life of your ancestor as you study his profession and learn about his guild. Even if you do not find your ancestor in guild records, you may still benefit from learning about his occupation and related guilds.

Other Occupational Records

If your ancestor served in the military, you may find rich sources of genealogical information documenting his service. Many Irishmen served in the British Army and Navy. There are numerous military documents such as pensions and discharge records that contain information of great worth to family historians. Most of these military papers are found at the National Archives in Kew, England.

If any of your Irish kin were in the clergy, you may find biographical information about them in the many Catholic, Church of Ireland, or Presbyterian church directories.

Many other occupations and professions have kept records of genealogical value. If your ancestor was in the printing trade, his own name might be preserved in print as well. Men in the printing trade are listed in Robert Munter's *A Dictionary of the Print Trade in Ireland, 1550–1775*. Some of the specific occupations mentioned in this compilation are booksellers, bookbinders, engravers, publishers, printers, stationers, papermakers, printsellers, and typefounders.

Finding Occupation Records

To find occupation records on your Irish ancestors, try searching the Family History Library Catalog (see Chapter 17, "The Family History Library," for instructions on using the catalog). The catalog usually lists occupation records under the following topic categories:

- Business records and commerce
- Church directories
- Directories
- Military history
- Military records
- Nobility
- Occupations
- Officials and employees
- Pensions
- Politics and government
- Religion and religious life
- Schools

In Summary

Occupation records might tell you where your ancestor lived, the names of family members, birth and marriage information, and more—it all depends on the particular occupation and the kinds of records that were kept. While a small farmer typically left little indication of his presence except in church, land, census, and civil records, people of many other occupations left paper trails created by their employer, the government, or their guild. The information preserved in these records might yield the genealogical clues you seek.

References and Selected Reading

Clark, Mary, and Raymond Refaussé, eds. *Directory of Historic Dublin Guilds*. Dublin: Dublin Public Libraries, 1993.

Herlihy, Jim. *The Royal Irish Constabulary: A Short History and Geographical Guide*. Dublin: Four Courts Press, 1997.

Munter, Robert. *A Dictionary of the Print Trade in Ireland, 1550–1775*. New York: Fordham University Press, 1988.

Internet Sites

It is not a secret if it is known by three people.
—*Irish proverb*

The Internet has fundamentally changed family history research. Billions of genealogy records are now accessible from home through the Internet, with millions of new records added daily. Genealogy is one of the most popular activities on the Internet, with tens of millions of people researching their ancestry online every month. Many of the family history records and researchers on the Internet are Irish. This chapter provides an introduction to some of the best Irish family history resources on the Internet.

Where to Start

There are lots of ways to find your Irish ancestors using the Web. Here are a few recommended activities:

- Search the best Irish family history websites
- Search the mega-genealogy websites
- Collaborate with Irish cousins using genealogy message boards
- Surf the entire Web for your Irish ancestors
- Find records in the Family History Library Catalog (see Chapter 17, "The Family History Library")

Search the Best Irish Family History Websites

A good genealogy website will help you along in your family history by showing you records on your ancestors, pointing you to other record sources, teaching you the nuances of research, or connecting you with other people researching your family lines. Each of the best Irish family history websites has strengths in one or more of these areas. Here are a few of the top websites for Irish genealogy:

Cyndi's List—Ireland and Northern Ireland
<www.cyndislist.com/ireland.htm>

While not an Irish website per se, Cyndi's List is the largest directory of genealogy and family history on the Internet. This website, created by Cyndi Howells, can help you find virtually everything about genealogy, whether online or offline. The huge section on Ireland and Northern Ireland has links to hundreds of websites that specialize in Irish family history. This is a great place to start if you want to explore the breadth of Irish family history on the Internet.

American Family Immigration History Center
<www.ellisisland.org>

Over 22 million people arrived in Ellis Island between 1892 and 1924. Many were Irish immigrants beginning a new life in America. The LDS Church indexed the names of all these Ellis Island immigrants from microfilms of the original passenger lists. The resulting computer database captures the greatest migration in recent history. Once you find your immigrant ancestor, you can view the original ship's manifest and discover your ancestor's birthplace, occupation, height, eye color, and cash on hand when disembarking at the port of New York. This collection of passenger records and ships' photos is the best immigration database ever created.

Irish Ancestors
<www.ireland.com/ancestor>

Much of John Grenham's classic how-to book, *Tracing Your Irish Ancestors*, has been converted to online articles on this website. Search this site to learn about Irish records in greater detail. You can also learn about specific record sources for each county in Ireland. Some databases and services are also available for a fee.

IrelandGenWeb Project
<www.irelandgenweb.com>

The IrelandGenWeb Project is part of WorldGenWeb, a grass-roots effort to build communities of family historians all around the world dedicated to local genealogical research. IrelandGenWeb is particularly focused on promoting websites for each of the thirty-two counties of Ireland and Northern Ireland. These county websites feature genealogical databases, research guides, and useful links centered on local family history.

The Irish Ancestral Research Association (TIARA)
<http://tiara.ie>

According to the home page of this website, "TIARA is a nonprofit organization established to develop and promote the growth, study and exchange of ideas among people and organizations interested in Irish genealogy and historical research and education." This website has many articles and links to Irish genealogy topics.

GENUKI
<www.genuki.org.uk>

GENUKI stands for "UK and Ireland Genealogy." The service was created to be a "virtual reference library," especially designed to help people researching their ancestors from England, Ireland, Scotland, Wales, the Channel Islands, and the Isle of Man.

Irish Family History Foundation
<www.irishroots.net>

The Irish Family History Foundation coordinates dozens of genealogy Heritage Centres in Ireland and Northern Ireland. These centres have indexed and computerized millions of genealogical records from parish registers, land records, censuses, civil registration, cemetery records, and more. This website is a gateway to the Heritage Centres for the thirty-two counties (see Chapter 18, "Irish Heritage Centres").

Irish Origins
<www.irishorigins.com>

Irish Origins offers many valuable collections of Irish genealogy online, including Griffith's Valuation, Griffith's survey maps, an 1851 census of Dublin City, the William Smith O'Brien Petition, an index of Irish wills, some Irish passenger list abstracts, and other premium databases for Irish genealogists. Many of these collections are accompanied by digital images of original documents.

Otherdays.com
<www.otherdays.com>

A relatively new website, Otherdays.com is building a good collection of online resources for Irish family history. The website has a number of searchable databases of Irish records, including a name index to Griffith's Valuation. Each name links to a digital image of the corresponding page of Griffith's Valuation. Each of these pages in turn links to a digital image of the associated Ordnance Survey map. New content is added regularly. This website offers access to Irish family history resources for a fee.

Irish Genealogical Society, Int'l
<www.rootsweb.com/~irish>

The Irish Genealogical Society is a non-profit, Minnesota-based organization dedicated to helping its members in finding their Irish and Scotch-Irish ancestors. The society publishes a journal, *The Septs*, which covers a wide variety of topics emphasizing Irish records and genealogical research standards. The website has articles, research guides, and basic genealogical information to help family historians get started with their Irish research.

Irish Genealogy
<www.irishgenealogy.ie>

Irish Genealogy allows you to search indexes of computerized records from many Irish Heritage Centres. Currently, eleven counties in Ireland are represented in this database: Armagh, Cavan, Derry (Londonderry), Donegal, Fermanagh, Leitrim, Limerick, Mayo, Sligo, Tyrone, and Wexford. More counties will be added to this index over time. You can search the index for free and see the basic details of records matching your query. To see complete details of these records, you can request the information, for a fee, from the corresponding Heritage Centre (see Chapter 18, "Irish Heritage Centres").

Eneclann

<www.eneclann.ie>

Eneclann is the largest family history research firm in Ireland. The research service is of the highest caliber. Eneclann is also involved in a number of unique digitization and indexing projects at major archives and libraries in Ireland. A number of record collections digitized by Eneclann are searchable for a fee on Irish Origins <www. irishorigins.com> (see above).

Search the Mega-Genealogy Websites

Three genealogy websites have each compiled searchable databases containing over one billion names. Ancestry.com is the largest, followed by Genealogy.com and FamilySearch <www.familysearch.org>. Each of these websites has millions of genealogy records on Irish and Irish-American families. On Ancestry.com and Genealogy.com, many of the most valuable collections have digital images of original sources; once you find your ancestor in one of these name indexes, you can click to view a digital image of the historical document. A fourth website, RootsWeb.com, deserves special mention because it provides access to hundreds of millions of records assembled in family trees.

Ancestry.com

<www.ancestry.com>

Ancestry.com has the largest collection of family history records on the Internet, with over two billion names. The *Ancestry World Tree* is the largest database of family trees in the world, with many hundreds of millions of names connected through the generations. Ancestry.com also offers Family Tree Maker™, the best-selling genealogy program in the world. Family Tree Maker™ can automatically search databases on Ancestry.com to find people in your family tree.

Ancestry.com has digitized and indexed all U.S. censuses, from 1790 to 1930. The website also has a huge U.S. records collection, a growing collection of U.K. and Ireland content, and a new set of passenger lists to help trace ancestors back to the old world. Ancestry.com adds new databases every day, averaging millions of new records each week.

The following record collections are representative of the kinds of genealogy sources available on Ancestry.com to help you trace your Irish ancestry. Some of these databases come from Irish records, some contain information on Irish immigrants arriving in America, and others provide details about Americans of Irish birth:

- U.S. Federal Census images and indexes, 1790–1930
- New York Passenger Lists, 1851–91
- New York, 1820–50 Passenger and Immigration Lists
- Boston, 1821–50 Passenger and Immigration Lists
- Philadelphia, 1800–50 Passenger and Immigration Lists
- Ireland 1766 Religious Census
- Irish Immigrants: New York Port Arrival Records, 1846–51
- Ireland Householder's Index, County Antrim

- Antrim, Ireland: Parish and Probate Records
- Down, Ireland: Parish and Probate Records
- Irish Marriages, 1771–1812
- Irish Records Extraction Database
- Louth, Ireland: Parish and Probate Records
- Ireland Biography and History
- Burke's Commoners of Great Britain and Ireland
- World War I Draft Registration Cards, 1917–18
- General Armory of England, Scotland, Ireland, and Wales
- Great Britain and Ireland: Picturesque Views of County Seats, Volume I-VI
- Ireland Visitation
- Irish Landed Gentry
- Irish Records Index, 1500–1920
- Irish Settlers in North America before 1850
- Landed Gentry of Great Britain and Ireland
- New England Irish Pioneers
- Scots-Irish: The Scot in North Britain, North Ireland and North America, Volumes 1 and 2
- Irish Quaker Immigration into Pennsylvania
- Ship Passenger Lists from Ireland to America: Miscellaneous Ships
- Ship Passenger Lists to New York: Miscellaneous Ships
- Irish Flax Growers List, 1796
- Ireland, The Royal Irish Constabulary, 1816–1921
- New York Emigrant Savings Bank, 1850–83

Genealogy.com

<*www.genealogy.com*>

Genealogy.com offers a wide variety of family history collections, from census to immigration records, online family history books, family trees, and an excellent collection of U.S. records. Most of the contents on this website require a subscription fee.

Major Irish collections searchable for a fee on Genealogy.com include:

- Irish and British Immigrants to America, 1860s–1870s Passenger and Immigration Lists
- Irish and British Immigrants to America, 1870–72, Volume 2
- Index to Griffith's Valuation of Ireland, 1848–64
- Ireland, 1831–41 Census Index
- Irish Flax Grower's List, 1796 International Land Records
- Scotch-Irish Settlers in America, 1500s–1800s Immigration Records
- Tithe Applotment Books of Ireland, 1823–38 (for the six counties of Northern Ireland)

FamilySearch

<www.familysearch.org>

This is the family history website of The Church of Jesus Christ of Latter-day Saints. With over a billion online records and an online catalog of the largest family history collection (and largest Irish genealogy collection) on the planet, you will find this website an indispensable resource for finding your Irish ancestors. The website is covered in detail in Chapter 17, "The Family History Library."

RootsWeb.com

<www.rootsweb.com>

RootsWeb.com is one of the oldest genealogy websites in existence, and all the contents are free. RootsWeb WorldConnect is a database of family trees submitted by hundreds of thousands of genealogy enthusiasts. Many of these family trees have Irish branches. RootsWeb has a number of unique family history databases, including thousands of message boards to help people work together in their family history.

Collaborate with Irish Cousins Using Genealogy Message Boards

Let's suppose a husband and wife in your ancestry gave birth to five children around the year 1820. Let's say each of their children had five children about thirty years later, and this pattern continued until the present time. How many descendants would the original couple now have? About 98,000! How many of these descendants would still be alive today? About 94,000! That's roughly how many living cousins you might have who descend from just one couple two hundred years back in your Irish ancestry. Many of these living relatives are also doing family history and would be thrilled to meet you, their cousin.

The Internet can connect you with distant and not-so-distant cousins and help you collaborate with them to find your shared ancestry. People learning about their family history are universally willing to share what they have found with others. Working with others increases the momentum and potential of your efforts.

Some of your cousins have already made some exciting discoveries about your ancestry. Others are currently searching, as you are. Some will begin looking into their family history, your family history, in the next few months or years. The Internet is one of the best ways to find living relatives and combine your efforts to find your Irish ancestors together. You can use message boards to connect with other researchers interested in the same ancestors and localities.

The largest and most popular family history message boards on the Web are found on Ancestry.com, RootsWeb.com, and Genealogy.com. Millions of messages have been submitted over the years, as people have shared their questions about their family history and connected with others who can help them out.

How to Craft a Message Others Will Find on the Message Boards

The best way to ask others for help with your family history is to post a query (or genealogy question) on a popular genealogy message board. Put a name, date range, and place in a message title, like this: "George Gilbert

> ↓
> **Internet**
>
> The best way to ask others for help with your family history is to post a query (or genealogy question) on a popular genealogy message board.

Love, born 1893, County Longford." In the body of your message, be concise while providing enough detail so that others will find your message. The best way to get a quick response is to reply to an existing message that may relate to the individual or family you are researching.

I have received excellent responses packed with information about my ancestors within hours of my original posts. Most replies come within a week, as people have time to find and respond to my messages. Some responses come years later and are well worth the wait.

Ancestry.com and Genealogy.com have the largest, most active genealogy message boards on the Web. These websites are a great starting point for broadcasting all your most challenging family history questions to a wide audience. Once you have posted a few of your Irish genealogy messages, just sit back and wait for others to respond.

Surf the Entire Web for Your Irish Ancestors

There are literally thousands of Irish family history websites. Finding your Irish ancestors online might seem like an impossible task considering the enormity of the Internet. How do you find all the Irish genealogy websites, and how do you search these quickly to find your ancestors? Search engines are the answer.

A search engine is a tool to find whatever you are looking for anywhere on the Web. Most search engines have you type in a word or two describing what you want to find—then they show you matching pages found across the entire Web. Google, Yahoo, and AltaVista are a few examples of successful search engines on the Internet. Since Google is currently the most popular and powerful search engine, and it's very easy to use, we will focus on searching the Web using Google. The search techniques we will demonstrate can be used with other search engines.

Here's a quick way to search for an Irish ancestor using Google:

1. Get on the Internet and go to <www.google.com>.
2. Type your ancestor's surname, followed by a space.
3. Type the word "genealogy."
4. Click the Search button.

You may be surprised at the large number of matching pages Google finds. The list of matches includes pages that contain your ancestor's surname and the word "genealogy." The pages are sorted by relevance, with the best pages usually listed first. Google has scanned a large percentage of the websites on the Internet and done the homework for you, finding every occurrence of your ancestor's name on millions of Web pages.

If Google returns a Web page that looks like a good match, click on that page and scan for details on your ancestor. If your first search is not productive, you will want to focus your search more precisely. You can do this by following these steps, or something similar:

1. Type your ancestor's surname, followed by a space.
2. Type your ancestor's spouse's surname.
3. Click the Search button.

This search will return Web pages listing both surnames—this is a great way to search for a marriage. If you get too many poor-quality matches, you may want to add more words to your search, like "genealogy" or "family history."

Fewer matches appear as you add more words to your searches, but the matches may be closer to what you are looking for. Try various combinations of names, places, and terms like "genealogy" or "family" until you begin to see quality matches appearing. This is how to do a basic search of the Web for your ancestors.

If you want to squeeze the best genealogy out of Internet search engines, you can try doing some power searches. For example, if your search for the name "Murphy" returns too many tens of thousands of results, try typing in the first and last name of your ancestor in quotes (e.g., "John Murphy"), then click the Search button. By using quotes, you are telling the search engine that you want to find all occurrences of the name "John Murphy" written exactly as you specified, with the first name followed by a space followed by the last name. Have some fun with the various combinations of your family names, using dates, places, and other details to refine your search.

One of the first things you will notice is that the same websites appear again and again in your search results. A number of large genealogy websites, many with a particular focus on Irish families, will consistently percolate to the top of your search results. This is not a coincidence—these websites have lots to offer as you do your Irish family history. Spend some time on each of these websites. Look beyond the pages you landed on and see what else these websites have to offer. Bookmark these websites in your browser so you can easily find them later.

In Summary

Irish family history is blossoming on the Internet. With so many people tracing their Irish roots online, so many Irish genealogy databases online, and an ever-growing collection of online images of Irish genealogy sources, there has never been a better time to use the Internet to find your Irish ancestors.

References and Further Reading

Howells, Cyndi. *Cyndi's List, A Comprehensive List of 70,000 Genealogy Sites on the Internet.* 2d ed. 2 vols. Baltimore: Genealogical Publishing Company, 2001.

———. *Netting Your Ancestors: Genealogical Research on the Internet.* Baltimore: Genealogical Publishing Company, 1999.

Porter, Pamela, and Amy Johnson Crow. *Online Roots: How to Discover Your Family's History and Heritage with the Power of the Internet.* Nashville: Rutledge Hill Press, 2003.

Raymond, Stuart A. *Irish Family History on the Web.* 2d ed. Bury, Lancashire, England: Federation of Family History Societies, 2004.

Warren, Paula Stuart, and James W. Warren. *Your Guide to the Family History Library.* Cincinnati: Betterway Books, 2001.

The Family History Library

And he shall turn the heart of the fathers to the children, and the heart of the children to their fathers.

—*Malachi 4:6*

The Family History Library has the most comprehensive collection of Irish genealogy in the world. In fact, the Family History Library houses the world's largest collection of family history, period. Every year almost one million people from around the world travel to Salt Lake City, Utah, to visit the Family History Library and discover their roots.

The Family History Library also has thousands of branch libraries known as Family History Centers in many parts of the world. Many people visit their local Family History Centers to learn more about their ancestors.

The Genealogical Society of Utah began microfilming records for the library in 1938. Hundreds of microfilming projects are currently underway around the world. The master microfilms are stored in a climate-controlled vault carved out of a mountain in Little Cottonwood Canyon, near Salt Lake City. This facility, the Granite Mountain Records Vault, preserves over 2.4 million microfilms acquired over the decades. Copies of most of these microfilms are available to the public at the Family History Library.

Most rolls of microfilm in the library contain unpublished documents such as church records, census records, vital records, land records, and court documents. Many microfilms also contain published works like family history books, county and town histories, census indexes, and genealogy how-to guides.

The Family History Library has genealogy consultants on the staff with expertise in many countries of the world. The staff at the British Reference Desk can help you with any research questions you have about Irish family history.

Beyond Irish records, the Family History Library also contains some of the best collections of American, British, Canadian, and Australian family history available anywhere in the world. If you are working on tracing your immigrant ancestor back to Ireland, the Family History Library has excellent resources to help you achieve your goal.

Irish Records Collections at the FHL

Over the years, the Genealogical Society of Utah has microfilmed records at many archives and libraries in Ireland, including the Genealogical Office, the General Register Office in Dublin, the General Register Office of Northern Ireland, the National Archives of Ireland, the National Library of Ireland, the Public Record Office of Northern Ireland, the Registry of Deeds, and the Valuation Office. All types of Irish records discussed in this book are available at the Family History Library. The details are outlined in table 17-1.

> **↓**
> **Library Tip**
>
> All types of Irish records discussed in this book are available at the Family History Library.

The Family History Library Catalog

The Family History Library Catalog is the key to finding collections in the Family History Library.

Most Irish records are fairly easy to find in the catalog. You can search the catalog by place, surname, keyword, title, film/fiche number, author, subject, and call number. Most of the time you will search by place to find the Irish records where your ancestors lived.

The Family History Library Catalog lists Irish records by country, county, or civil parish, depending on the specific record collection. For example, if you were searching for your Irish ancestors in Abbeylara, County Longford, you would find some records under *Ireland*, some under *Ireland, Longford*, and some under *Ireland, Longford, Abbeylara*. It is important to search under each level of locality.

Within each locality, the records are organized by topic. Some of the more important categories of Irish records are:

- Archives and libraries
- Bibliography
- Biography
- Business records and commerce
- Cemeteries
- Census
- Church directories
- Church history
- Church records
- Civil registration
- Court records
- Description and travel
- Directories
- Dwellings
- Emigration and immigration
- Gazetteers
- Genealogy
- History
- Land and property
- Maps
- Military history
- Military records
- Names, geographical
- Names, personal
- Newspapers
- Nobility
- Obituaries
- Occupations
- Officials and employees
- Orphans and orphanages
- Pensions
- Periodicals
- Politics and government
- Poorhouses, poor law, etc.
- Probate records
- Public records
- Religion and religious life
- Schools
- Social life and customs
- Societies
- Taxation
- Vital records
- Voting registers

Table 17-1: Irish Genealogy Sources at the Family History Library

Record Type	Available at the Family History Library	Only Available Elsewhere

Civil Registration	For all Ireland (before 1922):
	    Birth indexes, 1864–1921
	    Birth registers, 1864–March 1881; 1900–13
	    Non-Catholic marriage indexes, 1845–63
	    Marriage indexes, 1864–1921
	    Marriage registers, 1845–70
	    Death indexes, 1864–1921
	    Death registers, 1864–70
	
	For the Republic of Ireland:
	    Birth indexes, 1922–58
	    Birth registers, 1930–55
	    Marriage indexes, 1922–58
	    Death indexes, 1922–58
	
	For Northern Ireland:
	    Birth, marriage, and death indexes, 1922–59
	    Birth, marriage, and death registers, 1922–59
		For all Ireland (before 1922):
		    Birth registers, June 1881–99
		    Birth registers, 1914–21
		    Marriage registers, 1871–1921
		    Death registers, 1871–1921
		
		For the Republic of Ireland:
		    Birth registers, 1922–29
		    Birth registers, 1956–present
		    Marriage registers, 1922–present
		    Death registers, 1922–present
		
		For Northern Ireland:
		    Indexes, 1960–present
		    Registers, 1960–present

Church Records	One-third of all Catholic parish registers Few transcripts of Church of Ireland registers Few transcripts of Presbyterian registers Many Quaker registers	Two-thirds of Catholic parish registers Almost half of the parishes of the Church of Ireland have registers that survived the 1922 fire Most Presbyterian records are available on film at the Public Record Office of Northern Ireland
Censuses and Census Substitutes	Complete 1901 and 1911 censuses Nineteenth-century census fragments and transcripts Many census substitutes	
Land and Property Records	Tithe Applotments Books, 1823–38 Griffith's Valuation, 1847–64 Canceled land books, 1850s–1920s (often later) Registry of Deeds, 1708–1929	Registry of Deeds, 1930–present
Newspapers	Birth, marriage, and death announcements for many newspapers have been abstracted and are available on microfilm or in publications	Most surviving Irish newspapers are at the National Library of Ireland, the British Library, or in local custody in Ireland
Commercial and Social Directories	National, provincial, and local directories for certain years; Dublin and Belfast directories	Extensive collections of national, provincial, and local directories exist for many years
Wills and Administrations	Pre-1858 indexes; some pre-1858 wills from National Archives; post-1858 wills, administrations, and indexes	Will copies in private custody
Gravestone Inscriptions	Many transcripts of gravestone inscriptions are on microfilm or in published works	Most cemeteries have not been covered yet. Many have been by Heritage Centres and others.
School Registers	Registers of about 1,000 national schools in Northern Ireland and a few dozen schools in the Republic	National school registers for the Republic of Ireland are mostly in local custody, with a few dozen at the National Archives of Ireland
Occupation Records	Good collections for some occupations such as the Royal Irish Constabulary, schoolteachers, and guild members.	Many other professions maintained records of their members

Most people searching Irish records begin by looking under the four major record sources:

- Census
- Church records
- Civil registration
- Land and property

Feel free to explore the list of books and manuscript collections under each topic category, especially within the civil parishes where your ancestors lived.

Preparing to Visit the Family History Library

If you are planning a trip to the Family History Library, preparation is key. You can maximize your success by preparing for your visit well in advance.

It is best to have a plan for each family you are researching. The simplest way to build a research plan is to write down a goal, something you want to learn about an ancestor. Then search the Family History Library Catalog online to find the best sources to consult, sources that may help you achieve your research objective. When you find a promising record in the catalog, write down the title of the record, the location and time period covered, and the microfilm number or call number you need. As you assemble a list of records, you build a research plan. Doing all of this work in advance helps you use your time very efficiently when you arrive at the library. All your time is then available for finding your ancestors in the records. If you run into a snag, you can work with the experts at the reference desk to find out what to do next.

While at the library, you may want to attend some of the classes offered to the public throughout the day. These classes cover topics such as beginning genealogy, computers and genealogy, researching in specific types of records, and researching in specific geographic regions. You can check the schedule of classes—it's posted online on the website FamilySearch <www.familysearch.org>.

Family History Centers

The Family History Library has a network of almost forty-five hundred Family History Centers in about one hundred countries throughout the world. They are open free to the public. The majority of these centers are located in meetinghouses of The Church of Jesus Christ of Latter-day Saints. Some Family History Centers service large regions and have extensive holdings. The main purpose of Family History Centers is to offer everyone access to family history records and resources, including the millions of microfilms and microfiche listed in the Family History Library Catalog. For a nominal fee, you can order most any microfilm in the catalog to be delivered to your local or regional Family History Center. Some Family

Library Tip

The main purpose of Family History Centers is to offer everyone access to family history records and resources, including the millions of microfilms and microfiche listed in the Family History Library Catalog.

History Centers already have substantial Irish genealogy collections in books and on microfilm, microfiche, and CD-ROMs.

To find the Family History Center closest to your home, consult the website FamilySearch <www.familysearch.org>. You can search for all centers in your city, county, state, or country. Each listing includes the name of the center, the address, phone number, and hours when the center is open.

In Summary

The Family History Library is a Mecca for family historians researching their Irish roots. All kinds of Irish genealogy records are available at the Family History Library. You can also visit a local Family History Center to access Internet genealogy resources, search local collections of family history materials, get advice from research consultants, or order microfilms from the extensive collection of records listed in the Family History Library Catalog on FamilySearch <www.familysearch.org>.

References and Selected Reading

Ireland Research Outline. Salt Lake City: Corporation of the President, The Church of Jesus Christ of Latter-day Saints, 1997.

Smith, Frank. *Smith's Inventory of Genealogical Sources: Ireland.* Salt Lake City: Corporation of the President, The Church of Jesus Christ of Latter-day Saints, 1994.

Warren, Paula Stuart, and James W. Warren. *Your Guide to the Family History Library.* Cincinnati: Betterway Books, 2001.

The beautiful Irish coast.

18

Irish Heritage Centres

The Irish Genealogical Project, which is supported by [Irish and British] governments, is transferring handwritten records from local registers of births, deaths and marriages, on to computer. It uses modern technology to allow men and women, whose origins are written down in records from Kerry to Antrim, to gain access to them.

—Mary Robinson, President of Ireland,
addressing the Irish Parliament and Senate in February 1995

Each county in Ireland has one or more Heritage Centres with indexes of important genealogical sources. Most centres have at least partially indexed the church parish registers (Catholic, Church of Ireland, and Presbyterian) for their respective counties. Many Heritage Centres have also begun to index gravestone inscriptions, land valuation records, civil registration, and census records, transcribing literally hundreds of thousands of names, dates, and places from historical documents. A number of Heritage Centres have received access to church records that are difficult to obtain remotely—in many instances the Heritage Centres will provide the easiest access to these valuable church records.

Genealogy Services Provided

For a fee, Irish Heritage Centres will search their collections of family history sources to locate your ancestors. Staff members conduct these record searches themselves—the computer indexes are not available for public use.

Imagine how valuable an Irish Heritage Centre can be if you know only the county of origin for your immigrant ancestor. Rather than search all parish registers in the county yourself, you could commission the county Heritage Centre to search their database for your ancestor and report what they find.

The Killarney Genealogical Centre in County Kerry helped me learn more about my family, finding a record of the Catholic baptism of my great-uncle in their database of church registers. The baptism was performed in a different parish church than I expected, illustrating the value of consulting a Heritage Centre, which has records spanning an entire county.

> ### Library Tip
> If you know only the county of origin for your immigrant ancestor, consider commissioning that county's Irish Heritage Centre to search their databases for your ancestor.

The major Irish record sources indexed at Heritage Centres are:

- Civil registration of births, marriages, and deaths
- Church parish registers (Catholic, Church of Ireland, and Presbyterian)
- 1901 and 1911 census returns
- Griffith's Primary Valuation of Tenements
- Tithe Applotment Books
- Gravestone inscriptions

Other sources of family history information available at some Heritage Centres include:

- Census fragments before 1900
- Commercial directories
- Newspaper abstracts
- Regional censuses
- Registry of deeds
- Rental books
- School registers
- Voter lists
- Workhouse records

By early 2003, over fifteen million records had been computerized by these research centres. A few centres have computerized all their records. Although for most, this is a work in progress.

Most centres offer three types of genealogy services: preliminary family history reports, full family history reports, and searches of specific records; the latter is generally least expensive. The genealogy services differ somewhat from centre to centre, and the fees and waiting periods also vary. Check the website of the appropriate Heritage Centre to get current information. Contact information for each Heritage Centre is listed at the end of this chapter. A quick way to access most of the Heritage Centre websites is to go to <www.irishroots.net> and click on a county name. This will take you to that county's Heritage Centre home page.

Many of these Heritage Centre websites also provide sample reports, so you can see in advance how they would respond if you ordered a genealogical report for your ancestors. Try the Heritage Centre websites for Counties Clare and Laois <www.clareroots.com> and <www.irishmidlandsancestry.com>, respectively) to see what a typical commissioned genealogy report looks like.

A number of Irish Heritage Centres have provided indexes of their computerized records on a central website, Irish Genealogy <www.irishgenealogy.ie>. See Chapter 16, "Internet Sites," for more details about this website.

Ireland's Heritage Centres are listed below, county by county, with current addresses and contact information. Please be advised that phone numbers, e-mail addresses, and websites are always subject to change. Remember to check, before your visit, the hours each Heritage Centre is open.

Councy Heritage Centres

Antrim
Ulster Historical Foundation
Address: Balmoral Buildings, 12 College Square East, Belfast, BT1 6DD, Northern Ireland
Phone: (028) 90332288
Fax: (028) 90239885
E-mail: enquiry@uhf.org.uk
Website: <www.ancestryireland.co.uk>

Armagh
Armagh Ancestry
Address: 38A English Street, Armagh, BT61 7BA, Northern Ireland
Phone: (028) 37521802
Fax: (028) 37510033
E-mail: ancestry@armagh.gov.uk
Website: <www.armagh.gov.uk/history/ancestry.php3>

Carlow
Carlow Genealogy Project
Address: Old School, College Street, Carlow, County Carlow, Ireland
Phone: (0503) 30850
Fax: (0503) 30850
E-mail: carlowgenealogy@iolfree.ie
Website: <www.irishroots.net/carlow.htm>

Cavan
Cavan Genealogy Research Centre
Address: Cana House, Farnham Street, Cavan, County Cavan, Ireland
Phone: (049) 4361094
Fax: (049) 4331494
E-mail: canahous@iol.ie
Website: <www.irishroots.net/cavan.htm>

Clare
Clare Heritage and Genealogical Centre
Address: Church Street, Corofin, County Clare, Ireland
Phone: (065) 6837955
Fax: (065) 6837540
E-mail: clareheritage@eircom.net
Website: <www.clareroots.com>

Cork (City)
Cork City Ancestral Project
Address: c/o Cork County Library, Farranlea Road, Cork City, County Cork, Ireland
Phone: (021) 54699

Cork
Mallow Heritage Centre
Address: 27/28 Bank Place, Mallow, County Cork, Ireland
Phone: (022) 21778
E-mail: mallowhc@eircom.net
Website: <www.irishroots.net/cork.htm>

Derry (Londonderry)
County Derry or Londonderry Genealogy Centre
Address: Heritage Library, 14 Bishop Street, Derry City, County Derry, BT48 6PW, Northern Ireland
Phone: (028) 71269792
Fax: (028) 71360921
Website: <www.irishroots.net/derry.htm>

Donegal
Donegal Ancestry
Address: The Quay, Ramelton, County Donegal, Ireland
Phone: (074) 51266
Fax: (074) 51702
E-mail: donances@indigo.ie
Website: <http://indigo.ie/~donances>

Down
Ulster Historical Foundation
(Please see listing under County Antrim for details.)

Dublin (North)
Fingal Genealogy
Address: Swords Historical Society Co. Ltd., Carnegie Library, North Street, Swords, County Dublin, Ireland
Phone: (01) 8400080
Fax: (01) 8400080
E-mail: swordsheritage@eircom.net
Website: <www.irishroots.net/fingal.htm>

Dublin (South)
Dún Laoghaire Rathdown Heritage Society
Address: Moran Park House, Dún Laoghaire, County Dublin, Ireland
Phone: (01) 2806961 extension 238
Fax: (01) 2806969
E-mail: kcallery@dlrcoco.ie
Website: <www.irishroots.net/dunlghre.htm>

Fermanagh
Irish World
Address: 51 Dungannon Road, Coalisland, County Tyrone, BT71 4HP, Northern Ireland
Phone: (028) 87746065
Fax: (028) 87746065
E-mail: info@irish-world.com
Website: <www.irish-world.com>

Galway (East)
East Galway Family History Society
Address: Woodford Heritage Centre, Woodford, County
    Galway, Ireland
Phone: (0509) 49309
Fax: (0509) 49546
E-mail: galwayroots@eircom.net
Website: <www.irishroots.net/etgalway.htm>

Galway (West)
West Galway Family History Society
Address: Unit 3, Venture Centre, Liosbaun Estate, Tuam
    Road, Galway City, County Galway, Ireland
Phone: (091) 756737
Fax: (091) 753590
E-mail: galwaywestroots@eircom.net
Website: <www.mayo-ireland.ie/geneal/wtgalway.htm>

Kerry
Killarney Genealogical Centre
Address: Cathedral Walk, Killarney, County Kerry,
    Ireland
Website: <www.irishroots.net/kerry.htm>

Kildare
Kildare Heritage and Genealogy Company
Address: c/o Kildare County Library, Newbridge, County
    Kildare, Ireland
Phone: (045) 433602
Fax: (045) 431611
Website: <www.kildare.ie/heritage/genealogy>

Kilkenny
Kilkenny Archaeological Society
Address: Rothe House, 16 Parliament Street, Kilkenny
    City, County Kilkenny, Ireland
Phone: (056) 22893
Fax: (056) 22893
E-mail: rothehouse@eircom.net
Website: <www.kilkennyarchaeologicalsociety.ie>

Laois
Irish Midlands Ancestry
Address: Bury Quay, Tullamore, County Offaly, Ireland
Phone: (0506) 21421
Fax: (0506) 21421
E-mail: ohas@iol.ie
Website: <www.irishmidlandsancestry.com>

Leitrim
Leitrim Genealogy Centre
Address: County Library, Ballinamore, County Leitrim,
    Ireland
Phone: (078) 44012
Fax: (078) 44425
E-mail: leitrimgenealogy@eircom.net
Website: <www.irishroots.net/Leitrim.htm>

Limerick
Limerick Ancestry
Address: The Granary, Michael Street, Limerick City,
    Ireland
Website: <www.limerickancestry.com>

Longford
Longford Roots
Address: 1 Church Street, Longford, County Longford,
    Ireland
Phone: (043) 41235
E-mail: longroot@iol.ie
Website: <www.longfordroots.com>

Louth
Meath Heritage Centre
(Please see listing under County Meath for details.)

Mayo (North)
Mayo North Family Heritage Centre
Address: Enniscoe, Castlehill, Ballina, County Mayo,
    Ireland
Phone: (096) 31809
Fax: (096) 31885
E-mail: normayo@iol.ie
Website: <http://mayo.irishroots.net>

Mayo (South)
South Mayo Family Research Centre
Address: Main Street, Ballinrobe, County Mayo, Ireland
Phone: (092) 41214
Fax: (092) 41214
E-mail: soumayo@iol.ie
Website: <http://mayo.irishroots.net>

Meath
Meath Heritage Centre
Address: Mill Street, Trim, County Meath, Ireland
Phone: (046) 36633
Fax: (046) 37502
E-mail: meathhc@iol.ie
Website: <www.energa.com/meathhc/>

Monaghan
Monaghan Ancestry
Address: Clogher Historical Society, 6 Tully Street, Monaghan, Ireland
Phone: (047) 82304
Website: <www.irishroots.net/monaghan.htm>

Offaly
Irish Midlands Ancestry
(Please see listing under County Laois for details.)

Roscommon
County Roscommon Heritage and Genealogy Company
Address: Church Street, Strokestown, County Roscommon, Ireland
Phone: (071) 333380
Fax: (071) 333398
E-mail: info@roscommonroots.com
Website: <www.roscommonroots.com>

Sligo
County Sligo Heritage and Genealogy Society
Address: Aras Reddan, Temple Street, Sligo, Ireland
Phone: (071) 43728
E-mail: info@sligoroots.com
Website: <www.sligoroots.com>

Tipperary
Tipperary Family History Research
Address: Excel Heritage Centre, Mitchell St, Tipperary, Ireland
Phone: (062) 80555
Fax: (062) 80552
E-mail: research@tfhr.org
Website: <www.tfhr.org>

Tipperary (North)
Tipperary North Family History Research Centre
Address: Governor's House, Kickham Street, Nenagh, County Tipperary, Ireland
Phone: (067) 33850
Fax: (067) 33586
E-mail: tipperarynorthgenealogy@eircom.net
Website: <www.irishroots.net/ntipp.htm>

Tipperary (South)
Brú Ború Cultural Centre
Address: Rock of Cashel, Cashel, County Tipperary, Ireland
Phone: (062) 61122
Fax: (062) 62700
Website: <www.irishroots.net/stipp.htm>

Tyrone
Irish World
(Please see listing under County Fermanagh for details.)

Waterford
Waterford Heritage Genealogy Centre
Address: St. Patrick's Church, Jenkin's Lane, Waterford, Ireland
Phone: (051) 876123
Fax: (051) 850645
E-mail: mnoc@iol.ie
Website: <www.iol.ie/~mnoc>

Westmeath
Dún na Sí Heritage and Genealogical Centre
Address: Knockdomney, Moate, County Westmeath, Ireland
Phone: (0902) 81183
Fax: (0902) 81661
E-mail: dunnasimoate@eircom.net
Website: <www.irishroots.net/wstmeath.htm>

Wexford
Wexford Genealogy Centre
Address: Yola Farmstead, Tagoat, County Wexford, Ireland
Phone: (053) 32610
Fax: (053) 32612
E-mail: wexgen@iol.ie
Website: <http://homepage.eircom.net/~yolawexford/genealogy.htm>

Wicklow
Wicklow Family History Centre
Address: Wicklow's Historic Gaol, Wicklow Town, County Wicklow, Ireland
Phone: (0404) 20126
Fax: (0404) 61612
E-mail: whf@eircom.net
Website: <www.wicklow.ie> ; click on "Family History"

Fort ruins on the Aran Islands.

19

Archives and Libraries

You know that you are addicted to genealogy when you get locked in a library overnight and never even notice.

—Author unknown

A number of archives and libraries around the world have tremendous collections of Irish family history records. Governments, churches, and other institutions tend to preserve their most valuable records. These records often contain personal details about real people. In other words, they tell us about our ancestors.

The repositories included in this chapter are listed alphabetically within each country for the Republic of Ireland, Northern Ireland, the United States, England, Canada, and Australia. Please be advised that phone numbers, e-mail addresses, websites, and opening hours are always subject to change.

Archives & Libraries in the Republic of Ireland

General Register Office
Address: Joyce House, 8-11 Lombard Street East, Dublin 2, Ireland
Phone: (01) 6354000
Fax: (01) 6354440
E-mail: Use form on Web page <www.groireland.ie/contact_details.htm>
Website: <www.groireland.ie>
Holdings: Government registration of births, marriages, and deaths.

National Archives of Ireland
Address: Bishop Street, Dublin 8, Ireland
Phone: (01) 4072300
Fax: (01) 4072333
E-mail: mail@nationalarchives.ie
Website: <www.nationalarchives.ie>
Holdings: Many manuscript materials and microfilm collections of genealogical value, including the 1901 and 1911 censuses, 1821–51 census fragments, wills, estate papers, many Church of Ireland parish registers, Griffith's Valuation, Tithe Applotment Books, and other land valuation records.

National Library of Ireland
Address: 2-3 Kildare Street, Dublin 2, Ireland
Phone: (01) 6030200
Fax: (01) 6766690
E-mail: info@nli.ie
Website: <www.nli.ie>
Holdings: Roman Catholic parish registers, newspapers, landed estate papers, Irish history and genealogy publications.

Registry of Deeds
Address: Henrietta Street, Dublin 1, Ireland
Phone: (01) 670 7500
Fax: (01) 804 8393
E-mail: helen-queenan@landregistry.ie
Website: <www.landregistry.ie>
Holdings: Memorials, transcripts, abstracts, and indexes of deeds relating to property in Ireland from 1708 through the late twentieth century.

Religious Society of Friends Historical Library
Address: Swanbrook House, Bloomfield Avenue, Morehampton Road, Dublin 4, Ireland
Phone: (01) 6687157
Website: < www.quakers-in-ireland.org >
Holdings: Quaker records, minute books, and family lists. Registers of births, marriages, and burials from the 1600s to the present.

Representative Church Body Library
Address: Braemor Park, Churchtown, Dublin 14, Ireland
Phone: (01) 4923979
Fax: (01) 4924770
E-mail: library@ireland.anglican.org
Website: <www.ireland.anglican.org/library/index.html>
Holdings: Church of Ireland records for almost one thousand parishes, including baptism, marriage, and burial registers and vestry minutes from the seventeen to the twentieth centuries.

Valuation Office of Ireland
Address: Irish Life Centre, Abbey Street Lower, Dublin 1, Ireland
Phone: (01) 8171000
Fax: (01) 8171180
E-mail: info@valoff.ie
Website: <www.valoff.ie>
Holdings: Original land and property records for the Republic of Ireland dating back to the 1840s.

Archives and Libraries in Northern Ireland

General Register Office, Northern Ireland
Address: Oxford House, 49/55 Chichester Street, Belfast BT1 4HL, Northern Ireland
Phone: (028) 90252000
Fax: (028) 90252044
E-mail: gro.nisra@dfpni.gov.uk
Website: <www.groni.gov.uk>
Holdings: Post-1922 civil registration for Northern Ireland. The General Register Office website offers a service for ordering civil registration certificates online.

Linen Hall Library

Address: 17 Donegall Square North, Belfast BT1 5GB, Northern Ireland
Phone: (028) 90321707
Fax: (028) 90438586
E-mail: info@linenhall.com
Website: <www.linenhall.com>
Holdings: Genealogies, books, newspapers, and newspaper indexes. Library was founded in 1788 and is the oldest library in Belfast.

Presbyterian Historical Society

Address: Church House, Fisherwick Place, Belfast BT1 6DW, Northern Ireland
Phone: (01232) 322284
Website: <www.presbyterianireland.org/phsi/index.html>
Holdings: The oldest Presbyterian records of Northern Ireland are kept here.

Public Record Office of Northern Ireland

Address: 66 Balmoral Avenue, Belfast BT9 6NY, Northern Ireland
Phone: (028) 90255905
Fax: (028) 90255999
E-mail: proni@dcalni.gov.uk
Website: <www.proni.gov.uk>
Holdings: Most manuscript records relating to Northern Ireland genealogy, including church registers, wills, and estate papers.

Ulster Historical Foundation

Address: Balmoral Buildings, 12 College Square East, Belfast BT1 6DD, Northern Ireland
Phone: (028) 90332288
Fax: (028) 90239885
E-mail: enquiry@uhf.org.uk
Website: <www.ancestryireland.co.uk>
Holdings: Computerized databases of civil marriages for Antrim, Down, and Belfast (1845–1921); Catholic registers for Antrim, Down, and Belfast (pre-1900); civil births for Belfast (1864–1921); many Church of Ireland and Presbyterian registers; Griffith's Valuation; and Tithe Applotment Books for Northern Ireland.

Archives and Libraries in the United States

Allen County Public Library

Address: 200 E. Berry St., Fort Wayne, IN 46801
Phone: (260) 421-1225 (Genealogy Reference)
Fax: (260) 421-1386
E-mail: cwitcher@acpl.lib.in.us
Website: <www.acpl.lib.in.us>
Holdings: Extensive historical genealogy collection, with microfilms of many U.S. censuses, city directories, passenger lists, military records, and an enormous collection of published family and local history books. Irish records include copies of Griffith's Valuation, Tithe Applotment Books, nineteenth-century census fragments, and Ordnance Survey Maps.

Family History Library

Address: 35 North West Temple, Salt Lake City, UT 84150
Phone: (801) 240-2367 (for the British Reference Desk)
Fax: (801) 240-5551
E-mail: Use feedback form available on the website.
Website: <www.familysearch.org>
Holdings: Offers the largest collection of Irish family history records in the world. Most records are on microfilm, including censuses, census fragments, civil registration indexes and registers, registers for about one-third of all Catholic parishes, Church of Ireland records, Tithe Applotment books, Griffith's Valuation, canceled land books, Royal Irish Constabulary service records, and much more.

Library of Congress

Address: 101 Independence Avenue, SE, Washington, DC 20540
Phone: (202) 707-5537 (Local History & Genealogy Reading Room)
Fax: (202) 707-1957 (Local History & Genealogy Reading Room)
E-mail: Use website
Website: <www.loc.gov>
Holdings: Massive collection of published family histories, local histories, city and town directories, and much more.

National Archives and Records Administration

Address: 700 Pennsylvania Avenue, NW, Washington, DC 20408
Phone: (866) 272-6272
Fax: (301) 837-0483
E-mail: Use website
Website: <www.archives.gov>
Holdings: U.S. federal censuses, military records, immigration and naturalization records, passport applications, and much more.

Newberry Library

Address: Local and Family History Section, 60 West Walton St., Chicago, IL 60610
Phone: (312) 255-3512 (genealogy reference desk)
Fax: (312) 255-3658
E-mail: genealogy@newberry.org
Website: <www.newberry.org>
Holdings: Over seventeen thousand family histories, especially colonial America, New England, and gentry of the British Isles; local histories; census records for the United States, Quebec, and Ontario; U.S. military records; U.S. historical and genealogical periodicals.

New England Historic Genealogical Society

Address: 101 Newbury Street, Boston, MA 02116
Phone: (617) 536-5740
Fax: (617) 536-7307
E-mail: nehgs@nehgs.org
Website: <www.newenglandancestors.org>
Holdings: Over 200,000 books, periodicals, and microfilms and over one million manuscripts of genealogical materials, including vital records, censuses, church records, probate, naturalization records, military records, land records, city directories, and much more.

Archives and Libraries in England

British Library Newspaper Library
Address: Colindale Ave., London NW9 5HE, England
Phone: (0171) 4127353
Fax: (0171) 4127379
E-mail: newspaper@bl.uk
Website: <www.bl.uk/collections/newspapers.html>
Holdings: Largest collection of Irish newspapers in the world.

Family Records Centre
Address: 1 Myddelton St., London EC1R 1UW, England
Phone: (0845) 6037788
Fax: (01704) 550013
E-mail: certificate.services@ons.gsi.gov.uk
Website: <www.familyrecords.gov.uk/frc>
Holdings: Indexes of births, marriages, and deaths in England and Wales from 1837, census returns for England and Wales from 1841 to 1901, wills registered in the Prerogative Court of Canterbury, non-conformist registers, and more.

National Archives (formerly the Public Record Office)
Address: Kew, Richmond, Surrey, TW9 4DU, England
Phone: (020) 88763444
Fax: (020) 83925286
E-mail: enquiry@nationalarchives.gov.uk
Website: <www.nationalarchives.gov.uk>
Holdings: Birth, marriage, death registers and indexes from 1837, census returns from 1841 to 1901, wills, military records, and much more.

Archives and Libraries in Canada

Memorial University of Newfoundland
Address: Maritime History Archive, St. John's, NF A1C 5S7, Canada
Phone: (709) 737-8428
Fax: (709) 737-3123
E-mail: mha@mun.ca
Website: <www.mun.ca/mha>
Holdings: Microfilm copies of many Irish Roman Catholic parishes registers from Counties Kerry, Kilkenny, Waterford, Wexford, and Donegal; microfilm copies of many Church of Ireland parish registers from Counties Cork and Waterford.

Montreal Public Library—Salle Gagnon
Address: Salle Gagnon, 1210 Sherbrook St. East, Montreal, QC H2L 1L9, Canada
Phone: (514) 872-5923
Website: <http://www2.ville.montreal.qc.ca/biblio>
Holdings: Records for Ireland: Griffith's Valuation and Tithe Applotment Books on microform, with indexes. Records for Quebec: all Catholic and non-Catholic parish registers prior to 1900, province-wide marriage indexes, censuses, and fifty thousand family history books. Many more records for other provinces, England, Wales, and the United States.

Library and Archives Canada
(formerly the National Library of Canada and the National Archives of Canada)
Address: 395 Wellington Street, Ottawa, Ontario K1A 0N3, Canada
Phone: (613) 996-7458 or toll free 1 (866) 578-7777
Fax: (613) 995-6274
E-mail: cgc-ccg@lac-bac.gc.ca
Website: <www.collectionscanada.ca>
Holdings: Censuses, immigration and naturalization records, land grants, military records, and much more.

Archives and Libraries in Australia

Mitchell Library
Address: State Library of New South Wales, Macquarie Street, Sydney, NSW 2000, Australia
Phone: (02) 9273 1414
Fax: (02) 9273 1255
E-mail: library@sl.nsw.gov.au
Website: <www.sl.nsw.gov.au>

National Library of Australia
Address: Parkes Place, Canberra, ACT 2600, Australia
Phone: (02) 6262 1111
Fax: (02) 6257 1703
E-mail: www@nla.gov.au
Website: <www.nla.gov.au>
Holdings: Australian records: birth, marriage, and death indexes; convict transportation records; immigration and passenger lists; and microfilms of parish registers. Irish records: Griffith's Valuation and an index to the Tithe Applotment Books.

Society of Australian Genealogists
Address: Richmond Villa, 120 Kent Street, Sydney, NSW 2000, Australia
Phone: (02) 9247 3953
Fax: (02) 9241 4872
E-mail: info@sag.org.au
Website: <www.sag.org.au>
Holdings: Family histories and biographies; local and school histories; birth, marriage, and death indexes; shipping records; probate records; cemetery transcriptions; and parish registers.

References and Selected Reading

Helferty, Seamus, and Raymond Refaussé. *Directory of Irish Archives.* 3d ed. Dublin: Four Courts Press, 1999.

Maxwell, Ian. *Tracing Your Ancestors in Northern Ireland: A Guide to Ancestry Research in the Public Record Office of Northern Ireland.* Edinburgh: Stationery Office, 1997.

O'Neill, Robert K. *Irish Libraries: Archives, Museums and Genealogical Centres.* Belfast: Ulster Historical Foundation, 2002.

Warren, Paula Stuart, and James W. Warren. *Your Guide to the Family History Library.* Cincinnati: Betterway Books, 2001.

Visiting Ireland

For dear old Killarney tonight I am sighing,
In silence I wander far over the sea,
To the green fields and dells and the lakes of Killarney,
Back to the old home where I used to be.
—From the traditional Irish poem "Killarney,"
as sung by Deirdre Connolly on her album, A Song in Turn

So you're thinking about visiting Ireland! Ireland is one of the most incredible tourist destinations in the world. The lush green countryside, the ruins of ancient churches and ring forts, the melodious sounds of traditional music, and the friendliness of the people are all great reasons for visiting Ireland. Your trip is made even more memorable as you connect with your Irish roots. Perhaps you want to do some family history, searching records in Dublin, Belfast, or near your ancestor's home. Maybe you want to see your ancestor's house or hope to meet some relatives in Ireland. Go with a purpose, go prepared, and you will have a wonderful experience.

Basic Travel Preparations

Since Ireland is a popular vacation spot, you will find it easy to learn all you want to know about the country before you go. Contact the Irish Tourist Board, or *Fáilte Ireland*, to get a packet of information about traveling to Ireland. Their website <www.ireland.ie> has lots of great travel advice, including a section on genealogy research.

You can stay at hotels, bed and breakfasts, guest houses, elegant manors, hostels, or castles while visiting in Ireland. Choose the accommodations that best fit your plans, sense of adventure, and budget. A few travel agencies offer discounted travel packages including airfare, rental car, and bed-and-breakfast vouchers.

Bed and breakfasts offer warm and convenient accommodations throughout Ireland. You can choose from thousands of family homes and farmhouses as you develop your trip itinerary. You'll enjoy friendly hosts and hearty Irish breakfasts every day of your journey.

Some professional genealogists bring tour groups to Ireland each year for a week of family history research in Belfast or Dublin. If you would like to have some expert genealogy guidance, these tour groups will help you get the most out of the major archives and libraries.

Citizens of most western nations, including the United States, Canada, and Australia, need no visa to travel to either the Republic of Ireland or Northern Ireland. However, a passport is a necessity. You should apply for a passport well before your trip begins. If you already have a passport, it should be valid for at least six months after you plan on arriving in Ireland.

In 2002 the Republic of Ireland adopted the Euro (€) as its currency. However, Northern Ireland continues to use the British pound sterling (£)—also called the Northern Ireland pound—as its currency. Before you leave your home for Ireland you can exchange some of your local currency for either Euros or pounds. Banks give the best exchange rates. You will be more prepared when you arrive in Ireland if you have some spending money when you step off the plane.

Ireland has dozens of weather conditions, mostly ranging from wet to very wet. If you bring an umbrella, a light jacket, and wear layers of clothes that you can peel off as needed, you will feel more comfortable throughout your travels. You'll want to pack a good pair of walking shoes as well.

Family History Preparations

I have seen many people stroll into the National Library in Dublin with only the vaguest hint that they have Irish ancestors. They don't know their immigrant ancestor's birth date, birthplace, parents' names, or residence in Ireland. Fortunately, many others arrive armed with a knowledge of where their ancestors lived in Ireland and other family history details; they come prepared with specific goals they wish to achieve while at the library. Their advanced preparation really pays off.

To get the most out of your trip to Ireland, spend a few months doing family history before you get on the airplane. As demonstrated throughout this book, many Irish family history sources are readily available outside Ireland. Take the time to learn as much as you can about your Irish roots before you travel to Ireland. At a minimum, you need to know the county or parish where your ancestors lived. Ideally, you will find your ancestors in Irish civil registration, church records, censuses, and land records before you set foot on Irish soil.

> **⇥ Basic Principle ⇤**
>
> Spend a few months working on your Irish family history before traveling to Ireland. At a minimum, you need to know the county or parish where your ancestors lived.

Study the local history and geography, collecting historical and modern maps to help you find your ancestors' homes, the churches they attended, and the cemeteries where they were buried.

You may choose to order a search at the Irish Heritage Centre in your ancestor's county; do this before you go to Ireland, so you can review the results well before your trip. If you do your homework before you go, you will be amply rewarded with a more meaningful, productive, and rich genealogy experience in Ireland.

My personal preparations include creating a family history trip binder. I devote one section to each family, with all the family history details organized chronologically, like a time line. I have copies of all the maps I'll need and lists of all the place names in the vicinity of my ancestors' homes. I devote one page to each archive or library I intend to visit, listing what I want to find and the sources I want to search to learn more about my ancestors.

I also bring a notebook for documenting what I learn. I write down the name of each source I consult, even if I don't find anything in it. When I do find something of value, I make a genealogical abstract of each entry. I also make photocopies of whatever I'm allowed to copy.

Don't bring everything with you. Leave all your original family history documents at home. Do, however, bring copies of anything you would like to review while in Ireland.

Planning Your Genealogy Itinerary

A genealogy trip combines sightseeing with family history research. You'll want to strike the right balance between family history and Irish culture. Decide how you want to spend your time, whether it's visiting cemeteries, churches, archives, libraries, historical sites, Irish relatives, or your ancestor's home site. Find out the dates and places of Irish genealogy conferences, music festivals, cultural events, and holidays when planning your trip.

Ireland may look like a small country on the map, so it might seem that you can drive from Donegal in the far north to Waterford in the extreme south in one day. In reality, it's best to plan lots of extra time to drive from place to place. The same may also be said about the time you plan to spend in a city or at a records repository. If you cushion your itinerary with extra time in each place, you will avoid feeling rushed and wishing you had planned for just another half day here or there. Enjoy the Irish countryside, get to know the people, and drop by a pub to hear some traditional Irish music.

Visiting Irish Archives and Libraries

Irish archives and libraries contain many historical documents about our ancestors. When I first visited Dublin, I took the bus to the Representative Church Body Library to learn more about my grandfather and his family. I was warmly greeted by the staff and shown how to find the records I wanted to search. They brought me parchment manuscripts from the churches my ancestors attended. I examined parish registers, vestry minutes, photos of old churches, and many other valuable documents that told me of my ancestors in nineteenth-century Ireland. You too can learn about your ancestors as you visit archives and libraries in Ireland.

The most popular archives and libraries for genealogy research in Dublin are:

- **National Archives of Ireland**—censuses, wills, land valuation records, and many manuscript collections
- **National Library of Ireland**—Catholic parish registers and Irish newspapers
- **General Register Office**—government registration of births, marriages, and deaths
- **Valuation Office of Ireland**—land and property valuation records

- **Registry of Deeds**—memorials of deeds spanning the last three centuries
- **Representative Church Body Library**—Church of Ireland parish registers

The staff are very helpful and knowledgeable. For example, the National Archives and the National Library have professional genealogists who meet with first-time visitors to help them make the most of their time doing research at these facilities. They offer personalized guidance about which records to consult and how to use these records effectively.

Family historians traveling to Belfast usually visit these archives and libraries:

- **Public Record Office of Northern Ireland**—most manuscript records relating to Northern Ireland genealogy, including church registers, wills, estate papers, and much more
- **General Register Office**—government registration of births, marriages, and deaths
- **Presbyterian Historical Society**—Presbyterian church registers
- **Ulster Historical Foundation**—computerized databases of civil births and marriages for some counties, Catholic registers, many Church of Ireland and Presbyterian registers, Griffith's Valuation, and Tithe Applotment Books for Northern Ireland
- **Linen Hall Library**—genealogies, books, newspapers, and newspaper indexes

Most counties have at least one library or Heritage Centre. These local libraries will often have family history sources unavailable elsewhere. Robert O'Neill's book, *Irish Libraries: Archives, Museums and Genealogical Centres*, describes the genealogical holdings of the major archives and libraries throughout Ireland and Northern Ireland.

As you plan your itinerary and select the archives and libraries you'd like to visit, check when each of these institutions is open (see Chapter 19, "Archives and Libraries"), and then double check locally when you arrive. Do all you can to adjust your schedule so that the places you want to visit will be open when you arrive. It also makes a lot of sense to have a backup plan just in case the library is closed. Call ahead where advised, and get advanced permission to look at any restricted records.

Pens, backpacks, cameras, and other items are not permitted in certain reading rooms where you will be researching your ancestors. You will usually be allowed to bring paper and pencils, even laptop computers.

Visiting Your Ancestor's Home

One of the highlights of a genealogy trip to Ireland is a visit to your ancestor's home. Many family houses are still standing a hundred or more years after they were built. You might be surprised to find relatives living in your ancestor's home. On the other hand, some houses have fallen into disrepair, have been converted to barns, or no longer exist. My grandfather's house is now unoccupied and leans to the side a little, but I found it easily using an old map of the area. With the help of land records you can often identify the exact property, even the building where your ancestors lived (see Chapter 9, "Land and Property Records").

Other destinations include your ancestor's church or old schoolhouse, even the cemetery where your ancestors are buried. Chapter 10, "Gravestone Inscriptions," discusses how to identify the right graveyard to search and how to properly record gravestone inscriptions.

If you are fortunate, you will find living relatives in Ireland and establish lifelong friendships with these cousins. The three most common tools used to identify living relatives in Ireland are current phone books, newspaper queries, and the Internet.

Consult modern phone books (e.g., at <http://mmm.eircom.ie/phonebook> for people who have the same surname as your ancestors and who now live near where your ancestors used to live. Call or write in advance to see whether they are related.

You can send Irish newspapers a personal advertisement about your search for living relatives. Make sure to mention when you will be in town and give your contact information. This will improve your chances of receiving a positive response and getting to meet a relative during your stay in Ireland.

The Internet connects millions of people doing family history research, including a number of Irish citizens. If you post genealogy queries on the Internet you might meet an Irish cousin online. This is how one of my relatives in Ireland found me. See Chapter 16, "Internet Sites," for details on how to use the Internet to find living cousins.

In Summary

Visiting Ireland becomes more than just another vacation when you focus on finding your ancestors. May you find your Irish ancestors, feel your heart turn to them, and preserve your Irish heritage for your children and grandchildren. Enjoy the journey!

References and Selected Reading

Downs, Tom, et al. *Lonely Planet Ireland*. 6th ed. Oakland, Calif.: Lonely Planet, 2004.

Gerard-Sharp, Lisa, and Tim Perry. *Eyewitness Travel Guide: Ireland*. Rev. ed. London: Dorling Kindersley, 2003.

Helferty, Seamus, and Raymond Refaussé. *Directory of Irish Archives*. 3d ed. Dublin: Four Courts Press, 1999.

Maxwell, Ian. *Tracing Your Ancestors in Northern Ireland: A Guide to Ancestry Research in the Public Record Office of Northern Ireland*. Edinburgh: Stationery Office, 1997.

O'Neill, Robert K. *Irish Libraries: Archives, Museums and Genealogical Centres*. Belfast: Ulster Historical Foundation, 2002.

Registration Districts

The following list shows the Registration Districts (also known as Poor Law Unions) pertaining to each county in Ireland. The districts spanning more than one county are indicated in *italic* font. For example, if a person's death was registered in Ballymoney, the person likely lived within this Registration District, which is partly in County Antrim and partly in County Derry (Londonderry).

A typical entry in a marriage index might read "O'Brien, Mary. Mitchelstown. 5, 452." This entry tells us that Mary O'Brien was married in the year or quarter of the marriage index, with her marriage registered in the registration district of Mitchelstown. Checking the table below, we see that Mitchelstown is partly in County Cork and partly in County Limerick. The marriage is registered in volume 5, on page 452. We would need to look at the marriage register to find out the townland, parish, and county where the bride and groom were each living.

Registration Districts by County

Antrim: Antrim, Ballycastle, Ballymena, *Ballymoney*, *Belfast*, *Coleraine*, Larne, *Lisburn*, *Lurgan*

Armagh: *Armagh*, *Banbridge*, *Castleblaney*, *Dundalk*, *Lurgan*, *Newry*

Carlow: *Baltinglass*, *Carlow*, *Enniscorthy*, *New Ross*, *Shillelagh*

Cavan: Ballieborough, *Bawnboy*, Cavan, *Cootehill*, *Enniskillen*, *Granard*, *Kells*, *Oldcastle*

Clare: Ballyvaghan, Corrofin, Ennis, Ennistimon, Killadysert, Kilrush, *Limerick*, *Scarriff*, Tulla

Cork: Bandon, Bantry, Castletown, Clonakilty, Cork, Dunmanway, Fermoy, Kanturk, *Kilmallock*, Kinsale, Macroom, Mallow, Middleton, Millstreet, *Mitchelstown*, Skibbereen, Skull, *Youghal*

Derry (Londonderry): *Ballymoney*, *Coleraine*, *Londonderry*, Magherafelt, Limavady

Donegal: *Ballyshannon*, Donegal, Dunfanaghy, Glenties, Inishowen, Letterkenny, *Londonderry*, Millford, *Strabane*, Stranolar

Down: *Banbridge*, *Belfast*, Downpatrick, Kilkeel, *Lisburn*, *Lurgan*, *Newry*, Newtownards

Dublin: Balrothery, *Celbridge*, Dublin North, Dublin South, Dunshaughlin, *Rathdown*

Fermanagh: *Ballyshannon*, *Clones*, *Enniskillen*, *Irvinestown*, Lisnaskea

Galway: *Ballinasloe*, *Ballinrobe*, Clifden, Galway, Glennamaddy, *Gort*, Loughrea, Mountbellew, Oughterard, Portumna, *Scarriff*, Tuam

Kerry: Cahersiveen, Dingle, *Glin*, Kenmare, Killarney, Listowel, Tralee

Kildare: *Athy, Baltinglass, Celbridge, Edenderry, Naas*

Kilkenny: *Callan, Carrick-on-Suir,* Castlecomer, Kilkenny, *New Ross,* Thomastown, *Urlingford, Waterford*

Leitrim: *Ballyshannon, Bawnboy, Carrick-on-Shannon,* Manorhamilton, Mohill

Laois: Abbeyleix, *Athy,* Carlow, Donaghmore, *Mountmellick, Roscrea*

Limerick: Croom, *Glin, Kilmallock, Limerick, Mitchelstown,* Newcastle, Rathkeale, *Tipperary*

Longford: *Ballymahon, Granard,* Longford

Louth: *Ardee, Drogheda, Dundalk*

Mayo: *Ballina, Ballinrobe,* Belmullet, Castlebar, *Castlereagh,* Claremorris, Killala, Newport, Swineford, Westport

Meath: *Ardee, Celbridge, Drogheda, Dunshaughlin, Edenderry, Kells,* Navan, *Oldcastle,* Trim

Monaghan: Carickmacross, *Castleblaney, Clogher, Clones, Cootehill, Dundalk,* Monaghan

Offaly: *Edenderry, Mountmellick, Parsonstown, Roscrea, Tullamore*

Roscommon: *Athlone, Ballinasloe, Boyle, Carrick-on-Shannon, Castlereagh,* Roscommon, Strokestown

Sligo: *Ballina, Boyle,* Dromore West, Sligo, Tobercurry

Tipperary: Borrisokane, *Callan, Carrick-on-Suir,* Cashel, Clogheen, *Clonmel,* Nenagh, *Parsonstown, Roscrea,* Thurles, *Tipperary, Urlingford*

Tyrone: *Armagh,* Castlederg, *Clogher,* Cookstown, Dungannon, *Enniskillen,* Gortin, *Irvinestown,* Omagh, *Strabane*

Waterford: *Carrick-on-Suir, Clonmel,* Dungarvan, Kilmacthomas, Lismore, *Waterford,* Youghal

Westmeath: *Athlone, Ballymahon,* Delvin, *Granard,* Mullingar, *Tullamore*

Wexford: *Enniscorthy,* Gorey, *New Ross, Shillelagh,* Wexford

Wicklow: *Baltinglass, Naas, Rathdown,* Rathdrum, *Shillelagh*

Terms Used in Irish Family History

Abstract. A brief summary of the information found in a genealogical source (e.g., a name index); compare with *Transcription*.

Administration. Papers handling the distribution of property in the absence of a *Will* (see also *Intestate*).

Ancestry. An individual's parents, grandparents, and so on.

Anglican Church. The Church of Ireland.

Anglo-Norman. People from Normandy (now part of northern France) who invaded Ireland in the late twelfth century.

Barony. A long-obsolete land division often corresponding to ancient tribal or clan boundaries.

Calendar of Wills and Administrations. An annual listing of will and administration *Abstracts*, arranged alphabetically by name of the deceased.

Canceled Land Books. Also known as Revision Books, these records describe the occupancy and valuation of all properties in Ireland from the mid-1800s to the late 1900s.

Catholic Relief Acts. A series of British Parliamentary rulings enacted in the late 1700s to relax restrictions imposed by the *Penal Laws*.

Celtic. Of or related to the *Celts*.

Celts. An ancient race of warlike people who invaded Ireland about 500 B.C.; also known as Gaels.

Census. An official list of inhabitants; Irish national censuses named each person in each household on the day of the census.

Census Substitute. A name list from a source other than an official census, especially valuable for nineteenth-century Ireland since the national censuses were mostly destroyed.

Civil Registration. The official process of informing the government of births, marriages, and deaths.

Common Prayer, Book of. The prayer book of the *Anglican Church*.

Constable. Local law enforcement officer.

Cottier. A tenant who rented a small cottage (and possibly land) from a landlord.

County. One of the most basic land divisions in Ireland, similar in many ways to a state in the United States; Ireland consists of thirty-two counties.

Current Land Books. The most recent *Canceled Land Books*.

Deed. A legal contract, typically describing a change in land ownership.

Descendants. An individual's children, grandchildren, and so on.

Diocese. An administrative unit in either the Catholic Church or Church of Ireland, consisting of a number of church *Parishes* and presided over by a bishop.

Electoral Division. A subdivision of the *Poor Law Union*, consisting of a number of *Townlands* and used in some records such as the *Canceled Land Books*.

Emigrant. One who leaves a country to settle in another.

Established Church. A name for the Church of Ireland between 1536 and 1870, while it was the official state church.

Executor. An individual chosen to see that the estate of the deceased is properly settled.

Family History. The study of *Ancestors* and *Descendants*, the most popular hobby in the world.

Freeholder. One who holds property for life or with the right to pass on the property through inheritance.

Gaelic. Another name for the Irish language; synonymous with the term *Celtic.*

Gaeltacht, the. The remaining regions of Ireland where the Irish language is still commonly spoken.

Gazetteer. A dictionary of place names, often containing historical details of the geography and population.

Genealogy. The study of *Descendants*; often used synonymously with the term *Family History.*

Gentry. People of social standing just below *Nobility.*

Given Name. The name by which an individual is familiarly known, also called a first name, baptismal name, or Christian name in English-speaking countries.

Griffith's Valuation. Formally known as Griffith's Primary Valuation of Tenements and published between 1848 and 1864, this land valuation record lists all *Householders* and landholders in Ireland.

Householder. The head of a family or household.

Householders Index. An index of surnames for *Griffith's Valuation* and the *Tithe Applotment* survey.

Immigrant. One who arrives in a new country to settle there.

Intestate. Said of an individual who died without leaving a *Will* (see also *Administration*).

Kin. Individuals related by birth or by marriage.

Lessor. A landlord.

Marriage Banns. Public notice of a proposed marriage, announced over the pulpit for three consecutive Sundays.

Marriage License. A legal certificate empowering a couple to marry without requiring *Marriage Banns.*

Marriage License Bond. A document purchased from the Church of Ireland *Diocese* declaring that the couple was to be married by license.

Memorial. A gravestone or inscription placed in memory of the deceased; the term is also used to refer to a synopsis of a deed.

Nobility. People of high rank, title, or birth.

Non-Conformist. A Protestant who was not a member of the Church of Ireland (e.g., Presbyterian, Methodist). Catholics were also occasionally referred to as non-conformists.

Norman (See *Anglo-Norman*)

Old Age Pension Act. A pension program started in 1908 for senior citizens in Ireland.

Ordnance Survey. A government-sponsored survey of Ireland carried out in the early 1800s to facilitate the valuation of land, resulting in a detailed series of maps of the entire country.

Pale, the. A district of eastern Ireland, centered in Dublin, and considered an English stronghold centuries ago.

Parish. A civil or religious jurisdiction. There are three distinct types of parishes in Ireland: civil parishes, Church of Ireland parishes, and Catholic parishes. Civil parishes in Ireland are similar to counties in the United States. Church of Ireland and Catholic parishes have different congregations and boundaries. Catholic parishes are typically larger geographically than Church of Ireland parishes.

Pedigree. Synonymous with the term *Ancestry*; pedigree charts begin with an individual. The pedigree chart then lists parents, grandparents, and so on.

Penal Laws. A series of British Parliamentary rulings instituted in the late 1600s and early 1700s forbidding Catholics from public office, education, voting, bearing arms, and buying land.

Plantation of Ulster. English and Scottish settlement of Ulster beginning in the early 1600s, forcing many Irish-Catholic families from their lands.

Poor Law Union. Administrative areas created by the Poor Law Relief Act of 1838 for the purpose of collecting taxes for the relief of the poor.

Presbyterian Church. Any of a number of congregations in Ireland, especially in the north, based on the doctrines of Calvin and governed by presbyters (church elders).

Probate. The "proving" of a *Will* in court; more broadly, the legal system and documentation surrounding *Wills* and *Administrations*.

Province. Ireland consists of four provinces, roughly corresponding to regions dominated by four major Irish clans before the *Anglo-Norman* invasion.

Registration District. An administrative unit for *Civil Registration* of births, marriages, and deaths; essentially the same as *Poor Law Unions*, sharing the same names and boundaries.

Revision Books (See *Canceled Land Books*)

Session Minutes. Meeting records kept for the governing committee of a *Presbyterian* congregation.

Superintendent Registrar's District. Same as *Registration District*.

Surname. The family name passed on from a father to all children. The practice of inheriting surnames began in Ireland more than one thousand years ago, earlier than in most European countries.

Synod. A general council of the Catholic Church.

Tenement. The equivalent of a modern-day apartment complex.

Testator. One who leaves a *Will*.

Tithe Applotment. First detailed survey and valuation of agricultural land throughout Ireland, carried out between 1823 and 1838.

Townland. The most fundamental land division in Ireland. In rural areas, the townland name serves as the postal address even in modern times.

Transcription. A word-for-word copying of information, with effort to preserve even the format and punctuation of the original.

Vestry. Anglican Church members responsible for managing the temporal affairs of the parish.

Will. A legal document declaring the deceased's intent to distribute property to specific heir.

Recommended Reading

The following books are excellent general references for Irish family history. For recommendations on specific topics discussed in this book, consult the "References and Selected Reading" section of each chapter.

Begley, Donal F., ed. *Irish Genealogy: A Record Finder*. Minneapolis: Irish Books and Media, 1987.

———. *Handbook on Irish Genealogy*. Dublin: Heraldic Artists, 1987.

Grenham, John. *Tracing Your Irish Ancestors: The Complete Guide*. 2d ed. Baltimore: Genealogical Publishing Company, 1999.

Ireland Research Outline. Salt Lake City: Corporation of the President, The Church of Jesus Christ of Latter-day Saints, 1997.

MacConghail, Máire, and Paul Gorry. *Tracing Irish Ancestors*. Glasgow: Harper Collins, 1997.

Maxwell, Ian. *Tracing Your Ancestors in Northern Ireland: A Guide to Ancestry Research in the Public Record Office of Northern Ireland*. Edinburgh: The Stationery Office, 1997.

McCarthy, Tony. *The Irish Roots Guide*. Dublin: Lilliput Press, 1991.

Mitchell, Brian. *Pocket Guide to Irish Genealogy*. Baltimore: Clearfield, 1991.

Neill, Kathleen. *How to Trace Family History in Northern Ireland*. Belfast: Irish Genealogical Association, 1986.

Radford, Dwight A., and Kyle J. Betit. *A Genealogist's Guide to Discovering Your Irish Ancestors*. Cincinnati: Betterway Books, 2001.

Ryan, James G. *Irish Records: Sources for Family and Local History*. Salt Lake City: Ancestry, 1997.

Index